Transnational Urbanism

Transnational Urbanism
Locating Globalization

Michael Peter Smith

BLACKWELL
Publishers

Copyright © Michael Peter Smith 2001

The right of Michael Peter Smith to be identified as author of this work has been asserted in accordance with the Copyright, Designs and Patents Act 1988.

First published 2001

2 4 6 8 10 9 7 5 3 1

Blackwell Publishers Inc.
350 Main Street
Malden, Massachusetts 02148
USA

Blackwell Publishers Ltd
108 Cowley Road
Oxford OX4 1JF
UK

Library of Congress Cataloging-in-Publication Data
Smith, Michael P.
    Transnational urbanism : locating globalization / Michael Peter Smith.
      p. cm.
    Includes bibliographical references and index.
    ISBN 0−631−18423−6 (hc : alk. paper)—ISBN 0−631−18424−4 (pb : alk. paper)
    1. Cities and towns.   2. Urbanization.   3. Urban policy.   4. Urban economics.
  I. Title.
  HT119.S62 2000
  307.76—dc21   00−025866

British Library Cataloguing in Publication Data
A CIP catalogue record for this book is available from the British Library.

Typeset in 10/12pt Bembo
by Graphicraft Limited, Hong Kong
Printed in Great Britain by TJ International, Padstow, Cornwall

This book is printed on acid-free paper.

Contents

Preface and Acknowledgments

This book has benefited from the insightful comments of scholars at my own university and in the wider intellectual community. Several colleagues read drafts of one or more chapters and helped to sharpen my thinking on the current state of urban theory, the discourse on globalization, and the transnationalization of social networks. The extensive critiques of various chapters offered by Fred Block and Luis Guarnizo, my close colleagues and traveling companions on the Berkeley to Davis train, are especially appreciated. My departmental colleagues Ted Bradshaw, Frank Hirtz, Bernadette Tarallo, and Miriam Wells also provided helpful suggestions on individual chapters. Robert Beauregard of the Milano Graduate School of the New School for Social Research reviewed several completed draft chapters at a critical juncture. His suggestions influenced the final shape of the story arc of this book. Thanks are also due to Dennis Judd of the University of Illinois at Chicago for the encouraging commentary he provided in his review of several chapters. Finally, I am grateful for the enjoyable exchange of views I have had with planning theorist John Friedmann about his conceptualization of world cities and my formulation of transnational urbanism.

A number of other settings were fruitful contexts for receiving helpful commentary on draft versions of various chapters. These venues, which refined the final product, included the seminars and informal discussions I engaged in as a Visiting Fellow at the International Center for Advanced Studies at New York University, in Fall, 1998; my participation in the British Economic and Social Research Council sponsored conference on "New Approaches to Migration: Transnational Communities and the Transformation of Home" at the University of Sussex in September, 1999; and the following international meetings at which portions of the book were previewed as conference papers: the International Sociological Association World Congress in Montreal in August, 1998; the conference on "Civic Participation and Civil Society" at the Rockefeller Foundation Study and Conference Center, Bellagio, Italy in April, 1999; and the International Symposium on "Transnationalism: Perspectives from Spain, Latin America, and the US" at UCLA in May, 1999.

One of the most enjoyable stages in the production of this book consisted in the meetings I had with the design team of Elizabeth Siverts, Sharie Lesniak, and Laura Rioux, who created the exciting cover design for the book, turning my thoughts on cross-border connectivity into the collage of interconnected images that gives life to my concept of transnational urbanism. My warm thanks go out to them and to my friend and sushi mate Marc Russell of TBWA/ Chiat-Day Advertising in San Francisco for bringing together this creative team to work on the cover design.

In the final stages of preparing the book for publication I also received excellent copy-editing assistance from Jack Messenger of the Redshoes Cooperative in Upton-upon-Severn, UK, and much appreciated assistance in a variety of editorial matters from my graduate research assistant Shannon Seed Hardwicke. My thanks are also extended to my Blackwell editors Susan Rabinowitz and Ken Provencher for their support of this project.

Although most of this book is newly published, parts of some chapters have drawn upon extensively revised versions of work I have published elsewhere. I am grateful to the editors and publishers for permission to use selected materials from the following of my writings: "Postmodernism, Urban Ethnography, and the New Social Space of Ethnic Identity," *Theory & Society*, Vol. 12, No. 4 (1992): 493–531; "Can You Imagine? Transnational Migration and the Globalization of Grassroots Politics," *Social Text* (August 1994): 15–29; "Looking for Globality in Los Angeles," in Ann Cvetkovich and Douglas Kellner (eds), *Articulating the Global and the Local*. Boulder, Col. and Oxford: Westview Press, 1997, 55–71; "The Locations of Transnationalism," in Michael Peter Smith and Luis Guarnizo (eds), *Transnationalism from Below*. New Brunswick, NJ: Transaction Publishers, 1998, 3–34, with Luis Guarnizo; "The Global City: Whose Social Construct is it Anyway?" *Urban Affairs Review*, Vol. 33, No. 4 (March 1998): 482–8; and "Transnationalism and the City," in Robert A. Beauregard and Sophie Body-Gendrot (eds), *The Urban Moment*. Thousand Oaks, Calif.: Sage Publications, 1999, 119–39.

In closing, I would like to express my deep gratitude to my wife Pat. Only she can possibly know the many ways, large and small, in which she has made it possible for me to complete this work. This book is dedicated to her, with all my love.

Michael Peter Smith
Berkeley, California

The Social Construction of Transnational Urbanism

1

When we speak of landscapes of modernity, postmodernity, post-colonialism, consumerism, fear, marginality, or spectacle, we simplify just as radically, and perhaps with no more justification than did Burgess with his bland "commuter zone." [W]e would do well to remember that places and patterns are always more complex than is implied by the way we label them.

Richard Harris and Robert Lewis, "Constructing a Fault(y) Zone"

At the dawn of the twenty-first century we live in a time of accelerated economic and sociocultural change. New modes of global communication have penetrated to even remote hinterlands. New rounds of economic and political instability in what was once unproblematically described as the "periphery" of the "world system" have erupted with the end of the Cold War and the spread of the neoliberal variant of "globalization." These two transnational political developments have displaced millions of economic migrants and political refugees, thereby reconstituting the social structures of many putatively "core" centers of wealth and power.

Transnational flows of migration and cultural practices are inexorably enmeshing the everyday activities of many residents of both "sending" and "receiving" localities in dense and resilient migrant networks that some researchers are now calling "transnational social formations" (see, for example, Basch, Glick Schiller, and Szanton Blanc, 1994; Guarnizo, 1998). The literally overnight dissolution of that social formation we once called the Eastern Bloc has added to the complexity of the world-at-large, thus increasing our sense of confusion about the character of the global context in which "locality" is experienced and lived.

At the same time, despite the claims of some globalization theorists, the state has not withered away as a disappearing relic of the end of modernity. Instead, contemporary national and local states have differentially but ubiquitously mediated the flows of transnational investment, migration, and cultural production through their boundaries. Politically constructed state policies, legitimating discourses, and institutional practices are key elements through which transnational social formations are being constituted. This has added still another dimension of complexity to the picture.

In the face of this complexity, which some have deemed "disorienting," two recentering metaphors of late modernist thinking – the "global city" and the "postmodern city" – have been deployed in urban studies to impose periodicity and patterned regularity on a rapidly changing world. Both of these periodizing narratives assign a central role in urban change to the logic of capital accumulation and the agency of finance capital as instruments of postmodernization. Calling a city "global" or "postmodern" has become a way to invoke and often exaggerate the universalizing power of "late capitalism" (see, for example, Jameson, 1984; Harvey, 1989). In the prevailing discourse on late capitalism, "global" and "local" social process have been framed in binary opposition, as mutually exclusive and inherently antagonistic explanations for urban development which pit local cultures against globalizing economic transformations in the production of material commodities and commodity-signs (see, for example, Harvey, 1989; Castells, 1984, 1997).

This modernist way of framing urban analysis has a long history in urban studies. It reflects the persistence of binary thinking in the social sciences. In these binary frames the global–local binary has been conflated with the universal–particular and the economic–cultural dichotomies. Once these steps are taken we are left with little or no discursive space between various grand narratives of "globalization" – whose very universalism renders them ineffectual as explanatory frameworks for social change – and various postcolonial petite narratives of spontaneous resistance to the global reach of capitalist (post)modernity, whose deployment as markers of "localism" renders them unconvincing wish fulfillments.

It is important to recognize that constructions of the "global" and the "local" are discursively and practically constructed "positionalities" that are appropriated and deployed by specific social forces at particular times; globalization and localization are thus spatial and cultural metaphors embedded in historical time. The social actors and forces represented as operating "globally" (e.g. empires, religious and cultural movements, transnational capitalists) are different at different historical junctures. Moreover, many such actors and processes, both then and now, have actually operated at the more limited scale of historically specific transnational networks of social practice, rather than in a disembedded global space that urban theorist Manuel Castells (1997) has called the "space of flows." As urban geographer Murray Low (1997: 244) has pointed out, even in the economic sphere, "globalization is not a matter of the construction of a 'global' economic space or arena, but of the restructuring and extension of networks of flows (of money, goods, and people) and of their articulation with areal or 'regional' spaces at different scales."

Why Transnational Social Practices?

Like "globalization," other social processes that are dispersed across space and found in many places at the same time, like transnational migrant networks or neoliberal political coalitions, are also temporally and spatially particular, socially constructed relations of power and meaning. To understand social relations such as these with any precision requires us to consider their formation, deployment, and impact as they become localized in single places, articulated with other places in translocal communication circuits, and spread out across societies and national borders. When viewed in this way, the global–local interplay becomes a matter of "locating" both transnationalism and globalization on the ground in all of their untidy contingencies as various projects get constructed, deployed, accommodated to, or resisted in specific times and places.

In this book I make a clear conceptual distinction between "globalization" and "transnationalism." There are good reasons to insist on maintaining this conceptual distinction beyond the obvious one that these two social processes differ in scope, scale, and "reach." Anthropologist Michael Kearney (1995: 548) argues convincingly that discourses on globalization and transnationalism differ significantly in the key assumptions they make about the role of the state in the production of meaning, identity, and social outcomes. While the globalization discourse draws attention to social processes that are "largely decentered from specific national territories," as in the case of Manuel Castells' (1997) discussion of globalization(s) as taking place in a "space of flows," research on *transnational* processes depicts transnational social relations as "anchored in" while also transcending one or more nation-states. For this reason globalization discourses like the "global cities" discourse which I critique in this book, often explicitly assume the growing insignificance of national borders, boundaries, and identities. In contrast, the transnationalist discourse insists on the continuing significance of borders, state policies, and national identities even as these are often transgressed by transnational communication circuits and social practices.

Unlike the globalization discourse, which maintains a kind of zero-sum assumption, in which globalization and the nation-state are treated as mutually exclusive and antagonistically related conceptual categories, theorists of transnationalism tend to treat the nation-state and transnational practices as mutually *constitutive* rather than mutually exclusive social formations (Basch, Glick Schiller, and Szanton-Blanc, 1994; Smith, 1994; Smith and Guarnizo, 1998; Schein, 1998a, 1998b). For example, the anthropologist of transnational cultural formations, Louisa Schein, has effectively taken to task those who would conceptualize transnational practices by marking them and the nation-state as mutually exclusive entities or even as antagonistically locked in a competition for paradigmatic primacy. "Why instead," argues Schein (1998b: 169–70), "can these debates not work toward imagining nation-state and transnational as interlocked, enmeshed, mutually constituting? In the process nation and state would need to be vigilantly delinked, making room for the notion of deterritorialized nationalisms, loosed from their moorings in the bounded unit of the territorial state, and coalescing at both local and translocal levels."

In these transnational times what Albert Hirschman (1970) has termed the "exit option" has been especially prominent, as people experiencing untenable economic and political conditions in their places of origin engage in transnational migration to develop economic and cultural resources spanning national borders. Transnational households, kinship networks, and village-based information circuits have played an active and creative role in the social organization and channeling of these migration flows. Because these forms of exit are not permanent erasures of people's past social ties and because new means of communication and travel have facilitated back-and-forth flows of people, ideas, exchanges of material resources, and multi-sited projects, these social networks in migration "from below" have widely expanded the scope and geographical scale of translocal ties.

As we shall see in subsequent chapters of this book, social networks of transnational migrants comprise one of the key circuits of communicative action connecting localities beyond borders and constituting translocal ties across the globe. Hirschman has compared the exit option to what he calls the "voice option" as ways in which business firms deal with perceived threats in their organizational environments. His distinction may be applied fruitfully to the ways in which other micro-level actors such as households, neighborhoods, ethnic minorities, grassroots political organizations, and other putatively "marginal" social interests cope with perceived threats to their members' lives and livelihoods. For example, the political activities of networks of local households often constitute self-organized grassroots initiatives giving voice to demands for redress when the essential fabric of everyday life is jeopardized by perceived threats such as the environmental or economic effects of global capital restructuring. Examples include food riots and other mobilizations on city streets, university campuses, and rural town squares as forms of popular resistance to the state policies enacted in response to IMF austerity policies. The Zapatista rebellion in Chiapas, Mexico and its transnational ripple effects further illustrate that political voice is now often exercised by groups capable of *jumping scales* of social practice and transcending political borders, moving from the local to the transnational scale as new means of communication like faxes, e-mail, and the internet enable the connection of differently situated "local" actors with other "local" actors who share their objectives to constitute "transnational" communication circuits and political projects. (For other lucid examples see Keck and Sikkink, 1998.) The operation of social networks "from below" through the mechanisms of transnational migration and political mobilization thus provides one important answer to the more general question of how sociocultural and political–economic forces articulate with the politics of everyday life at local, national, and transnational scales throughout the world.

Why "Transnational Urbanism"?

I have chosen to use the metaphor "transnational urbanism" rather than "transnational localism" or "glocalization" to designate the articulations under consideration in this book. It captures a sense of the wide range of possibilities for social change that we usually associate with urban life, even though some of the particular changes discussed in this book are taking place in Mexican villages (Goldring, 1998; R. Smith, 1998), or in Chinese factory towns (Smart and Smart, 1998), or in the countryside (Schein, 1998a), as well as in urban centers throughout the world. This metaphor was chosen because the forging of *translocal* connections and the social construction of transnational social ties generally require the maintenance of social relations that are sustained in one of two ways. Either (a) transnational social actors are materially connected to socioeconomic opportunities, political structures, or cultural practices found in cities at some point in their transnational communication circuit, (e.g. transnational cities as sources of migrant employment, the means to deploy remittances, the acquisition of cultural and physical capital, consumption practices, political organizing networks, or lifestyle images); or (b) they maintain transnational connections by using advanced means of communication and travel, which because of their simultaneity, indirectly implicate transnational actors in an orbit of cosmopolitan ideas, images, technologies, and sociocultural practices that have historically been associated with the culture of cities. "Transnational urbanism" is thus a cultural rather than a strictly geographic metaphor. I use the term as a marker of the criss-crossing transnational circuits of communication and cross-cutting local, translocal, and transnational social practices that "come together" in particular places at particular times and enter into the contested politics of place-making, the social construction of power differentials, and the making of individual, group, national, and transnational identities, and their corresponding fields of difference.

Why Agency-oriented Urban Theory?

A central purpose of this book is to place the study of urbanization and urbanism squarely within an agency-oriented theoretical perspective that concretely connects macro-economic and geopolitical transformations to the micro-networks of social action that people create, move in, and act upon in their daily lives. It is a central assumption of this book that the accumulation strategies of capitalist logics, structures, and actors, to which many urban analysts devote so much attention, are not the sole, or at times even the most important, agencies in the constitution of urban life. As important, if not more so, has been the impact of ordinary women and men – their consciousness, intentionality, everyday practices, and collective action – on the social construction of urban life.

This does not mean that investigating the "agency" of ordinary men and women is a transparent social process. People's intentions and actions, and the meanings given to them, are derived from human experience. As positioned subjects, occupying multiple social locations, people often experience inner tensions and conflicts in forming their own sense of agency. As Meaghan Morris (1993: 39) has noted, "there is something tinny about theories of 'agency', and demands for theories 'of' agency, that enunciatively erase a sense of the messiness of living and acting in the mediated world of today."

Despite the difficulties involved in sorting out all of the untidy contingencies involved in moving from acting subjectivity to conscious human agency, the quest for an agency-oriented urban research and practice is nonetheless preferable to resolutely maintaining a global gaze which focuses our consciousness disproportionately upon the global economy, reified as a pre-given "thing," existing outside of thought, whose developmental logic not only fully explains the development of cities but even determines the subjectivity of their inhabitants, without ever interrogating them about what they are up to. As Stuart Hall (1991: 58–9) has said:

> People are not cultural dopes. . . . They know something about who they are. . . .
> And that notion of politics which . . . increasingly is able to address people
> through the multiple identities which they have – understanding that these
> identities . . . are frequently contradictory, that they cross-cut one another, that
> they tend to locate us differently at different moments, conducting politics in
> light of the contingent, in the face of the contingent – is the only political game
> that the locals have at their disposal.

The historically and ethnographically grounded studies discussed throughout this book have been selected for discussion precisely because they take seriously Stuart Hall's call for a contingent political analysis of the practices of everyday life and more importantly because they stretch that analysis to encompass a transnational imaginary. Let me briefly illustrate the theoretical relevance of such practically grounded narrative interventions into the often all too abstract realm of urban theory. Nestor Rodriguez and Jacquelyn Hagan (1992; see also Rodriguez, 1995; Hagan, 1994) have conducted ethnographically grounded, historically situated, and insightful studies into the everyday life experiences of transnational migrant men and women moving back and forth between various localities in Central America and Houston, Texas in the last two decades of the twentieth century. Their research efforts well illustrate the usefulness of human-agency driven urban ethnographic research while also recognizing the importance of contingent circumstances in the production of urban life. Their studies pay close attention to an ever changing transnational context as well as to the local practices by which people make sense of and act upon that changing context. Viewed contextually, in the 1980s over 100,000 undocumented Salvadorans, Guatemalans, Nicaraguans, and Hondurans, fleeing Cold War inspired economic and political turmoil in their countries of origin, migrated to metropolitan Houston. This period of transnational migration precisely coincided with a sharp decline in Houston's oil-based economy driven by an over supply of oil on world markets. The migrants were largely absorbed into Houston's secondary labor market, which continued to expand despite the decline of the city's overall economy. Working in this historical context, in one of their collaborative studies Rodriguez and Hagan chose a participant-observation ethnographic approach to study closely the evolving interactions between groups of long-time black, white, and Latino residents of an apartment complex on Houston's west side and a group of newly arrived Central American transnational migrants who had been attracted to the complex by the lowered rents offered by its owners and managers as the Houston economy went into decline. Hagan became a tenant in the complex prior to their two-year study. Rodriguez and Hagan's study describes in detail how the new transnational migrants used their social networks to take advantage of the opportunity provided by the lowered rents. These social actors developed strategies such as expense sharing, complex new household formation, and teaching newcomers how to negotiate established institutions to enable themselves not only to survive in an inhospitable economic climate but to appropriate neighborhood space for their own uses.

Subsequently, as Houston's overall economy began to rebound, the owners and managers of the apartment complex tried to restructure its occupancy a second time by selectively upgrading units and amenities and raising rents, while downgrading facilities in the building where most of the new migrants lived. The most fascinating part of Rodriguez and Hagan's study deals with the various ways in which the transnational migrants moved beyond the boundaries of their transnational networks by forging social relations with the locally-based networks of established residents to frustrate, circumvent, and at times even to openly resist the landlord's efforts to displace them. In Rodriguez and Hagan's study a single apartment complex on Houston's west side became a kind of imploded social space where the Central American transnational migrants became a group acting for itself, and in coalition with established residents, adapted to and resisted broad structural changes impeding their everyday lives. By their local social actions the transnational migrants living in this complex both materially and symbolically modified their everyday conditions of existence.

Other ethnographic research conducted separately by Hagan (1994) and Rodriguez (1995) has carefully documented the ways in which transnational migrants living in Houston in the 1980s and 1990s actively maintained social relations with kinship and locality-based social networks in their communities of origin in Guatemala and El Salvador, as well as Mexico. These studies detail numerous socioeconomic and political changes in the "sending" communities attributable to the flow of money, goods, ideas, and meanings circulated by means of these transnational networks of social practice. Taken together, the multi-sited ethnographic research efforts of Rodriguez and Hagan reveal a few facets of the complex, criss-crossing, contingent character of "place-making" in transnational times that I have chosen to call "transnational urbanism." In subsequent chapters I will flesh out other facets of the social process of transnational place-making and its implications for urban theory and research.

On Social Constructionism

A word or two is in order at this point about my use of "social constructionism" in this book. As I understand this approach to theory-building, I view social constructionism as a meta-theoretical approach to social analysis that makes four key assumptions about the relationship between social theory, social practice, and our understanding of the world in which we live. First, the social theories we use are largely constitutive of the reality we see, tell stories about, and act upon. My reading of social constructionism is thus comfortable with Anaïs Nin's insight that "We don't see things as they are, we see things as we are." Second, it follows from this that, unlike other social theories deployed in urban studies, whether neo-Marxist or neoliberal in inspiration, my approach assumes that the "structures" which social analysts represent as pre-given contexts for social action, e.g. the market (Tiebout, 1956), globalization (Castells, 1984, 1997; Sassen, 1991), the world system (Wallerstein, 1979), late capitalism (Jameson, 1984), or the postmodern urban form (Soja, 1989; Dear and Flusty, 1998), as well as the agents deemed to be important makers of these structures, e.g. the global capitalist class (Sklair, 1998) or state-centered agencies (Gurr and King, 1987), are *both* socially constructed understandings of how the world works. These understandings are produced by historically specific discourses and practices, including not only the discourses and practices of social theorists, but those of political and economic elites, as well as ordinary men and women, all situated in different "subject positions" (Laclau and Mouffe, 1985) at the nodal points of heterogeneous circuits of communication. Discursively and practically constructed understandings of how the world works, when widely accepted as truths in contests over power, meaning, difference, and identity, can produce, reproduce, or transform the contours of the patterned regularities we call "structures." Put differently, social subjects give meaning to their lives through the networks of communication in which they are involved and through which they constitute themselves, their identities, and their relations to social structures. The "structures" in turn are thus constituted by social practices informed by intersubjective understandings.

Given these assumptions, my own practice of social constructionism in urban theory requires a third move, namely a theoretical effort to uncover the explicit and implicit assumptions about how the world works found by close observation of the actual practices of social actors, including their theoretical, discursive, and material practices. The means of close observation that I have chosen to deploy include not only close textual analyses of the works of urban social theorists, but also the use of political, historical, and ethnographic vignettes to narrate and draw theoretical lessons from the socioeconomic, political, and cultural practices of those social actors that I think are constructing the transnational world we are ushering in as the new millennium begins.

My fourth guiding assumption in writing this book is that the project of social constructionism does not end with a deconstruction of the urban social theories I have chosen to critique. Nor does it end with a close mapping of the discourses and practices that constitute the world of social practice that I seek to understand and narrate. In my view, the careful practice of social constructionism also entails a responsibility to offer an alternative construction of how the world works and an epistemological way forward for studying this construction. In short, my aim is to create a new discursive space for social inquiry into a key dimension of human existence and social practice that I am seeking to explicate, namely, the changing social forms, cultural practices, and politics of urban life at the present historical moment.

The Architectonics Ahead

This book is divided into two major parts. The first is deconstructive of the globalization discourse in urban theory. The second is reconstitutive of a transnational imaginary in urban research. Part I, "Locating Globalization," consists of three chapters. Part II, "Reconstructing Urban Theory," consists of four chapters. The book ends with an epilogue in which I use the epistemological imaginary developed in Part II to take the reader on a brief tour of some of the new sites of transnational urbanism revealed by deploying this imaginary, and tease out the connections constituting transnational urban politics in New York and Los Angeles.

Locating Globalization

The central purpose of Part I of this book is to critically deconstruct three key globalization discourses that have been influential in urban theory. These discourses have three elements in common that led to their selection for critical scrutiny. In explaining "globalization" each privileges economic over political and sociocultural processes. In discussing opposition to economic globalization each also privileges class over all other social relations and identities, as if the social relations of class, ethnicity, race, and gender were easily separable parts of lived experience. Finally, because each, in different ways, focuses resolutely on structural transformations while giving scant attention to the discursive and material *practices* by which people create the regularized patterns that enable and constrain them, these discourses lack an effective theory of political agency, or any other kind of agency. In chapters 2 through 4 I focus on the three major strains of urban theorizing that have equated the "global" with the space of top-down political–economic power relations and reduced the "local" to a site of either class polarization or ineffectual cultural resistance to the inexorable march of global capitalism. These chapters deconstruct the central theoretical motifs found in the writings of David Harvey, John Friedmann, Saskia Sassen, and the Los Angeles school of urban studies that have become virtual mantras to the omnipotence of capital in the formation of cities and the constitution of human subjectivities. These are the "time-space compression" imaginary, the "global city" metaphor, and the "postmodern urbanism" paradigm. Each of these motifs has been an influential theme in urban theory, having been invoked by numerous urban researchers to give their empirical work a theoretical gloss, while devoting scant attention to the theoretical origins of these ideas, the constraints entailed in their use as conceptual frames, or the practical political implications of their frequent use.

In chapter 2 I turn my attention to the intellectual confines of David Harvey's urban theory and try to offer some useful ways to move beyond these confines in both urban theorizing and everyday political practice. I focus critical attention foremost on Harvey's meta-theoretical quest for "foundational" knowledge which leads him to posit a functionalist theory of capital accumulation and a superstructural conceptualization of "culture" which radically separates economic from cultural practice and subordinates the latter to the former. For Harvey, the deeper economic "imperatives" of the global reorganization of capitalism have produced a new urban spatiotemporal experience which he terms the condition of postmodernity. This new age of hypermobile economic, spatial, and cultural change is depicted as producing a social and psychic state of "time-space compression" which causes people, independently of their social locations, to experience a sense of malaise and ontological insecurity often expressed in episodic outbursts of identity politics. Harvey discounts these forms of oppositional politics as purely "local" moves that lead to political dead-ends because they frustrate the development of a putatively universal or global class consciousness.

In my view, "culture" is an ever-changing product of human practices rather than a reflection of "deeper" economic imperatives. In chapter 2, starting from this assumption, I critique David Harvey's silences and dismissals of cultural and spatial practices "from below" that may be interpreted as creative adaptations to changing structural opportunities and constraints. Harvey, for example, reduces the practices of transnational migrant networks which celebrate their ethnic identities to the epiphenomenal status of "ritual" participation in "staged" urban ethnic festivals which, in his view, necessarily sap migrant political energies and mask their "real" class interests. This instance is one case in point of Harvey's easy dismissal of the political significance of all of the so-called "new social movements" that deploy discourses on behalf of race, ethnic and gender formations, environmentalism, human rights, or other identities. I fault Harvey's political theorizing for failing to come to terms with people's situatedness in the world – the situatedness of their knowledge as well as their unique positionality *vis-à-vis* the "discursive spaces," i.e. the social networks, political institutions, and social relations of race, ethnicity, and gender, as well as class – through which they become acting social and political subjects. Harvey's theoretical privileging of class over all other possible social relations and identities causes him to dismiss many potential political allies as weak, partial, irrational, and worse still as purely local.

My critique of David Harvey calls attention to the contingent construction of political identities as solidarities and oppositions are formed in and through people's interactions in particular discursive spaces, i.e. in particular networks and circuits of communication that are both media and outcomes of their practices (M. P. Smith, 1989). Viewed in this light, oppositional politics becomes more than a zero-sum game: ethnic and gender consciousness does not automatically subtract from class awareness. In actual practice, connections are often made by new political subjects between their class, ethnic, gender, and cultural identities and the politics of production, status, power, and culture. Lacking both a theory of the state and civil society and an understanding of the situated character of knowledge production and, hence, political agency, Harvey casts his global gaze upon the dynamics of capital, viewed as a whole and anthropomorphized as a unitary agent, which, by means of "globalization" and the fashioning of an "interrelated and ultimately global network of cities" realizes "*its own agenda* of accumulation for accumulation's sake" (emphasis added). A world socially constructed in this way views reality in terms strangely reminiscent of modernization theory, as a necessarily binary opposition between the advanced and the underdeveloped, the global and the local: the global as the triumphal space of top-down restructuring by anthropomorphized capital and the local as a backward site of "place-bound identities" and a "reactionary politics of aestheticized spatiality" (Harvey, 1989: 305).

There is little or no room in this kind of world to ask such questions as: What new oppositional spaces might be opened up by global economic restructuring? What "local" subjectivities, practices, or projects might partake in or even be partially constituted by transnational practices and processes initiated by actors other than multinational capitalists, e.g. migrant networks, religious movements, human rights advocates? How are spaces for new political possibilities being created in historically specific places as people discursively constitute the complex interplay between local, national, and transnational conditions and effects? These questions, which cannot even be raised within the confines of David Harvey's urban theory, will be addressed, and I hope at least partly answered, in subsequent chapters of this book.

Chapter 3 addresses a second major strand of globalization theory in urban studies, the "global cities" discourse, particularly as found in the work of John Friedmann and Saskia Sassen. These global cities theorists deploy a grand narrative of global capital restructuring that is less explicitly rooted in Marxist analytical categories than is the work of David Harvey. Particularly in the case of Sassen, these theorists offer empirical evidence in support of their theoretical claims. Nevertheless, the global cities theorists provide an incomplete social construction of globalization which privileges the functional logics of global capital "from above" while failing to address, or even acknowledge the presence of, myriad local and transnational practices "from below" which now cut across urban landscapes, producing disorderly, unexpected, and irretrievably contingent urban outcomes that do not sit well with the metaphors of urban hierarchy and social polarization envisioned in the global cities discourse. My critique of Friedmann and Sassen's urban theories recognizes some useful aspects of their work, but faults their functionalist reasoning and their tendency to reify the "global city" as if it were a "thing" existing outside of thought, rather than a socially constructed and hence unavoidably partial way of representing urban change.

Moving beyond economism, my argument in chapter 3 turns next to a discussion of the limits of economic globalization. My discussion seeks to situate and thus "locate" contemporary processes of "globalization" politically. Important limits upon the "global reach" of multinational capital which undermine key assumptions of the global cities discourse are identified. In order to historicize the analysis of "global cities," the theorized "newness" of factors deemed to be driving forces in the emergence of global cities is called into question. The global cities discourse is then viewed within the contemporary historical context of the wider discourse on "global governance" driven by those who would legitimate the ideology of neoliberalism as a worldwide public philosophy.

Chapter 3 ends by offering a series of vignettes intended to capture some of the flavor of an alternative, more dynamic approach to urban studies that I call "transnational urbanism." These vignettes highlight several transnational political developments that found expression in the 1990s. I discuss, in turn, the formation of a cross-border political coalition of international unions, NGOs, and transnational grassroots activists who successfully imposed restrictions on a major transnational corporation; the enmeshment of the recently deposed Suharto regime in Indonesia in the contradictions of neoliberalism because of transnational pressures "from above" and "from below"; and the political impacts of a recent round of anti-IMF protests in Seoul, Korea which directly challenged IMF austerity policies imposed on the South Korean state and indirectly contributed to the creation of an international political climate that has forced both the IMF and the World Bank to reconsider their rigid pursuit of the neoliberal global governance agenda. These vignettes clearly illustrate that transnational social space is a contested terrain rather than an exclusive preserve of multinational capital.

Perhaps no metropolis in recent memory has been subject to more labels intended to capture its essence than contemporary Los Angeles. It has been deemed a paradigmatic "global" or "world city," labeled the twentieth-century "capital of capital," inscribed as a decentered "postmodern" hyper-space, and decried for its social climate of fear, loathing, and spectacle. In chapter 4 I question these efforts to represent Los Angeles as something entirely new in the history of capitalism and urban development. The top-down social imaginary shared by the global cities theorists and the LA school of urban studies theorists alike, depicts contemporary Los Angeles as an economic and sociocultural resultant of the workings of "the global economy," conceived as an external reality, rather than as a process constituted by thought. In place of this imaginary I offer a more historicized political–economic and sociocultural reading of Los Angeles "from the ground up" that attempts to capture key features of LA's transnational urbanism, while freeing our theoretical imagination from the need to represent urban change in terms of evolutionary "stages" of economic development.

My telling of the LA story pays close attention to the past influences of state policy changes, particularly the legacy of US foreign and military expansionism during the Cold War, the impact of defense downsizing since the Cold War's end, the permissions and constraints of US immigration policies, Mexican state policies affecting the character of transnational migration from Mexico, and the effects of transnational neoliberal initiatives like NAFTA. Starting from a poststructuralist emphasis on the ubiquity and multi-positionality of power relations, I focus on the interplay of the macro-politics of such state policy-making, the cultural politics of transnational media representations of

Los Angeles, and the micro-politics of transnational migrant social networks in reconstituting the racial and ethnic landscape of contemporary Los Angeles. My approach seeks to explain the contemporary sociospatial diversity of Los Angeles in terms of a criss-crossing of heterogeneous, sometimes linked and sometimes disjointed, social processes, rather than viewing the city's spatial decentering and multicultural complexity as a differentiating mask deployed by multinational capital to conceal the underlying economic unity of the postmodern metropolis.

Once this framework for viewing social change in contemporary Los Angeles is established, the second half of chapter 4 turns to two dimensions of LA's "transnational urbanism" that are constituting the kind of city it is becoming at the beginning of a new century. I first try to deconstruct the dynamics of ethnic, class, and gender relations within the emergent "ethnic economy" of contemporary Los Angeles. My purpose here is to move beyond romanticized images of "communitarianism" sometimes used to characterize the economic arrangements found in business clusters owned by transnational migrant entrepreneurs, or to erase the modes of surplus extraction, gender inequality, and class, cultural, and political differentiation found in hetero-geneous ethnic enclaves mislabeled as "transnational communities" (e.g. in the recent work of Portes, 1996a, 1996b). Chapter 4 ends with a narrative account of the social construction and transformation of one such ethnic formation, the Los Angeles neighborhood of "Koreatown," over the past three decades. The story narrates the contradictions of transnational entre-preneurialism, depicts the transnational dimension of localized struggles over livelihood and place-making, and describes forms of transnational grassroots social activism that infuse our understanding of everyday life in contemporary Los Angeles with a degree of social dynamism "from below" that contradicts LA school representations of "immigrant labor" in the city as an occupation-ally manipulable "subject population" (Soja, 1986: 266).

Reconstructing Urban Theory

Chapter 5 shifts from the global to the local level of analysis. The chapter revisits what has sometimes been termed the "locality" debate in urban theory. In seeking to move urban studies firmly beyond naturalistic and communitarian conceptions of "locality," I begin my analysis by showing that the conceptual-ization of the global–local interplay by leading urban theorists David Harvey and Manuel Castells tends to reify the terms in this dialectic. This reification thereby produces a binary framework in which the global is represented as the site of history's dynamic flows and economic driving forces, while the local is seen as an inexorable site of the production of cultural meanings, leading to the creation of social movements of reaction (Harvey) or resistance (Castells).

I then show that this way of representing locality overlooks the extent to which transnational networks of social practice are constituted by their interrelations with and groundedness *within* localities.

My reconstruction of localities as sites of transnational connections builds upon (but departs in important ways from) the work of feminist geographer Doreen Massey. Likewise my effort to rethink the connections between place and culture draws upon but also critically reformulates selected dimensions of cultural anthropologists Akhil Gupta and James Ferguson's efforts to develop a mode of transnational ethnographic practice suitable for investigating the shifting borders and boundaries of difference-generating power relations across transnationally linked spaces. Their analysis of the contingent construction of "community" and "otherness" within and across local social formations is a useful antidote to binary constructions of "authentic community" vs. "staged capitalist landscapes" too often informing discourses like the "heritage debate" in urban theory (e.g. see Harvey, 1989 and Zukin, 1991). Yet my own interpretation of the work of Massey, Gupta, and Ferguson suggests that even these imaginative and nuanced scholars at times impose a theoretical *a priori* hierarchical ordering upon the power relations they seek to understand, rather than viewing them as contingent and changeable outcomes of struggles over the politics of representation.

Later in chapter 5 I turn to some of the everyday realms of representational politics where imagined communities are being constituted by an interplay of local and transnational discourses and practices such as those now coming together in British Muslim urban neighborhoods and in New York's Chinatown. My purpose is to free the notion of everyday life from its frequent association with purely local processes or with a fixed local level of analysis. My discussion of the social construction of these imagined communities, as in the case of my earlier discussion of Koreatown in Los Angeles, illustrates key points of articulation in contemporary urban politics and culture, where "placemaking" within bounded political jurisdictions overlaps with a transnationalized, network-based conception of politics and social life. The final step in my critical examination of the role of locality in urban theory turns to the realm of urban research, with the aim of developing a carefully historicized political–economic and ethnographic imagination, capable of capturing the socially constructed character of urban political life under conditions of contemporary transnationalism.

This epistemological project is continued in chapter 6, which enters into and attempts to reshape the debate on postmodernism in urban theory. The chapter sets aside, for the sake of clarity, the issue of postmodernism as an aesthetic and literary style. This is because, in my view, a carefully scripted social theoretical argument, that some may view as decidedly "modernist," is required to reach my intended audience of urban scholars in the social and human sciences. Since I have already comprehensively critiqued postmodernism as a teleological periodizing device in earlier chapters, I turn to the question of postmodernism as an epochal totality only briefly at the beginning of chapter 6. The main questions addressed in this chapter are the usefulness of a post-structuralist theoretical approach in urban theory and the limitations of the turn to "postmodern ethnography" as a method of urban research. My aim is to show that, despite the hyperbolic uses of the discourse on postmodernity in urban studies, some of the poststructuralist conceptual and epistemological innovations in the social sciences, also sometimes loosely deployed under the rubric "postmodern," provide us with an opportunity to imagine cities as dynamic crossroads of human practice.

In chapter 6 I draw upon the insights of such poststructuralist social theorists as Ernesto Laclau, Chantal Mouffe, and Michael Shapiro, as well as the work of selected critical anthropologists, to engage and reconfigure the discourse on the social construction of "new subject positions," "situated knowledges," and "identities put at risk," so that these theoretical formulations may articulate usefully with the field of urban studies at the current transnational moment. My aim is to rethink the project of postmodern ethnography by examining how ethnographic research projects are actually being reconfigured at the dawn of the millennium into a multi-sited, translocal, and transnational mode of research practice capable of making sense of the socially constructed *networks of power and meaning* which account for the shifting boundaries of place and identity.

Chapter 6 further extends the discussion begun in chapter 5 of how we might combine such a workable mode of transnational ethnographic practice with a truly historicized political economy of urban change to move urban studies along a navigable path in the years ahead. In advocating this recombinant methodological approach, I argue that it is important that we not lose sight of the presencing of the past in the worlds people come to "know," or of the fact that the discursive and material practices through which intersubjective knowledge is formed are always embedded in social relations of power and meaning that readily privilege some representations of the "out there" while impeding others. It is important to keep this in mind to avoid the easy privileging of "intersubjective dialogue" or sanctifying the "postcolonial subject." In my view, some postmodern ethnographers have displaced old master narratives of colonialism and capitalist hegemony with a new master narrative in which populist voices "from the margins" are released from bondage by the skillful ethnographer and become decontextualized, ventriloquized voices of postcolonial resistance. It is thus crucial, I argue, to become aware of the circuits of communication and theoretical practice in which not only the ethnographic subject but also the "subject position" of the researcher is constituted.

The valorization of "hybridity" as a basic marker of postcolonial subjectivity is a key theme in postmodern cultural studies. In the final section of chapter 6, I address the tension between the postmodern conception of identity formation as free-floating and the research findings in the growing field of transnational studies in which the identities formed in and through transnational families, translocal social networks, cross-border social movements, and multilateral interorganizational coalitions are very much embedded in socially structured and politically mediated processes of group formation and collective action. By distinguishing between the level of individual consciousness and the level of structured fields or discursive venues, I show that it is possible to view individual selfhood as fragmented and in contention, precisely because in forming a "self" people move over time and across space through different socially structured discursive spaces (e.g. village space, occupational space, neighborhood space, metropolitan space, racialized and gendered space, and the spaces of policing, enjoyment, education, consumption, worship, and alternative venues of political life) which affect the construction of personal consciousness of self and others, and hence of collective identities and projects. As in other chapters, key theoretical arguments advanced in chapter 6 are supported by reference to historicized vignettes illustrating how subjectivity and collective action are socially constructed by everyday social practices in diverse translocal contexts. Examples include the emergent subject positioning linking civil disobedience on the streets of New York City to political activities in Guinea, and the ethnic and class identities formed by indigenous Mixtec transmigrants moving back and forth between localities in California and Oaxaca, Mexico, in the emergent political venue anthropologist Michael Kearney (1995) terms "Oaxacalifornia."

Kearney's reconceptualization of spatial scales provides an excellent example of social theorist Alberto Melucci's (1995) more general argument, voiced in the epigram to chapter 7, that the emergence of a transnational dimension to issues and social agents "is a sign of the fact that human action is now capable of culturally creating its own space." While the jumping of political scales from the local to the transnational social scale is no easy task, the aim of chapter 7 is precisely to rethink the locations of "grassroots" social movements.

Chapter 7 begins by revisiting the localist and communitarian assumptions about grassroots politics found in Manuel Castells' influential book *The City and the Grassroots*. Moving beyond Castells' binary local–global social imaginary, the chapter takes the study of grassroots politics from the local to the transnational scale of analysis and social practice. I argue that the spatial dispersal of cultural production and reception through such mechanisms as transnational migrant networks, globalization of the media of mass communications, and the forging of transnational political connections, has opened up a new social space for conducting urban research. This new space is a translocal, multi-sited, spatially reconfigured world of cross-cutting social networks "from below" as well as "in between," formed by social actors engaged in a reterritorialized politics of place-making. How and why migrants, exiles, refugees, diasporas, ethnic formations, political activists, and other "transnationals" actively maintain the socially extended social relations around which they orchestrate their lives is a central question driving this new mode of research on transnational grassroots politics. How actors situated in such transnational political networks interact with actors, networks, and structures of power that are more locally and nationally based is a second key question that locates the first squarely within the domain of transnational urbanism.

To address these interrelated questions concretely, the second half of chapter 7 pays close attention to the actual practices of several transnational grassroots movements that emerged in the 1990s. The purpose of this turn to the realm of practice is to move our political imaginary beyond the confining limits of the global–local binary in urban social theory, in which the global economy is opposed to local culture and urban politics is reduced to the glib slogan "Think globally, act locally." Through a close analysis of the transnational political practices of Guatemalan refugees, opponents of US military interventionism in Central America, the Mixtec political formations in the US and Mexico discussed earlier, and a coalition of immigrant, refugee, and women's rights organizations in many transnational cities throughout the world, I show that the world in which we are now living is much more complex and interwoven than this duality would suggest. Some of the social activists in the stories I tell in chapter 7 "think locally" while jumping scales and acting globally. Others are bifocal border crossers, coalescing from many national and local geographical locations to think transnationally while acting multi-locally. Still other "transnationals" practice what I call "the politics of simultaneity," working to genderize the political discourse on human rights and the legal framework in which it is deployed internationally and within particular urban and national formations. In this mode of political practice single political acts are orchestrated toward multiple targets at a variety of institutional and geographical scales. The global media of mass communications are appropriated by a transnational coalition of rights organizations to enact a multi-scaled political project simultaneously. In the world that is unfolding as the new millennium begins, the state and its monopoly over the means of coercion have certainly not disappeared. But the construction of new scales of political practice has certainly complicated state-centered projects which rely solely on force to command loyalty.

The changing role of state and nation under conditions of transnational urbanism is one of the key themes taken up in chapter 8. This chapter brings together the various strands of my argument that transnational urbanism, while more complex and at times even elusive, is nonetheless a more fruitful optic for guiding urban research than the global cities, "time-space compression," and postmodern urbanism frameworks. Starting from a multidimensional conception of contemporary transnationalism, chapter 8 addresses four interrelated themes: the agency of transnational networks, the rise of translocalities, the continuing significance of the state and nationalist projects in the social construction of transnationalism, and the development of a comparative urban research agenda suitable for studying transnational urbanism.

In addressing the first theme I foreground the continuing significance of cities as sites of transnational practices, contexts of transnational network formation, socially structured settings for social interaction, and mediators of the power, meaning, and effects of transnational flows "from above" as well as "from below." In my discussion of the rise of translocalities I highlight the need to focus upon historically specific "translocal" (i.e. local to local) social relations of power and meaning when studying the actual origins and effects of transnational social networks, economic ties, or political mobilizations. It is these translocal relations that form the multifaceted connections linking transnational actors, the localities to which they direct flows (of meaning, remittances, investment, political pressure, etc.), and their points of origin. The specificity and contingency of these ties is discussed by comparing the findings of a growing body of ethnographic, political–economic, and historical research on transnational connections. (Compare, for example, Smart and Smart, 1998, with Mitchell, 1993, 1996, on different translocal circuits of Hong Kong Chinese investment along the Pacific Rim; and Smart and Smart 1998, in turn, with Schein, 1998a, on different modes of transnational penetration of different regions and localities in China.)

The third theme of chapter 8 questions those theories of transnationalism (e.g. Appadurai, 1996) that have suggested that we are now moving into a "postnational" phase of the global cultural economy. Nationalism is very much alive as a political project not only of state formations but of transnational political diasporas and ethnic formations within existing states. Nationalism can be seen as well in the current efforts by many nation-states that have experienced substantial out-migration in recent decades to go to great lengths to develop discourses and institutional mechanisms designed to actively promote the reincorporation of transnational migrants into their state-centered projects – to "recapture," so to speak, migrant remittances, investments, and loyalties, as state agencies themselves transnationalize the meaning of nationhood. (For discourses and practices developed in this respect by India, Mexico, Columbia, El Salvador, and Haiti, see Lessinger, 1992; Goldring, 1998; Guarnizo, 1998; M. P. Smith, 1994; Mahler, 1998; and Glick Schiller and Fouron, 1998.) Moreover, agents of receiving states remain quite capable of reconstituting the meaning of transnational flows of people, cultural practices, ideas, and even money entering their political jurisdictions as undesirable "boundary penetrations" that must be controlled. Paradoxically, then, the expansion of transnational connections has contributed to the reigniting of essentialist nationalisms in both sending and receiving localities and states.

In the final analysis, how do we make sense of the paradoxes of transnationalism in urban studies? In the second half of chapter 8 I propose a comparative historical and ethnographic research agenda to provide a clear direction for the epistemological approach I have sought to develop in this book. I recommend three modes of comparative analysis: comparing the practices and effects of different transnational networks in the same city; comparing the practices and effects of particular transnational networks in different cities across space; and comparing different localizations of the neoliberal project of fiscal austerity and global governance. Each of these modes of comparative research is fleshed out by reference to either existing transnational ethnographies or my own historicized reading of the political economy of neoliberalism, both of which have been written to "locate" transnationalism on the ground as different transnational networks, practices, and projects currently unfold before our eyes, ears, and imaginations.

PART I

Locating Globalization

The Local as Globalism's "Other": The Confines of the Master Narrative of Time-Space Compression

2

Any transformation of capitalism opens up a range of possibilities that are not just determined by the endogenous logic of capitalist forms, but also by the latter's constitutive outside and by the whole historical situation in which those logics operate. Inasmuch as capitalism always has a constitutive outside, its domination can never be merely imposed through the internal development of its logic, but must be imposed through the hegemonization of something radically exterior to itself. In which case, capitalism must be seen . . . as a system of power. . . . The more dislocated is the ground on which capitalism operates, the less it can rely on a framework of stable social and political relations and the more central this political moment of hegemonic construction will be; but for that very reason, the more extensive the range of political possibilities opposed to capitalist hegemonization will also be.

Ernesto Laclau, New Reflections on the Revolution of Our Time

David Harvey is among the most influential urban theorists of the past three decades. Harvey's political–economic theorizing has produced the most comprehensive and consistent body of structural Marxist urban theory in the literature of urban studies. His writings on the urban impacts of economic globalization have deeply inscribed the concept of time-space compression as a metaphor for the way in which contemporary capitalism has increased the pace of life and overcome spatial barriers to capital accumulation by globally reorganizing processes of production, consumption, and exchange. His cultural theorizing, derived from his political–economic model, is preoccupied with the global spread of the cultural condition of postmodernity as a consequence of this "annihilation of space by time." Harvey's work thus may be read as a dystopian form of modernist social theory, one that links and at times conflates the processes of modernization, globalization, and urban development.

In Harvey's urban theory, as in the case of earlier theories of modernity, a powerful cultural logic, closely connected to capitalist development, is depicted as sweeping the world, eventually absorbing all human subjects into its frame of reference, regardless of their situatedness in historical time and geographical place. Ironically, therefore, as a cultural theorist, the logic of David Harvey's reflections on the postmodern urban condition thus resembles Max Weber as much as Karl Marx. In place of Weber's projection of the iron cage of rationalism, instrumental reason, and bureaucratization of the life-world as dominant cultural dimensions of early twentieth-century modernity, Harvey envisions irrationalism, fragmentation, and flexible personality development as dominant cultural imperatives of late twentieth-century postmodernity. Moreover, Harvey represents postmodernity as the latest stage of capitalist development, as the cultural logic of late capitalism, rather than as a radical break with modernity. My critique of Harvey's urban theory is thus a key component of my larger critique of the economism and lack of agency underlying much of the effort in urban theory to explain urban development entirely in terms of various global narratives of epochal transformation, whether modernist or postmodernist in inspiration and style.

At least since the publication of *The Urbanization of Capital* (1985b) the language that Harvey has deployed in urban theory has viewed cities as key sites within a systemic "urban process" reflective of the larger evolution of capitalism on a global scale. Cities and regions are given meaning as production sites of accelerated capital accumulation and storehouses of "social surplus value." Cities are key parts of the "spatial fix" by which capitalism survives and reproduces itself. It is these functional imperatives of capital accumulation rather than any actors or agents offering contested representations of the urban future that are invested with historical agency. In this way structure and agency are completely reversed. Functionalist explanations like Harvey's exegesis of "the urban process" ultimately reduce urban politics to the requirements and logic of capital accumulation. This, in turn, diverts attention from situational contingencies as well as political processes that may inhibit or even jeopardize capitalist development and lead to new modes of social change or urban transformation (see M. P. Smith, 1994).

Thus it is crucial not only to critique the assumptions underlying David Harvey's theory of urban change but to closely examine the very metaphors through which he speaks. In the following analysis several of Harvey's key metaphorical moves will be highlighted, though they by no means exhaust the discursive constructions which limit what he sees and can say about cities and urban life. These include: (a) the use of functionalist metaphors to convey the "systemic needs" of global capitalism; (b) the use of binary oppositions to depict culture as epiphenomenal; (c) the use of anthropomorphic language to empower capital and marginalize state–society relations; and (d) the deployment of a set of metaphors that, taken together, construct a universal "postmodern subject," fraught with cognitive confusion, emotional malaise, and ontological insecurity. In Harvey's view the political agency of this universalized subject can only be recovered through a reassertion of the Enlightenment project of taking control of the disruptive forces of capitalism, urbanization, and nature through class struggle. It will be shown that an underlying technological determinism informs each of these metaphorical turns.

Beyond Technological Determinism

In David Harvey's (1990) essay "Between Space and Time: Reflections of the Geographical Imagination," reality is defined in terms that privilege technological and economic forces and downplay the potentially creative force of socially constructed concepts of space and time, being and becoming. Harvey first argues that the "roots" of socially constructed concepts of space and time "lie in the mode of production and *its* characteristic social relations." He goes on to make an apparent concession to the social constructionist perspective by stating that structurally "rooted" social constructions of space-time nonetheless "operate with the full force of objective facts to which *all* individuals and institutions *necessarily* respond" (Harvey, 1990: 418, emphasis added). By expressing the issue in this way Harvey elides the materialist–social constructionist debate in urban theory by erasing the very idea that reality itself is socially constructed. Instead, social constructs only have social force because they are "rooted" in a deeper and more penetrating material reality: the mode of production. "Mode of production," a historically contingent and socially constructed conceptual category, is thus enshrined in a privileged position in the master discourse that Harvey calls "geographical–historical materialism." This way of structuring his argument about time, space, and geographical imagination makes it easy for him to draw the conclusion that culture is produced not by people's practices but by systemic features of political economy. Thus, for example, Harvey asserts that cultural revolutions in "social conceptions of space and time" are "associated with" the speedy turnover time of capital, driven by technological development and rapid economic change. Since, in his view, "all" individuals and institutions "necessarily respond" to conceptions of space and time that are functional to the "underlying" mode of production, history is made not by people and the institutions they create but by structural imperatives. Whether intentionally or not, Harvey turns on its head Marx's famous aphorism. By the logic just deconstructed: "Structures make history, people don't." How else are we to interpret the following passage other than as a brief for technological determinism? According to Harvey (1989: 425): "The turnpikes and canals, the railways, steamships and telegraph, the radio and the automobile, television and telecommunications, have altered space and time relations and *forced us* to new material practices as well as to new modes of representation of space."

David Harvey's discussion of economic globalization and its relationship to cultural change closely follows this functionalist schema. He begins by arguing that the reconstruction of the global space economy by capital "has been one of the main means to permit the survival of capitalism into the twentieth century" (ibid.). Deploying a crisis theory of capitalist development, Harvey argues that the elimination of spatial barriers to capital accumulation, which "annihilates space by time," has been an especially prominent feature of capitalist development that becomes particularly acute during periodic crises of over-accumulation. These crises initiate new types of spatiotemporal "fix" which compress time and space. In Harvey's view, the current instantaneous diffusion of information by computers and global media, along with the intro-duction of flexible production practices on a global scale, while intended to overcome accumulation crises, have disruptive sociocultural and psychic con-sequences. They heighten people's sense of transience, delocalize their experi-ence, and render them ontologically insecure (see Bondi, 1990: 156–67). They engender a quest for roots and security, an obsession with identity politics, and a retreat into the local as a response to economic globalization.

For Harvey (1989: 426–7) the political–economic crisis of 1973 "forced" a worldwide revolution in "production techniques, consumption habits, and political economic practices." This change in material practices involved greater speed, fragmentation, and "time-space" compression in the social organization of economic production. For Harvey this restructuring of the global economy "betokened" a transformation in what Raymond Williams calls the "structure of feeling." Just as the speed and simultaneity of political–economic change in 1848 "called for" a new modernist mode of representation, à la Baudelaire, so too the time-space compression since the 1970s has generated new experi-ences of time and space from which new postmodern modes of representation "are squeezed." In Harvey's view, the economic "penetration" of the realm of cultural production has become particularly attractive to capital because "the lifetime of consumption of images, as opposed to more tangible objects like autos and refrigerators, is almost instantaneous" (Harvey, 1989: 427).

In the face of the global production of commodities and the commodification of signs as a kind of globalization of desire, Harvey envisages a return to the local as an ontological space of meaning and a key site of identity politics. He states: "There is still an insistent urge to look for roots in a world where image streams accelerate and become more and more placeless." Following Kern (1983), Harvey sees the return to the localism of place, ethnicity, and other "fragmentary" identities as provoked precisely by "the reduction of the power of spatial barriers to separate and defend against others." He thus constructs a binary dialectic of place vs. space in which place, like the "local" in modernist discourses, is a static, if not reactionary, site of the quest for ontological security and space, like the "cosmopolitan" is the dynamic realm of global capital circulation, deployment and consumption of image streams, and penetration of place-bound life-worlds. In this sort of binary logic "placeless" people find little room for maneuver except to return to the local, viewed by Harvey as globalism's Other, the site of a sedentarist metaphysics of "being." (For insightful critiques of this metaphysics of place see Massey, 1994b; Malkki, 1995.)

In *The Condition of Postmodernity* this underlying logic is even more directly stated. In this work Harvey's prime mover, his uncaused cause, like an omnipotent and omniscient god who produces the chaotic condition of postmodernity, is anthropomorphized as "the circulation of capital restlessly and perpetually seeking new ways to garner profits" (Harvey, 1989: 107). The perpetual motion machine of capitalism is transposed in Harvey's language from a structure and a process to an actor and a historical agent. "Restless" capital is represented as the only efficacious agency of social change, creating new needs, cultivating "imaginary appetites," generating fantasy, and increasingly shaping human desires.

Cities, in this story, are not discrete entities but spatial concentrations of the "social surplus product" of advance capitalism. The people inhabiting cities are not historical agents but passive objects "pushed," "squeezed," "penetrated," and "conditioned" by capital accumulation and manufactured desire. The state, no less than its subjects, is engulfed in the globalization of capital. Like a drowning man, the state "struggles" to contain the "fluid," "spatially open," virtually unstoppable process of borderless capital circulation. Despite its struggle, the state is given little or no autonomy in Harvey's discourse, often being reduced to the role of symbolic representation of state power through myth-making, the mystification of its own lack of autonomy from capital, and the aestheticization of politics. In the final analysis, Harvey's state apparatus serves the long-term interests of capital by stifling "progressive working-class revolutions."

Cultural Reductionism

As Steven Connor (1993: 230) has pointed out in a trenchant critique of David Harvey, despite significant differences in tone, breadth, and thematic focus, Harvey's corpus of writings on the city consistently rest upon another binary opposition in which political economy is seen as providing "grounding, depth, radicality, and foundation" against the "airy insubstantiality or miasmatic opacity of the cultural." The view of culture as an epiphenomenal result of deeper political–economic determinants is most clearly evident in *Consciousness and the Urban Experience* (1985a), where Harvey sketches out a theory of urban culture which reduces cultural practices to *effects* of underlying political–economic determinants such as the evolving capital–labor relation, the state's role in ideological production, and the structuration of the capitalist family. He does this, as Andrew Sayer (1987: 397–9) has shown, while ignoring the actual content of cultural practices as a historical force and eliding the fact that social relations, whether class, gender, or racially constituted, are historically constructed in particular times and places, rather than timeless and universal.

This same reductionist schema which views culture as an effect of more substantial political–economic realities informs the very structure of Harvey's *Condition of Postmodernity* (1989). His book is organized into four parts designed to connect four simultaneous phenomena: the cultural transition from modernity to postmodernity, the economic *origins* of this cultural change, the psychic consequences of the time-space compression unleashed by the economic globalization, and the fragmented aesthetic *responses* to this time-space compression that have displaced the political imperatives of class politics.

Both as a whole and within each part of *The Condition of Postmodernity* the argument follows a "logic of accumulation" formula in which culture is produced by economy, the former is chaotic, the latter coherent, and both ultimately are driven by the logic of capital. Thus, for example, consider an early chapter entitled "Postmodernism and the City: Architecture and Urban Design." In this chapter Harvey discusses recent changes in intellectual trends in architecture and urban design that have been subsumed under the rubric "postmodern." In describing postmodernism as an architectural style Harvey singles out its eclecticism, appropriation of vernacular traditions, multivalency, and the "confusions" of its "interior maze," as in the case of the Musée d'Orsay. He treats these as symptomatic of the "fragmentation" of culture under conditions of "flexible accumulation." Similarly, contemporary urban design is depicted as "dispersed," "deconcentrated," "decentralized," and "chaotic," as urban designers respond to such social forces as "taste cultures" and "the Heritage Industry." He further argues (Harvey, 1989: 87) that the trend in architecture and urban design to build urban spaces that appropriate collective memories and play upon the "nostalgic impulse" is reflective of a wider cultural "preoccupation" with the personal and collective roots of identity that has emerged in recent years "*because of* widespread insecurity in labor markets, in technological systems, and the like." Thus not only "taste cultures" but the wider cultural politics of identity construction are reduced to epiphenomenal status, as by-products of the psychic insecurity produced by capital's deployment of flexible accumulation on a global scale.

It is instructive in this regard that Harvey's analysis of cultural production in the putatively postmodern epoch focuses almost entirely on elite cultural production in media, the arts, architectural forms, and literary genres of the post-Enlightenment West. He says next to nothing about the ways in which cultural and spatial practices are produced by the daily life experiences of ordinary men and women in different times and places, North, South, East, or West. For someone as focused as Harvey is on the experiences of time, space, and class this is no small omission.

Even within the contemporary "West" the question still remains how differently situated social actors experience and act upon the sea change of time-space compression that Harvey says the universal "we" experience and that he views as the "singularly important mediating link" connecting economic and cultural processes. What Harvey says about ordinary people's practices is consistent but limited. He implicitly, albeit equivocally, asserts the passivity of "the general public" in the face of the sea change in cultural production ushered in by aesthetic and cultural elites. Posing the issue of the social base of postmodern cultural forms Harvey (ibid.: 59) states:

> This raises the most difficult of all questions about the postmodern movement, namely its relationship with and integration into the culture of daily life. . . . There are innumerable points of contact between producers of cultural artifacts and the general public: architecture, advertising, fashion, films, staging of multi-media events, grand spectacles, political campaigns, as well as the ubiquitous television. It is not always clear who is influencing whom in this process.

When Harvey moves from the subject position of "the general public" to discuss the new cultural spaces now being created in many cities by intensified transnational migration his analysis is limited and unidirectional. Discussing the daily practices of migrant social networks, Harvey denies the vibrancy and autonomy of these transnational urban spaces. He fits them instead into his general theme that capital has everywhere commodified culture. For instance, in the following passage the spatial practices of different cultures expressed in migrant neighborhoods are represented as a startling "pot-pourri of internationalism" (ibid.: 87) that,

> when accompanied by strong migration streams (not only of labour but also of capital) . . . produces a plethora of "Little" Italies, Havanas, Tokyos, Koreas, Kingstons, and Karachis as well as Chinatowns, Latino barrios, Arab quarters, Turkish zones, and the like. Yet *the effect,* even in a city like San Francisco where minorities collectively make up the majority, is to draw a veil over *real geography* through construction of images and reconstructions, costume dramas, staged ethnic festivals, etc.

Harvey's representation of transnational urban neighborhoods limits our view of their residents to the ritual recuperation of lost origins which provides a disorienting spectacle to the urban tourist. Even this limited view raises a number of intriguing questions. Who produces and who experiences the effect that Harvey sees? What "real geography" is hidden by the multicultural urban mosaic? Who are the cultural brokers staging reconstructive ethnic festivals? What effects do these reconstructions have on the *participants* rather than on synoptic spectators? If the producers of these cultural ceremonies are members of transmigrant networks, might not these activities more appropriately be viewed as signs of popular power to transform urban space? Even if ethnic festivals are sponsored by local governments in the name of multicultural urbanism are not they at least indicative of the salience of transmigrant ethnic networks in urban politics? In either case, as we shall see in subsequent chapters discussing transmigrant localities, they are far more than the stuff of spectator sport, or the epiphenomenal cultural artifacts of a capitalist reconstruction of taste. They are part and parcel of the socially constructed character of political "interests."

Postmodern Subjectivity, Political Fragmentation, and Identity Politics

The second half of *The Condition of Postmodernity* is permeated by both class reductionism and a tendency to repeat key themes, especially the centrality of the psychic experience of time-space compression, a state of disoriented consciousness driven by the logic of capital accumulation and symptomatic of the cultural turn to postmodernity. At this stage of his argument David Harvey departs from a complex exposition of the transition from modernity to postmodernity in various elite fields of contemporary culture and a useful synthesis of the literature on post-Fordist forms of "flexible accumulation" in the economic sphere. His analysis gives way, instead, to a forced, highly repetitive, and ultimately unconvincing effort to reduce the multiplicity of cultural transformations of the past three decades across the globe to a single explanation, one consonant with the discursive framework of historical materialism. In this respect Harvey's projection onto the world at large of a psychic inability to focus because of the confusions wrought by postmodern social and political fragmentation closely resembles Marxist theorist Frederic Jameson's projection onto the world of a generalized cognitive incapacity of ordinary people "to map the great global, multinational and decentered communication network in which we find ourselves caught as individual subjects" (Jameson, 1983: 25; see also Jameson, 1984: 146). In both cases nothing seems to stand between the confused individual and the swirling sign-systems of late capitalist political–economic development. Neither social networks nor political institutions, nor gender, racial, or ethnic differences come into play to locate people's encounter with postmodernity, situate their subjectivity, and differentially mediate their experience of globalization and time-space compression.

This failure to grasp the situated character of people's being-in-the-world distorts more than it reveals. Starting from a generalized fear of postmodern subjects caught in a decentering maelstrom of ephemeral, opaque, and confusing cultural imagery, the text of *The Postmodern Condition* often regresses into a ritual incantation of historical materialism viewed as an antidote to the confusions of late capitalist hyperspace, one capable of restoring clarity to the project of universal mapping. However, as feminist urban theorist Rosalyn Deutsche (1991: 22–3) has pointed out, "A commandeering position of the battleground of representation – one that denies the partial and fragmented condition of vision – is an illusory place. . . . Representations are produced by situated not universal subjects, the world is not so easily mapped any more."

Harvey's answer to people's putative confusion is expressed in a decidedly pugnacious masculinist rhetoric which affirms his membership in the once dominant discursive community of Marxist urban studies. Harvey depicts the postmodern turn to deconstructive politics as a "weak" relativism that merely plays language games and thereby avoids confronting the "hard" realities of political economy and the "material" circumstances of global power. This is reminiscent of his earlier defense of Marxian urban analysis (Harvey, 1987) in which the "tough rigor" of dialectical theorizing is contrasted with "looser" realist logic, "casual" empiricism, and "soft" structurationism. In insisting on the superiority of his preferred theory of urban political economy, Harvey fails to recognize that contemporary theories of political economy and globalization are themselves situated systems of representation, contested readings that give alternative meanings to the "out there" of political economy and global restructuring.

To salvage the intellectual viability of the discursive community of Marxist urban geography in which he is a leading light, Harvey offers basically structural explanations for urban sociospatial change. Changes in urban architectural forms, production systems, and (à la Jameson) transformations in the very "cultural logic" of postmodern cities produce, in Harvey's view, excessively flexible and accommodative postmodern personality types. In making this move he fails to consider, or perhaps even to comprehend, the full force of the new voices that have emerged in the making of transnational urbanism discussed elsewhere in this book. In Harvey's discourse the postmodern project of cultural politics and the political possibilities offered by emergent non-class based social movements are repeatedly dismissed as "local," "partial," "ineffectual," and even "irrational." They are constructed as part of a neo-Heideggerian unholy trinity of romanticism, aestheticized politics, and fascism. The trinity is first feminized and then condemned as too local and particularistic to do battle with capital.

In an essay in the influential collection *Mapping the Futures* Gillian Rose (1993) has written lucidly on the gendered language by means of which Harvey represents the modernist–postmodernist divide. In Harvey's language the modern is represented as "heroic, rational, progressive, universal, seminal, thrusting, and armed." The postmodern, in contrast, is depicted as "frothy, seductive, fecund, disruptive, charismatic, local, passionate, titillating, bound into places, and blind to the global gaze." Rose concludes that Harvey seems to make sense of postmodernism "only by constituting it as a feminine Other." Numerous feminist theorists (Massey, 1991b; Deutsche, 1991; Rose, 1993; Morris, 1993) have thoroughly dissected this limit of David Harvey's thinking. His synoptic gaze clearly celebrates those masculinized aspects of modern capitalist urbanization as "command over nature" (Harvey, 1989: 109) and technological advances "in productive force" that have opened up "new vistas" for "human development and self-realization" (ibid.: 110). He offers precise representations of economic globalization in which intensified international competition, fiscal crises, and related pressures have ushered in more flexible work processes like out-sourcing, job sharing, subcontracting, sweatshops, and "just in time" inventory flows. When he turns, however, to the realm of the popular consumption of postmodern cultural production Harvey (ibid.: 156) offers little more than rhetorical condemnation and a rather opaque view of the postmodern, feminized, cultural Other. He sees a confusing postmodernized cultural world in which "the relatively stable aesthetic of Fordist modernism [*sic*] has given way to all the ferment, instability, and floating qualities of a postmodern aesthetic that celebrates difference, ephemerality, spectacle, fashion, and the commodification of cultural forms."

As Michael Dear (1991a: 543) has correctly concluded, Harvey's economism is most apparent and least supported by careful argument when he claims that the economic fragmentation of flexible accumulation is mirrored in the disunity, dispersal and fragmentation of politics, philosophy, and social theory (see Harvey, 1989: 320). Since his gaze remains so clearly focused on the global level of analysis, Harvey fails to closely describe let alone explain the emergence of postmodern theory or politics in any particular time or place. At times he appears to link economy to culture through a vaguely stated psychodynamic, as when he states that the cultural impact of capitalism's time-space compression has been "the impulsive turn to postmodern cultural practices and philosophical discourses."

Harvey's writing is preoccupied with the theme of cultural fragmentation and the attendant decline of class politics. His critique of postmodern identity politics as something that has displaced class politics is most acidly stated in his essay "Three Myths in Search of a Reality in Urban Studies." This essay may be seen as a kind of abstract of the core political argument of *The Condition of Postmodernity*. The essay succinctly captures the image of political impotence underlying Harvey's social construction of the postmodern cultural "condition." Postmodern philosophy, Harvey states,

> urges us: to revel in the *fragmentation* and *cacophony of voices* through which the dilemmas of the modern world are understood. It has us accepting the reifications and *partitionings*, actually celebrating the *fetishisms* of *locality, place,* or *social pressure group,* without recognizing that history, geography, community, etc. are being dominated, *penetrated* and then recuperated under contemporary capitalism as pastiche. So are we to sit here lauding our local discourses in the face of a Brazilian debt-wipeout that brings the world to the edge of political–economic chaos?   *(Harvey, 1987: emphasis added)*

Harvey specifically faults poststructuralist social theorist Michel Foucault for advocating "localized resistance" to the institutionalized means of organized repression by such identity-based political groupings as "feminists, gays, ethnic and religious groupings, regional autonomists, etc." (Harvey, 1989: 45–6). He argues that such "localized" forms of resistance to repressive power–knowledge venues overlook capitalist strategies of systemic class domination and, by rejecting any "holistic theory of capitalism," fail to address "the question of the path whereby such localized struggles might add up to a progressive . . . attack upon the central forms of capitalist exploitation and repression."

Even if one were to accept, hypothetically, Harvey's central argument concerning the totally dislocating and disruptive effects of the new economic regime of "flexible accumulation," it would still be necessary to historicize the new political spaces opened up as well as the old political spaces displaced by this restructuring. Feminist theorist Jane Jenson has pointed out that ruptures in the economic and political realms such as those produced by global economic restructuring "can become moments of profound societal crisis and restructuring if new or reconstituted actors take advantage of the 'space' opened up in the universe of political discourse to demonstrate alternative meaning systems and institute alternative practices" (Jenson, 1990: 58). But the discursive spaces that give meaning to alternative practices occur not in the domains of technology or economy but in the communications expressed in and through informal social networks based on family, kinship, ethnicity, and other socially constructed discursive communities as these intersect with the wider political spaces of civil society; for example, political parties, interest groups, social movements, policy intellectuals, international organizations, NGOs, and local, national, and global public opinion. (See, for example, the discussion of the urban political changes produced by this interplay in Pahl, 1990: 719.)

Much is lost by Harvey's obsession with the imputed localism of identity politics and the political fragmentation he assumes to follow from a decline in class consciousness. For example, in *The Condition of Postmodernity* the feminist effort to turn political attention from issues of economic exploitation in the workplace to an analysis of the social relations of domination in the domestic sphere and implicitly, if not explicitly, to the history of power relations between working-class men and their wives and families, is avoided by Harvey by a rhetorical invocation of a hoped for "rainbow coalition." When he does construct a political space for women it is as part of a string of marginal "others" such as blacks and ethnic minorities viewed as economically exploited, albeit "marginal segments" of the working class in the public sphere, and hence, implicitly as potential allies of working-class males in the grand working-class struggle against capital. By this construction Harvey avoids having to deal with the question of how gender inequalities in the household may have affected the politics of class consciousness and working-class collective action in the public sphere.

Essentializing Class and Marginalizing Gender

This very issue of reducing gender struggles to a marginal component of a putatively more universal class struggle has been brilliantly explored in Nicky Hart's historical study of the relationship between the changing gender division of labor in the household and the rise and fall of class politics in Britain. Hart (1989) shows that from the mid-nineteenth century until the end of World War II, when material inequality within households was high and was exceptionally gender-based, British male working-class consciousness was most pronounced. She documents the wide range of gender inequalities within households that spanned the entire course of everyday life, encompassing income allocation, consumption patterns, property rights, and freedom of movement. Men enjoyed higher living standards than their wives by virtue of the privileged treatment of the male "breadwinner" in the distribution of such material resources as food, heat, disposable personal expenditure, and access to leisure time in the "masculine republic" of the British pub (ibid.: 38–9). As Sidney Mintz (1985: 214) has shown, more generally, during the heyday of class politics, wives and children within working-class households "were systematically undernourished because of culturally conventionalized stress upon adequate food for the 'breadwinner'." Nicky Hart expands this picture by painting a carefully documented portrait of the personal expenditure of men devoted to alcohol, tobacco, and working-class pub life. This contrasts sharply with the complete lack of household spending for the individual benefit of working-class wives. Challenging the romantic imagery of the pub as a "cozy communitarian institution," Hart shows that wasteful expenditure by men engaged in the male-bonding rituals of pub life produced the endemic cash-flow problems of working-class families. On top of low wages, wasteful male-bonding practices forced working-class housewives to make ends meet by resorting to that other old style "communitarian institution," the pawn shop (Hart, 1989: 33).

The most intriguing part of Hart's analysis is her discussion of the relationship between gender stratification in the household and the politics of class formation and consciousness. Against the tendency for the material inequality within households to diminish male class consciousness by taking the edge off "the class actor's perception of material deprivation," Hart (ibid.: 39) argues:

> We must weigh the influence of "male bonding" facilitated by the inequalities of access to the labor market and household expenditure. . . . The fact of common masculinity has been ignored as an ingredient of the transformation of the "class in itself to the class for itself." However, masculinity as it came to be defined during the first industrial century was important to the growth of industrial camaraderie. The dominant tendency in the sexual division of labor established by the second half of the nineteenth century made the status of breadwinner a *sine qua non* of masculinity.

Hart demonstrates that gender inequality is a central but missed ingredient in the rise of class politics. Her analysis suggests that the current decline in gender inequality in Britain may well explain the decline of class politics. The convergence between the material goals of working-class men and their wives, the domestication of the British working man, the decline of the pub as a "masculine republic," and the movement of men from the "public house" to the private house have all been viewed by British Marxists as negative signs of commodity fetishism. Hart (ibid.: 46) offers the following trenchant rejoinder to this view:

> The process of "privatization" need not be seen as a wholly negative development. . . . Though it may dilute the force of class as an agency of change, it has contributed to an equalization of the life chances of men and women. . . . Masculinist theory must bear part of the blame for the end of class as a force for change. It has encouraged a view of human liberation occurring only through the agency of men, while it has ignored or dismissed the significance of women's material deprivation and social degradation as a significant realm of oppressive social relations.

Hart's analysis of the interplay of class and gender relations in the rise and fall of working-class consciousness has several implications for David Harvey's urban theory. First, it suggests that not only is the politics of private life an important domain in its own right, it is intimately connected to social actions in public life in ways that profoundly challenge the binary separation of public and domestic space. More precisely, it challenges the tendency, as in Harvey, to privilege class struggle as a universal, omnipresent discourse of public life over against gender struggle viewed as a purely private, partial, and "local" form of oppositional politics. Second, Hart shows that class consciousness is not a pregiven resultant of the occupancy of a position within the mode of production, but a resultant of the interplay of discourses (in this instance about class and gender, exploitation and oppression, public and private life) enacted in historically specific times and places. Third, Hart's study is a pointed illustration of how political identities are socially constructed as contingent outcomes of experienced solidarities and oppositions formed and reformed by social interactions taking place in and through particular networks and circuits of communication (in this instance the "male bonding" allowed by gender-segregated working-class pub life). Fourth, studies like Hart's suggest the need for a more nuanced and historicized analysis of the interaction of various social identities in urban politics, rather than assuming, as Harvey does, that advancing particular "localized" interests (whether gender-, ethno-racially, or neighborhood-based) in urban politics automatically reduces the political will and energy available for advancing class interests more generally. Finally, by offering an alternative explanation for the decline of class politics, one rooted in historically specific social relations of class and gender, Hart's study provides a useful counterweight to David Harvey's vision of postmodern culture as the culprit accounting for the general decline of class politics in the West.

During nearly a decade of criticism of his views on feminist cultural theory and postmodern cultural politics, David Harvey offered numerous lively rejoinders to his critics (Harvey, 1990, 1992, 1993, 1995). First appearing in academic journals, these writings culminated in Harvey's latest major work, *Justice Nature, and the Geography of Difference* (1996). How has Harvey answered his critics? Has his more recent work addressed any of the concerns I have raised above and, if so, with what effects? Have his views on the political geography of difference and postmodern identity politics become any less binary or more historicized? How does he currently address the issue of the contingent construction of class and other political identities in urban time-space?

The Political Geography of Difference

David Harvey's *Justice, Nature and the Geography of Difference* is a wide ranging and ambitious work that spans topics as diverse as the metaphysics of G. W. Leibniz, the nature of nature, the social construction of space and time, and the "worlding" of possible urban futures. Among the notable strengths of this remarkably dense work are lucid chapters discussing the languages by which "nature" has been socially constructed in social theoretic discourse and the political values of global environmentalism inscribed in ideological discourse (see Harvey, 1996: 117–204). These chapters are largely textual in content, presenting various social theoretic and ideological points of view as self-contained positionalities; little attempt is made to explore the intertextuality of the former or the actual social practices (beyond writing) by which the latter are produced and change. Nevertheless, Harvey's overall discussion of "the nature of environment" represents his recent thinking at its most original.

This part of *Justice, Nature and the Geography of Difference* is only loosely connected to the rest of the book. When Harvey moves beyond metaphysics and debates on environmentalism, much of the rest of this work can be read as a reincarnation of his intellectual and political struggle to inscribe capital accumulation as the central driving force of human existence and class politics as the only universal, and hence the only legitimate form of political struggle. In the process of revisiting this leitmotif, Harvey attempts to answer the many critiques that have been made of his work by feminists, social constructionists, postmodern anti-foundationalists, and advocates of identity politics. Along the way he returns to the same arguments, and at times even the same passages, deploying the binaries of modernity vs. postmodernity, space vs. place, and global universalism vs. local particularism as tropes which simultaneously marginalize race, gender, and new social movement struggles and recenter class struggle against capital as the only viable form of urban politics. In the process Harvey continues to demonize postmodern culture as the central culprit responsible for the decline of class politics. He ignores more plausible explanations for that decline to be found in his own narrative depictions of urban social change.

Consider first Harvey's revisitation of key themes. At the outset he announces that his overall intention in writing the book is to "define a set of workable foundational concepts for understanding space-time, place, and environment (nature)" as a stable anchor against "the flood of chaotic images, ephemeral representations, contorted positionings, and multiple fragmentations of knowledge within which *we* now have our collective being" (ibid.: 2). Against this construction of the chaos of postmodern culture, global capitalism continues to be represented as a focused historical agent "always restlessly searching out new organizational forms, new technologies, new lifestyles" (ibid.: 240). Turnpikes and canals, radio and automobile, television and telecommunications, now joined by "containerization" and "jet cargo transport" are still "forcing new modes of representation of space" (ibid.). Time-space compression continues to be envisaged as a universal psychosocial process, the late twentieth-century equivalent of Weber's iron cage, a way of apprehending modernity engineered by capitalism that "forces all of us to adjust our notions of space and time and to rethink the prospects for social action" (ibid.: 243). In short, postmodern culture is still viewed as an epiphenomenon of capitalist development, a "response to the recent speed-up and acceleration of capital turnover time" (ibid.: 245) that is particularly pernicious because, in his view, unlike the consumption of cars or refrigerators, cultural consumption "is almost instantaneous" (ibid.: 246).

In restructuring urban space, capital is omniscient and omnipotent. An anthropomorphized capital "*produces* a geographical landscape (of space relations, of territorial organization, and of systems of places linked in a 'global' division of labor and of functions) *appropriate to its own dynamic of accumulation* at a particular moment of *its* history, only to have to destroy and rebuild that geographical landscape to accommodate accumulation at a later date" (ibid.: 412, emphasis added). The technological shifts in capitalist production have "allowed a radical shift in the way that space is organized and therefore opened up radically new possibilities for the urban process" (ibid.). As a result of global economic restructuring, "the development of an interrelated and ultimately global network of cities drawing on a variety of hinterlands *permits* an aggregate urban growth process radically greater than that achievable for each in isolation" (ibid.: 413). Despite the different "needs" and agendas of different fractions of capital, through globalization, capital as a whole "*realizes its own agenda* of 'accumulation for accumulation's sake, production for production's sake' against a background of the technological possibilities it itself has created" (ibid.: 414).

In the face of this relatively unitary view of "capital," Harvey returns to his key theme that postmodern cultural production has fragmented political resistance to the exploitative and oppressive social relations entailed in capitalist urbanization. In one of the most historically situated discussions in his book Harvey condemns the fact that the contemporary news media, along with the women's movement, and racial, ethnic, and environmental groups, paid little attention to a devastating fire in the Imperial Foods chicken-processing plant in the town of Hamlet, North Carolina in 1991, caused by corporate negligence, which led to the deaths or serious injury of scores of workers. Harvey explains the inattention given to this fire in terms of a supposed fragmentation of "progressive" politics stemming from the postmodern valorization of identity politics. Harvey complains that the rise of special issue politics and "the so-called new social movements focusing on gender, race, ethnicity, ecology, sexuality, multiculturalism, community and the like . . . often become a working and practical alternative to class politics of the traditional sort and in some instances have exhibited downright hostility to such class politics" (ibid.: 341). He further argues that the "militant particularisms" of these modes of identity politics preclude a quest for universal norms on the basis of which one could convincingly "register political anger" against the social injustice entailed in the Imperial Foods fire.

Harvey acknowledges in passing that the decline in working-class politics in the United States has several causes, including the erosion of working-class institutions and the geographical dispersal of industrial production to remote areas. Yet he devotes the most attention and vents the most hostility toward the alleged particularism of new social movements. He claims that women's organizations active at the time of the fire were "preoccupied" with issues of sexual harassment and the Clarence Thomas appointment to the US Supreme Court, "even though it was mainly women who died in the North Carolina fire." Likewise, he criticizes black and Latino organizations for remaining "strangely silent on the matter," and accuses "some ecologists" of exhibiting "more sympathy for the chickens than for the workers." On the basis of these alleged sins of omission, silence, and indifference, Harvey concludes that "the general tone of the media, *therefore,* was to sensationalize the horror of the 'accident,' but not to probe at all into its origins and certainly not to indict capitalist-class interests, the Republican Party, the failures of the state of North Carolina or OSHA as accessory to a murderously negligent event" (ibid., emphasis added). The media, according to Harvey, framed only "static pictures of the aftermath of the North Carolina fire," while obsessing on "the graphic video of the beating of Rodney King and the soap operatic Clarence Thomas hearings" (ibid.: 340). In short, Harvey blames the new social movements for somehow influencing the media content and tone which sensationalized racial and gender questions while marginalizing class relations. In his view, then, media representations and social movement politics are treated as zero-sum games in which concern for racial and gender oppression automatically reduces concern for class exploitation.

In constructing his argument in this way Harvey downplays a far more plausible explanation for the lack of class mobilization and media coverage of the class relations of the chicken factory fire, one that he mentions here only in passing: the systematic decentralization of industrial production that he has so trenchantly discussed elsewhere as part of the new spatial fix of postmodern capitalism. The industrial sites of capitalist exploitation are no longer largely concentrated in a few large industrial US cities. They have been relocated to rural, suburban, and offshore production sites far from the urban crowd that marched down Broadway to vehemently protest a New York City textile factory fire in 1911, the contrasting example that is framed in Harvey's discourse as a model of a once vibrant class politics that is now lost. These relocations, along with the multiple new sites of transnational immigrant labor working in new sweatshops that have reappeared in major cities throughout the world, create particularized expressions of late twentieth-century capitalism and of capital–labor, ethno-racial, and gender relations, embedded in localized cultural, gender, political, and social relations. It is these relations that must be examined to explain the presence or absence of workplace-related struggles under conditions of transnational urbanism.

Hence, rather than decrying the absence of working-class struggle in Hamlet, North Carolina, if Harvey had paid closer attention to the transnational processes by which social relations have become transnationalized and then relocalized, he might just as easily have found viable examples of ethnically and gender inflected workplace struggles in the labor campaigns against sweatshop conditions among immigrant workers in Los Angeles and New York

City. Likewise, if he had paid closer attention to the extensive media coverage devoted to the campaign against sweatshop conditions in El Salvador in textile factories producing clothing for The Gap, he would have been able to link these "local" struggles to the transnational connections being forged between labor activists in El Salvador and political coalitions organizing consumer boycotts against The Gap in cities like San Francisco and New York. All of these struggles have become cultural as well as economic struggles, engaging an array of actors and networks in addition to labor activists in the US and El Salvador, including the regional and national media, local, national, and transnational reference publics, transnational political actors linked by the internet, and political administrations in the US and El Salvador. Analyzing these developments is clearly more complicated than analyzing the social and political relations of production in more nationally bound contexts. But in the age of transnational urbanism it is crucial to engage in such analysis if we are to hope to understand, let alone change, the world that we are making.

Political theorist Iris Marion Young (1998) has raised a related point in a recent critique of Harvey's analysis of the chicken factory fire:

> Why did Americans focus on the Hill–Thomas hearings and the beating of Rodney King, and not the Imperial Food fire? . . . Is it because progressives have become more interested in gender and race oppression than in class exploitation? . . . I think that simple *location* more plausibly accounts for the facts. . . . Few people care about what happens in Hamlet, North Carolina; they care a lot more about what happens in Washington and Los Angeles. The media are headquartered in the latter places and have to haul their equipment to a dingy motel in Hamlet, hardly worth the trouble when their audience cares more about LA. It's a lot easier to mobilize tens and thousands of people for a rally in DC or LA than to load them onto buses bound for Hamlet.

David Harvey is so eager to condemn postmodern cultural politics that he uses deficient reasoning to hold racial and gender consciousness responsible for the end of class politics. Harvey starkly opposes the universalism of class-based political organization to the "militant particularism" of racial, gender, ecological, and other social movements. This binary logic has clear historical shortcomings. Labor unions, the putative voice of universal class interests, frequently have behaved particularistically, as in their exclusion of people of color and insensitivity to the everyday conditions of working-class women. Conversely, women, environmentalists, and postcolonial subjects have often forged political movements advancing claims based on such universalistic values as political democratization, gender equality, ecological survival, and respect for human rights. Why then is one type of movement assumed to be more universal than all of the others?

Social movements, including the labor movement, are historically particular expressions of social actors in real time that lay claim to universal categories of human existence; each is also an alliance of forces temporarily forged into a cohesive social force by the complex construction of a socially specific political identity extracted from the multiplicity of people's situatedness in the world. As Young (ibid.: 38, 39) cogently argues,

> Like working-class movements, each of these movements is universalist at the same time that it exposes divisions of interest based in structural social relations. When the claims of all these movements are asserted together, they expose privileges and differences within each other. . . . [Therefore] class-based anti-capitalist politics cannot be achieved by asserting some unity that transcends differences of gender, race, region, religion, sexuality, and so on, but rather . . . such politics must be the outcome of careful coalition-building which affirms social specificity.

Ironically, therefore, as long as David Harvey insists on condemning all political identities but class identity as forms of "militant particularism" (Harvey, 1995: 524), the careful coalition-building required to pursue his anti-capitalist politics is bound to elude him.

Many feminist urban geographers and sociologists have begun to explore the links between production politics and identity politics in the growing urban service sectors of major cities throughout the world (see Gilbert, 1997). Perhaps it is not surprising, given his deprecatory view of identity politics, that David Harvey's urban theory fails to take into account this growing body of literature. If it did, he would encounter, for example, Savage's (1998) urban political analysis of significant achievements made in the 1990s by the Service Employee's International Union (SEIU) in organizing women, people of color, and immigrants in US cities. Savage studied SEIU's national organizing campaign "Justice for Janitors." After reviewing the various local successes of this national union campaign, Savage (ibid.: 20–1) concludes that "along with a greater attention to the local political economy and the spatial organization of the workplace, labor unions need to actively and creatively engage with the many identities held by workers and commit resources to fight the racism and sexism that deeply affect workers' lives and are directly linked to their economic positions." This is a pointed lesson for urban theory as well as union activism in the new millennium.

An Alternative View of Urban Politics

Throughout his writings David Harvey expresses a very limited and negative view of cultural politics. He consistently equates class politics with universalistic politics and relegates gender-, ethnicity-, and place-based politics to the particularistic pole of a universalist–particularist conceptual duality. Universalism, in turn, is conflated with progressivism and cognitive rationality, while particularism is equated with regressiveness and irrationality. Consider the following passage from *The Condition of Postmodernity*: "We can no longer conceive of the individual as alienated in the classical Marxist sense," in postmodern culture, Harvey (1989: 53) states, "because to be alienated pre-supposes a coherent rather than a fragmented sense of self from which to be alienated. It is only in terms of such a centered sense of personal identity that individuals can pursue projects over time, or think cogently about the produc-tion of a future significantly better than time present and time past."

In my view, Harvey's modernist vision of identity politics fails to recognize the discursively and socially constructed character of the interests that people actually pursue in urban politics, whether those interests are based on class, race, gender, locality, or a hybrid recombination of such socially constructed political identities. When identity and interest are defined in cognitive rather than discursive and situated form, as Harvey does above, then, as Kian Tajbakhsh (1991: 1,934) has pointed out, an institution or group, whether a vanguard party or a group of geographical–historical materialists, "can claim to possess this knowledge." Harvey's very project of linking the universal interest with a single sociological category – class – posits interests as objectively grounded in absolutist class relations rather than discursively and practically formed in historically situated experiences. It thus privileges the knowledge possessed by one group of intellectual elites – geographical–historical materialists – who rationally perceive the universal interest.

The race, gender, and neighborhood dimensions of urban politics, to say nothing of the emergence of new discursively and practically formed com-munities based on transnational networks, are subordinated in David Harvey's modernist imagination to the master discourse of class struggle. He thereby refuses the more radical claim informing this book that reality ought not to be conflated with material existence and that there is thus no deeper rational, as opposed to political, basis for choosing between competing social construc-tions of reality (see Bondi, 1990). In my view the "outside" world is a realm of material existence. People, institutions, cities, and states, like trees, do materially exist. But their *meaning*, and hence the "reality" of their existence, is socially constructed by the meaning-making practices of differently situated discursive communities. Accordingly, contending political "interests," includ-ing those that constitute urban politics, are social products having no social force "independently of the consciousness of the agents who are their bearers" (Laclau and Mouffe, 1987: 96). These interests emerge in and through polit-ical contestations rather than preceding them. Put differently, "meaning is only constituted in the contexts of actual use . . . every identity or discursive object is constituted in the context of an action" (ibid.: 83).

What is needed, then, is a theoretical imagination focused upon a close analysis of *representational power* rather than a recentering of urban analysis around the master discourse of Marxism and the historical agency of class (on

this question see Bondi, 1990). Key concerns informing this capacity to imagine transnational urbanism would include such questions as: Who has the
power to give meaning to things, to name others, to construct the character of
collective identities, to shape the discourses of urban politics? When sufficient
attention is given to the politics of representation, what are the appropriate
boundaries of urban politics? How global, transnational, national, or local are
the circuits of communication and networks of power that "come together"
in particular urban formations? How do the relations between state and market, political economy and culture, vary from place to place and time to time?
How do old and new discursive communities collude and collide in answering
this question? What meanings do the participants in these communication
circuits give to their social actions and practices as well as to the actions and
practices of others with whom they interact? What new voices in urban
politics are rendered silent, invisible, or subordinate when class politics is taken
as the only rational form of urban politics?

Along with other radical urban geographers, David Harvey has consistently
sought to refocus analytical attention within urban analysis from time and
history to space and geography. Edward Soja, for example, has denounced all
historical analysis using the pejorative label "historicism." Harvey's treatment
of social history is less sweeping, but his theoretically filtered attention to the
history of city formation has led to an underdeveloped theory of the state and
the role of politics and state policies in the formation of cities. Sociologist
Charles Tilly (1988) points out that Harvey's inattention to both the structure
and the agency of the capitalist (or any other) state leads Harvey to leap
deductively from the mere existence of particular capitalist interests to their
full materialization in urban space. As Tilly expresses the issue, lacking a
theory of the state, Harvey "minimizes the autonomous influence of states on
urban processes and moves very quickly from the existence of a capitalist
interest to its realization in a particular feature of cities, without wasting much
effort on the process by which the interests generate their own realization"
(ibid.: 395). When the state is explicitly mentioned, its role is reduced to that
of an instrument of capital whose chief purpose is ideological mystification.

Not only is there no space for state autonomy in Harvey's urban theorizing,
there is no theory of state–society relations. Harvey's treatment of this question lacks historical specificity, fails to address the mechanisms by which
different uses of urban space are developed by politics and the state, and how
different urban regimes differ from society to society, place to place, and time
to time.

In short, what David Harvey leaves out of his theoretical discussions of the
relationship between the global economy and postmodern culture is *politics*,
i.e. the analysis of power in all of its criss-crossing forms, not just the power of
capital. It will not do to bemoan "the pulverization of space by private
property" (Harvey, 1985a: 34) as if property relations were social actors rather

than social constructions constituted by the social relationships between specific actors in historically specific states and societies. Missing from Harvey's
modernist generalizations about the power of capitalist production and exchange to shape urban consciousness are five basically political questions:

1 How is the power to use and control urban space shaped and legitimated
   in particular social systems? (political process).
2 By whom? (agency).
3 How do the policies of the national and the local state influence the
   character of particular cities? (role of the state).
4 How do such state policies, viewed as outcomes of state–civil society
   relations, differ *between* and *within* societies as well as *trans*nationally, over
   time? (historical specificity).
5 What is the changing role of specific cities in this state–civil society
   dynamic? (localization).

Social theorist Nicos Mouzelis (1988) has underlined the need to examine
the character of historically particular civil societies in addressing questions
such as these. He points out that in weakly organized civil societies, states
have historically been more important than markets in establishing the rules of
the game governing societal (and by implication urban) development. According to Mouzelis (ibid.: 118):

> If the state in capitalist formations is defined as an instrument of the econom-
> ically dominant classes, or as performing the functions of capital, or even as an
> arena of class struggle, this evidently rules out the investigation of cases where
> the holders of the means of domination/coercion have the upper hand over the
> holders of the means of production, or cases where state policies hinder rather
> than promote the enlarged reproduction of capitalism. . . . Cases of this kind are
> all too common in the capitalist periphery, where civil society in general and
> classes in particular are weakly organized and where, very often, the logic of
> domination prevails over the logic of the market, or to put it differently, the
> polity's reproductive requirements are relatively incompatible with those of the
> economy – in which case the latter gives way to the former.

At the present time, when the practice of neoliberalism has spread to
remote and peripheral social spaces and many academics tout a "postnational"
epoch of globalization, some might consider Mouzelis's comments naively
dated. But historical and contemporary developments suggest otherwise. For
example, consider the political logics and processes underlying the role of the
Chinese state in shaping the incorporation of Chinese cities into the global
political economy; the role of the British colonial administration, and now
the Chinese state, in brokering the urban development of Hong Kong (see
Henderson, 1989); the historical and contemporary politics of the French state

as an institutional agency in the development of Paris as an international capital of culture (White, 1998); the continuing role of the Japanese state bureaucracy and state developmental policies in shaping Japanese urbanization processes, in the face of transnational neoliberal calls for a smaller state and larger market role in Japanese economic development (Hill and Fujita, 1995; Kristof, 1999); and, in contrast, the national and local politics of neoliberalism in the United States, from national "empowerment zones" to local tax cuts to attract capital, which have discursively justified taxation and social policy retrenchment as "required" by economic globalization (M. P. Smith, 1988).

These developments suggest that Mouzelis's main line of argument needs to be expanded rather than abandoned. Not only in states with weakly developed civil societies (like China or Belarus), but also in those with more developed civil societies (e.g. Japan or the US), the state–society relation is central to the way different social formations respond to global capitalist imperatives. Part of the meaning given to "globalization" in historical practice thus can be found by comparative-historical analysis of different modes of incorporation or resistance of state formations to the political requirements of economic globalization. Likewise the extent to which particular cities have circumvented their own state's mediation of global economic relations is an intriguing question that also must be answered by comparing case studies rather than by assuming, as Harvey does, the universal spread of flexible specialization, hypercompetitive localities, and urbanized capital.

Even the role of "capital" *per se* in urban politics must be historicized rather than theoretically assumed. David Harvey views cities as means of capital accumulation in the form of land rents, reduced costs of production generated by urban concentration, and outlets for the investment of surplus capital in the built environment. Urbanization is thus viewed as a solution to general capitalist crises of overproduction and surplus accumulation. Theoretically, Harvey assumes that an "urban class alliance" of various capitalist fractions has converged on this urban "spatial fix" for reproducing capitalism. He leaves historically unexamined the mechanisms by which real estate capital, industrial capital, and finance capital might actually converge with enough coherence in particular cities to constitute a political "alliance." Indeed, as Charles Tilly (1988) has cogently shown, Harvey's discussion of the interplay of these capitalist factions in his own study of the urban development of nineteenth-century Paris suggests that their conflicts have been more important than their convergences in the social production of Parisian urban space. Harvey's failure to reconcile his historical story with his general urban theory is no small oversight. For if the actions of major capitalist factions that have interests in urbanization sharply contradict each other, "theories that trace urban form to the operation of an abstract, unified 'capital' no longer apply" (Tilly, 1988: 396).

In the final analysis, David Harvey's reductionist view of urban politics as "the powerful and innovative but in the end disciplining arm of uneven

accumulation" (Harvey, 1985: 126–7) leaves little room for contingent outcomes, let alone for the analysis of representational power in urban politics.
Rhetorical gestures calling for the formation of "relatively autonomous" non-
capitalist class alliances, while downplaying or even criticizing non-class based
social movements, do little to alter the technological determinism underlying
Harvey's urban vision.

Beyond Binary Dualities

The language that David Harvey has deployed in urban theory limits his
vision of urbanization, city life, and urban politics. Starting from a set of
functionalist assumptions about the inexorable logic of global capital accumulation, Harvey invests capitalism with too much systemic coherence and
capitalist class actors with too much unitary subjectivity and hegemonic power.
Despite numerous attempts to deal with the question of historical agency,
Harvey's approach offers an underdeveloped theory of the state, a highly
selective view of urban politics, and a non-autonomous interpretation of
culture. He fails to grasp that identities and interests are socially constructed
outcomes of political processes rather than pregiven positions derived from the
prevailing mode of economic production and its dominant cultural logic.

As a consequence of his representation of this cultural logic – postmodernity
– as inevitably fragmenting political identities and interests, Harvey concludes
that only class-based identities are capable of pursuing a mythical universal
reason. Class politics are inscribed with rationality, universalism, and global
vision, while ethnic, racial, gender, ecological, sexual, and locality-based social
movements and identities are deemed fragmented, particularistic, and narrowly local. The former is represented as desirably modernist and progressive;
the latter as undesirably postmodernist and reactionary. Harvey's insistent commitment to these linked binary dualities essentializes class while marginalizing
all of the rest of urban politics, particularly the ethnic, racial, and gender
struggles that became the stuff of late twentieth-century urban politics around
the globe.

This chapter has tried to show how limited and partial David Harvey's
effort to construct a foundational urban theory actually is and how much of
the dynamics of urban politics it inadvertently excludes or deliberately
marginalizes. The next chapter turns to a second influential strand of "structuralist" urban theorizing: the global cities discourse. Like Harvey, the most
prominent global cities theorists proffer a structural analysis of urban change
that gives scant attention to questions of agency, historicity, and the social
construction of meaning. The global cities theorists posit a grand narrative of
global capital restructuring less explicitly rooted in Marxist analytical categories.
Nevertheless, their theorization of the local and national impacts of the

"globalization" of capital leaves little space for historically contingent national or urban responses to globalization, let alone for creative initiatives by states or social networks and political movements operating transnationally in our putatively global epoch. In the end, as we shall see, the optic of "global cities" offers an incomplete social construction of reality which privileges a synoptic, economistic view of globalization "from above," while failing to address the myriad transnational practices of politics and culture that now criss-cross the landscapes of transnational cities throughout the world, inexorably irrigating their politics and social life.

The Global Cities Discourse: A Return to the Master Narrative? | 3

The metaphor of a (smooth and spherical) "global city" first developed as a fertile image to signify the city, its characteristics, and functions, and the (mainly socio-economic and financial) space of the world-economy in which it is embedded is too unitary, neutral, and balanced for the fragmented, scarred, and lopsided social and economic contradictions which the city contains.

Anthony King, Representing the City

Debates about "the global city" have taken on a recognizable, if not formulaic, character, poised somewhere on a conceptual and epistemological borderland where positivism, structuralism, and essentialism meet. The tendency to focus this debate around positivist taxonomies, urban hierarchies constructed on the basis of these taxonomies, and empirical efforts to map or even to formally model the "real" causes and consequences of global cities, leads participants in the debate to overlook the fact that the global cities discourse takes place within a wider public discourse on "globalization," which is itself a contested political project advanced by powerful social forces, not some "thing" to be observed by scientific tools. The global cities discourse constitutes an effort to define the global city as an objective reality operating outside the social construction of meaning. The participants in this debate argue about which set of material conditions are attributes of global cities and which cities possess these attributes. The debate generates alternative positivist taxonomies said to be occurring entirely outside our processes of meaning-making.

My own position on this debate about globalization and global cities is framed within the wider epistemological and ontological debate about social constructionism and the critique of ideology. The basic starting point of my argument is this: there is no solid object known as the "global city" appropriate for grounding urban research, only an endless interplay of differently articulated *networks, practices,* and *power relations* best deciphered by studying the agency of local, regional, national, and transnational actors that discursively and historically construct understandings of "locality," "transnationality," and "globalization" in different urban settings.

The global city is best thought of as a historical construct, not a place or "object" consisting of essential properties that can be readily measured outside the process of meaning-making. Discourses on the essence of global cities are reminiscent of earlier debates over the "essence of place" (see Massey, 1994a: 111). In both discourses certain internal features of this or that place constitute its essential status. In the case of global cities that status is the possession of a cumulative number of economic attributes and production functions that add up to its "global" status positioned within a stratified world hierarchy of cities.

The global cities literature varies in its specification of the financial, informational, and migratory flows that intersect to constitute a global city. Representations of global cities nonetheless share a common conceptual strategy in which these global flows are envisaged as "coming together" within the jurisdictional boundaries of single cities like New York, London, Paris, Tokyo, or Los Angeles. This strategy thus localizes within the boundaries of particular cities highly mobile, transnational processes of capital investment, manufacturing, commodity circulation, labor migration, and cultural production. In so doing, the strategy sharply demarcates an "inside" from an "outside" and largely highlights what goes on inside global cities. When the global cities framework addresses relations among global cities it imposes a hierarchical ordering on the economic functions and production complexes assumed to be "integrating" the global cities across space. By hierarchically nesting criss-crossing transnational connections and imposing an economic ordering mechanism on global cities, the effort to construct a global urban hierarchy belies the often marked disarticulation among the financial flows, political alliances, media-scapes, and everyday sociocultural networks now transgressing borders and constituting what I term transnational urbanism (see, for example, Appadurai, 1990, 1996).

Viewed in this light, the attributes taken as signs of economic globalization and global city status are widely agreed upon. They are most clearly stated in the analyses offered by John Friedmann (1986, 1995) and Saskia Sassen (1991). They include the following nested economic attributes:

1 Globalization of the international economy, accompanied by increased economic transgression of national borders.
2 Heightened capital mobility, the deployment of which is concentrated in a handful of global cities.

3   The shift from manufacturing to business and financial (or producer) serv-
    ices in major "core country" cities.
4   The concentration within the global cities of "command and control"
    functions which are coordinated on a global scale by these cities' expanded
    producer services sectors.
5   The hierarchical organization of these cities into a global system of cities
    whose purpose is the accumulation, control, and deployment of interna-
    tional capital.

The argument I advance in this chapter is constructed in the following
order. The first section reviews and critiques the representations of the global
city found in the work of John Friedmann and Saskia Sassen, arguably the two
most influential proponents of the global cities thesis. Structuralism, economism,
and inattention to questions of culture and agency are identified as key weak-
nesses of their approach to urban theory. While my critique recognizes some
useful aspects of their work, it stresses their tendency to reify the global city as
a fabricated by-product of the structural transformations of global capitalism in
the late twentieth century. The next part of my argument situates and localizes
the contemporary process of globalization politically. In the process, I identify
important limits to the "global reach" of multinational capital which undermine key assumptions of the global city thesis. Once this is accomplished, the
critique of the global cities thesis is completed by addressing the following
questions: (1) How new are the general processes of economic globalization
identified as key driving forces in the production of global cities? (2) How and
by whom has "globalization" been used as a legitimating ideology of neoliberal
capitalism? (3) What difference do these questions make for how we think
about transnational processes and how we might reconceptualize both cities
and global space as contested terrains?

Reconsidering the Global City Thesis

The theoretical writings on global city formation by John Friedmann and
Saskia Sassen clearly privilege economic and technological explanations for
global city development at the expense of political and sociocultural dynamics.
This has important consequences for the limited and derivative way in which
their theories conceptualize urban politics and culture. In light of the unavoidable interplay of economic processes with political and sociocultural dynamics,
it is important to contextualize the emergence of the global city thesis as a
social science research paradigm. Emerging in the 1980s, as David Ley (1998)
reminds us, the global city thesis

> coincided with the height of the Reagan–Thatcher hegemon, with its geopoli-
> tics of America first, and its political economy of deregulation, welfare-state

downsizing, and the emancipation of the profit motive. In these circumstances it was scarcely surprising that world-city theorizing would be broadly economistic, assume the obsolescence of the nation-state, and extend the American free-market model to the ends of the earth.

Viewed from our current vantage point, global city assumptions about the systemic coherence of the urban hierarchy, the transterritorial economic convergence of global command and control functions, and the declining significance of the nation-state, are more difficult to maintain than they once were. For better or worse, cities have different histories, cultural mixes, national experiences, and modes of political regulation of urban space. These must be taken into account in any nuanced analysis of the localization of global processes. Their absence weakens the usefulness of the global cities thesis.

Consider first the key conceptual assumptions underlying John Friedmann and Goetz Wolff's (1982) now-classical essay "World City Formation: An Agenda for Research and Action." Friedmann and Wolff argue that an emerging world system of production and markets is spatially articulated in and through a global network of cities, assumed but not shown to be hierarchically interconnected. The cities comprising this global hierarchy are said to be important because "most of the world's active capital is concentrated" within this global matrix (ibid.: 309). Unlike other analysts (e.g. Sassen), the urban regions or hinterlands in which the "world cities" identified by Friedmann and Wolff are located are also assumed to "play a part in the great capitalist undertaking to organize the world for the efficient extraction of surplus" (Friedmann and Wolff, 1982: 309).

In this grand narrative of capitalist urbanization it is clear that the global cities have a single, unitary author: transnational capital. For Friedmann and Wolff, world cities are material manifestations of the organizational control exercised by transnational capital, which has constructed a "linked set of markets and production units" across the globe (ibid.: 311–12). The world cities are transnational capital's banking and financial centers, administrative headquarters, production sites for global products, "safe" havens for investment of surplus capital in real estate, strong components of the global market, and/or global capitalist "ideological control" centers. Not every world city, to be sure, is deemed to be integrated into the global system of cities in all of these respects. Nevertheless, Friedmann and Wolff's inclusive list of modes of insertion into the global capitalist hierarchy allowed them to generate a list of 16 "world cities in the making" that manifest one or more pattern of integration into the globalized economy.

In a subsequent article entitled "The World City Hypothesis," John Friedmann (1986) elaborates upon the view of world cities he developed with Goetz Wolff. This analysis is more qualified. Friedmann describes his project as the advancement of a "framework for research" rather than a fully developed urban theory or even a universal generalization about urbanization processes. He acknowledges that world cities can be expected to differ among themselves because of their historical past, national policies, cultural influences, and mode of integration into the world economy. Friedmann nevertheless retains the central economistic assumption underlying his general research framework. He concludes that despite such differences, "the economic variable, however, is likely to be decisive for all attempts at explanation" (ibid.: 69). Consistent with this assumption, Friedmann views urban political conflict in world cities as originating not in political or cultural structures, nor in the social relations of race, ethnicity, or gender, but "in the global system of market relations" (ibid.: 89).

Starting from this core assumption Friedmann advances several interrelated theses on global city formation. I will try to capture their underlying logic. First, Friedmann asserts that any structural changes occurring within world cities will be decisively determined by "the functions *assigned* to the city in the new spatial division of labor" (emphasis added). He then makes clear just who is doing the assigning and how the functions are being organized, i.e. "global capital" uses key cities throughout the world as "basing points" in the spatial organization of production and markets. These cities, he argues, have been arranged by multinational capital into a complex urban spatial hierarchy. He proceeds to map this hierarchy by distinguishing, à la world systems theory, among "core primary world cities" (New York, London, Tokyo, Paris, Los Angeles, and Chicago), "semi-peripheral primary world cities" (Rio, São Paulo, and Singapore), "core secondary world cities" (San Francisco, Houston, Miami, Toronto, Madrid, Milan, Vienna, Sydney, and Johannesburg), and "semi-peripheral secondary cities" (Mexico City, Caracas, Buenos Aires, Seoul, Taipei, Hong Kong, Bangkok, and Manila). In addition to this classification, Friedmann identifies Rotterdam, Frankfurt, Zurich, and Brussels as part of the world city hierarchy, assigning the first three "first-rank" status and relegating Brussels to the status of a "secondary" world city.

Having thus mapped out a hierarchy linking the global system of cities, Friedmann turns to what goes on inside the global cities, arguing foremost that the leading production and employment sectors in world cities perform "global control functions." The controlling sectors he discerns include corporate and international finance headquarters, global transportation and communications sectors, high-level business services, and in the case of the top world cities, a sector responsible for "ideological penetration and control." Citing Sassen's early work (Sassen-Koob 1982, 1984a, 1986), Friedmann further argues that the high-paid professionals in these sectors are the leading driving force in the production of an array of low-paid service jobs catering to elite whims and producing a polarized income structure in the world cities.

Friedmann's theses further mark world cities as major sites for the attraction of international capital and for the concentration of domestic and/or international migrants. He notes, however, that there are several exceptions to these "patterns." The leading global city of Tokyo is an exception in both instances because of state policies limiting global investment and immigration. Singapore also has significantly reduced international migration through restrictive immigration policies. Less successfully, so too have Western European states sought to restrict the flow of transnational migrants to their world cities. Furthermore, IMF austerity policies, capital flight, and other factors have made Latin American semi-peripheral world cities net exporters rather than attractors of capital. Thus, by the time Friedmann finishes discussing his "globalization" theses linking international capital flows to labor migration, the exceptions he describes loom larger than the imputed patterns.

Friedmann's final theses address sociopolitical consequences of global city formation. He argues that world city formation produces spatial and class polarization. He depicts spatial polarization as emerging at three scales: at the global scale between core and peripheral economies and societies; at the regional scale, in terms of uneven development within regions, especially in the semi-periphery; and at the metropolitan scale within the global cities in terms of spatially segregated residential neighborhoods, based on income and class. Friedmann attributes the spatial segregation and social polarization within world cities largely to the changing employment opportunity structure. He draws upon Sassen's work on urban employment trends in pursuit of "global control capacity" to reach his conclusion that social polarization is an unavoidable by-product of emergent trends in capitalist economic development. Oddly, given his emphasis on financial services, global communications, and business services, both spatial and social polarization are depicted as "major contradictions of *industrial* capitalism" (Friedmann, 1986, emphasis added).

Friedmann finally argues that the social costs of world city development exceed the fiscal capacity of the state to address them. State budgets, he argues, offering no evidence, will reflect the "general balance of political power," and will thus allocate resources for the economic infrastructure needed by transnational capital and the urban amenities desired by the new professional elite strata at the expense of the social reproductive needs of urban migrant and immigrant labor. The fiscal crises that follow, he concludes, will generate a crisis of social reproduction in the global cities, met more often by police repression of the low-income migrant sector than by social policy initiatives.

In a retrospective review of the achievements and limits of world city research published a decade after his initial formulations, Friedmann (1995) has little to add to his basic argument. His more recent essay does however change the tone of the discourse, elaborate upon old theses, and introduce one new theme. Reflecting the often contentious effort by scholars and urban planners and policy makers alike to insert new contenders into the contest for global city status, Friedmann concludes that while it is still possible to arrange the commanding urban nodes of the global economy into a "hierarchy of spatial articulations," once the top of the hierarchy, namely New York, London, and Tokyo, are taken into account, "establishing such a hierarchy once and for all may . . . be a futile undertaking" (ibid.: 23). He argues that the world economy may be too volatile to allow a stable hierarchy to be constructed. Thus he revises his project away from the assignment of clear hierarchical rank to one of accepting a "rough notion" of differences in rank and then investigating the articulations of particular world cities with each other. This move enables him to consider historical changes that have eliminated some world cities from his list and added new contenders to the picture.

In my view this is a laudable move. It begins to open up the space for the investigation of a wider range of patterns of transnational urbanism. Yet because Friedmann's core assumptions remain economistic, the new path forward that he maps out is limited. Instead of exploring political and cultural differences among world cities stemming from their differing histories and the unique articulations of contemporary economic, political, and cultural flows coming together within their borders, Friedmann's new vision of world city politics stresses competition among would-be global cities to capture "ever more command and control functions" (ibid.). His new representation of cultural conflict in world cities produces a new universalism, a sharply demarcated duality that pits the "economic space" of the transnational capitalist class, whose interests are defined as the smooth functioning of global accumulation, against the "life space" of subaltern classes in the global cities, whose interests, à la David Harvey, are assumed to be "typically more territorial and local" (ibid.: 25). Once again a dynamic but placeless logic of global economic flows is opposed to a static image of place and local culture, now valorized, following Habermas and Heidegger, as the "life space" of being-in-the-world. Lost in this formulation are the cultural construction of economic spaces, the embeddedness of economic action, the transnationalization of urban culture, the war of position for "respect" among the putatively unitary "subaltern" classes, and the issues of power and conflict underlying these social constructions.

The quest for a fixed urban hierarchy should be abandoned, in my view not only because, as Friedmann has begun to recognize, hierarchical economic taxonomies are too static a formulation in the face of the volatility of capital investment flows, but also because of the multiple and often contradictory compositions of these flows (e.g. speculative vs. direct fixed investment). More importantly, this quest for a hierarchical ordering mechanism is fruitless because the local cultural spaces that are sites of transnational urbanism are also far less static than Friedmann and Harvey assume. Far from reflecting a static ontology of "being" or "community," localities are dynamic constructions "in the making." They are multiply inflected conjunctural sites of cultural and political as well as economic flows, projects, and practices. The cultural and political processes that go into their constant making and remaking are simply too dynamic to predict the course of urban development in advance of the actual political struggles through which contending spatial practices and cultural conflicts that constitute transnational urbanism are played out.

If in John Friedmann's view the actors decisively shaping world cities are constructed narrowly in terms of global bi-polar class relations, his framework at least leaves open a space for agents who socially construct global cities and relations of power that define their uses. The same cannot be said for the way in which the global city is represented in the writings of Saskia Sassen, particularly in her influential book *The Global City* (Sassen, 1991). Though not always consistently, Sassen represents global cities as material manifestations of a structural process of "globalization" operating largely behind people's backs to transform the economic functions, class composition, urban landscapes, and cultural patterns of global cities. The language of Sassen's discourse is infused with functionalist terminology. Global cities, as command centers, locations for financial and other specialized producer services, sites for the production of financial and technological innovations, and markets for these innovations, are seen as "required" by the new "global dynamic" because they concentrate control over vast resources. Economic globalization has ushered in a territorial dispersal of economic activity which, in turn, "creates a need for expanded central control and management." Thus, "key structures of the world economy are *necessarily* situated" in the global cities (ibid.: 4). Global cities are described as "modern molecules" of economic globalization. They follow a "new logic for concentration" (ibid.: 5). This logic, for Sassen, reflects a "fundamental dynamic," namely that "the more globalized the economy becomes, the higher the agglomeration of central functions in a relatively few sites, that is, the global cities" (ibid.).

Following this logic, Sassen locates three key cities, New York, London, and Tokyo, within "a set of global processes," which, in her view, underlie parallel changes in their economic base, spatial organization, and social structure in the 1980s, despite their different histories, culture, and politics. Much of her effort to document these changes is spent detailing the extent to which the three cities have become concentrated locations for global financial services, production sites for postindustrial producer services, and transactional spaces of direct foreign investment. This focus moves her beyond Friedmann's (1986) and my own early concern (Feagin and Smith, 1987; Smith and Tardanico, 1987) with global cities as nodal points for economic restructuring and spaces of political conflict, to a preoccupation with the theme of global cities as concentrated production sites for postindustrial services and financial goods. This shift in emphasis is precisely the point at which Sassen rejects a discursive space suitable for assessing power and agency in favor of one restricted to the language of the structural–functional logic of capitalist urbanization. There can be no question that this is an intentional move on her part. In her words (Sassen, 1991: 6):

> I am seeking to displace the focus of attention from the familiar issue of the
> power of large corporations over governments and economies, or supracorporate
> concentration of power through interlocking directorates or organizations such
> as the IMF. . . . My focus is not on power, but on production, the production of
> those inputs that constitute the capability for global control and the infrastruc-
> ture of jobs involved in this production.

The globalization narrative in *The Global City* is virtually devoid of historical actors. Indeed it explicitly *rejects* the actor, powerful or otherwise, as a unit
of analysis (ibid.: 325). We are thus left with a complex mapping of what
might be termed a *structural potential* for global command and control of
economic production and exchange. Using Sassen's own terms, she has pains-
takingly documented the global control "capability" of New York, London,
and Tokyo. Yet we cannot even be sure that the actors constructing this
infrastructural capacity might reside there or anywhere else, since it is not
social actors but "globalization" itself that "has given major cities a key role in
the management and control of such a global network" (ibid.: 324). When the
structural features of the global urban system are represented as dictated by the
functional "needs" of the leading economic sectors, then as Lipietz (1986) has
observed, it becomes difficult to see historical change at any point within the
system as open-ended.

In Sassen's view the production of the financial and organizational "inputs"
constituting the capacity for global economic control (e.g. international legal
and accounting services, management consulting, financial services) has consequences for the nation-state. By enabling the management of global production processes and "global markets for inputs and outputs," the rise of the
global cities is redefining the relation between city and nation. The national
urban system is becoming disarticulated from the global urban system, Sassen
argues, as older manufacturing cities in the United States, Great Britain, and
Japan decline due to the investment decisions made in the global cities.
Moreover, because "these cities constitute a system rather than merely competing with each other . . . what contributes to growth in the network of
global cities may well not contribute to growth in [their respective] nations"
(Sassen, 1991: 8–9). Sassen thus introduces a version of the postnationalist
discourse into her global cities narrative. Apparently, in her view, global cities
are globally and locally embedded but nationally disembedded.

Curiously, despite explicitly raising the question "Is there a global urban
hierarchy?" and entitling a chapter of *The Global City*, "Elements in a Global
Hierarchy," Sassen devotes very little attention to either ranking cities other
than New York, London, and Tokyo in terms of their financial or transactional functions, or mapping a network of cities tied together by global flows
of economic transactions. She does suggest a rather simplistic division of labor
among these three cities in which New York, and through it the US, becomes

the world's leading recipient of global financial flows such as direct foreign investment; Tokyo the leading net exporter of capital investment; and London the world's leading "throughput" of financial transactions (ibid.: 35–63, 327).

When the financial crisis in Japan in the late 1990s slowed Tokyo's export of capital to a trickle compared to that of the 1980s, Sassen's overly neat depiction of the new "transterritorial marketplace" in which New York, London, and Tokyo "fulfill distinct roles and function as a triad" (ibid.: 327) could be seen for what it is, a time-bound reflection of the historically specific position of the Japanese national economy at a time when its industries were generating surplus capital and financial markets around the globe were being deregulated by political means. The steadfast refusal of Japanese corporate managers to engage in corporate downsizing of their professional and managerial strata as a response to Japan's deepening financial crisis (*New York Times*, June 17, 1998) further suggests that territorially specific national corporate cultures continue to matter in the realization of global control capacities. These examples speak to the extent to which global economic processes are unavoidably embedded in historically specific political and sociocultural processes.

Sassen's treatment of class and spatial polarization in New York, London, and Tokyo, while also broadly economistic, is more historicized than her analysis of global finance-scapes and their inscription in global cities. She envisages social polarization as a structural feature of the new urban growth and restructuring trends. Sassen argues, and provides evidence, that major growth industries in business and financial services have a bi-polar employment and pay structure. She claims that the high-income gentrification occasioned by the rise of financial and other producer services "requires" low-wage service jobs providing luxuries, personal services, and construction. She notes that as a result of immigration, sweatshops and industrial home-work proliferate in the global cities. The emergent social order of the global city, in her view, shrinks the middle of the class structure and increases social and spatial polarization.

While focusing largely on economic restructuring trends to explain the polarization she discerns, Sassen nonetheless situates these trends coherently within a changed political context, one in which the power of trade unions has declined, the Fordist social compact of the postwar period has become unglued, the social wage has shrunk, and Keynesian economic growth policies of publicly subsidized suburban development are no longer in fashion. This move enriches Sassen's analysis of urban dualism. Yet having moved from the economism of financial transactions to the political economy of urban migration and the social geography of urban consumption, Sassen's bottom-line explanation for the changed political context she describes is structuralist rather than political–economic or sociocultural. She claims (Sassen, 1991: 333) that the generalized dismantling of the welfare state has come about because the social compact on which it was based "rested ultimately on an economic necessity" that is no longer present, namely, "the fact that the consumption capacity of a critical mass of workers was of central importance to profit realization for the leading industries in the economy." Since, in her view, postindustrial financial services have displaced the centrality of industrial manu-facturing and globalization has bypassed the nation–state as a cohesive unit of economic organization, the functional basis for the Keynesian welfare state has been transformed. In the last instance, for Sassen, changing economic func-tions rather than political power struggles determine urban outcomes. While urban and national politics may matter, they do not matter for much.

For Sassen, not only politics but also the structures of everyday urban life are decisively shaped by "the cultural forms accompanying these [economic] processes" (ibid.: 331). When culture is taken into account it is thus viewed in functionalist terms as a force holding the global city system together. As in the case of Harvey, cultural change is viewed as a by-product of economic restructuring, insuring reproduction of the system's major locational and allocational outcomes. Viewed in this light, urban poverty and social polariza-tion in the global cities are unavoidable by-products of economic restructuring alone.

The Limits of Global Economism

The global cities thesis centrally depends on the assumption that global eco-nomic restructuring precedes and determines urban spatial and sociocultural restructuring, inexorably transforming localities by disconnecting them from their ties to nation–states, national legal systems, local political cultures, and everyday place-making practices. In the past decade extensive research ques-tioning this core assumption on empirical grounds has opened up the dis-course on global cities and globalization more generally (Grosfoguel, 1995; Abu-Lughod, 1995; Ward, 1995; Cox, 1997a; Scott, 1997). After building my critique of the global cities discourse based on this research I will extend the argument by advancing a social constructionist analysis which exposes the entire discourse of globalization as a "tightly scripted narrative of differential power" (Gibson-Graham, 1996/1997: 1) that actually creates the powerless-ness that it projects by contributing to the hegemony of prevailing globalization metaphors of capitalism's global reach, local penetration, and placeless logic.

Many economic geographers have begun to reassess the claims made by exponents of the globalization thesis in terms of the empirical adequacy of the evidence for economic globalization. While not always concerned with global cities *per se*, this research has raised questions about the persistent power of "locality" even when processes of economic globalization are considered apart from their wider political and cultural contexts. This literature is well represented in Kevin Cox's *Spaces of Globalization: Reasserting the Power of the Local* (1997). In this book, studies by Cox (1997a, 1997b), Storper (1997), Gertler (1997), and Herod (1997) specify important national and local constraints on capital mobility experienced by multinational capital which limit its "global reach." These include the need for global industrial and service firms and real estate capitalists, in particular, to deal with (a) established economic relations within particular national and regional markets; (b) differing national cultural attitudes about worker–technology relations; (c) differing local workplace norms and worker attitudes; (d) locally specific producer information networks (e.g. in real estate); and (e) particular relations with local suppliers and dealers. A key question guiding this research approach, well summarized by Michael Storper (1997: 19) is: "How territorialized are particular types of economic relations?" Tracing out the research implications of these territorial and (re)territorializing constraints, Cox concludes that:

> The globalization debate has to take into account not just the deterritorializing forces, the emergence of a world of enhanced locational substitutability, but also the territorializing: those conditions, those social relations that result in enduring commitments to particular places, which can in turn be a source of competitive advantage and so serve to reinforce those commitments. *(Cox, 1997a: 19–43)*

Political and economic sociologists also have generated considerable research germane to the global cities thesis. This research likewise tends to reassert the power of the "local" in globalization. Rejecting the view that capitalist logic and global control capability are self-generating mechanisms, these researchers have devoted considerable attention to documenting the local political particularities characterizing putatively global cities. For example, Janet Abu-Lughod (1995) sensibly interrogates the character, causes, and consequences of the spatial and class polarization said to characterize and assumed to follow from the "globalization" of global cities. She sees a need to differentiate between the income inequality produced in such places by changes in state taxation and transfer policies and the inequality engendered by local and global labor market restructuring. (For a related critique, see White, 1998.) Moreover, New York, Los Angeles, and Chicago, all subject to processes of economic globalization, have different ethnic/racial hierarchies and varying degrees of spatial segregation as both causes and consequences of social inequality. Comparative-historical and grounded ethnographic investigation of such differences can help sort out the different forms and degrees of social and spatial inequality in these cities, and the local, national, and global determinants of these disparities. Not surprisingly, in sorting out these differences, local politics clearly matter. Differences in local civic cultures and political processes significantly mediate the inequalities observed in New York, Los Angeles, and Chicago. These local processes of political inclusion and exclusion, for example, help account for the difference between a new immigrant political incorporation process in New York City that is so thoroughly transnationalized that Mayor Rudy Giuliani regularly travelled to Santo Domingo, Dominican Republic to campaign for his re-election, while, in contrast, the political climate of Los Angeles was so exclusionary as to stigmatize Mexican and Salvadoran transnational migrants as politically unworthy "illegal aliens," thereby adding fuel to the multi-ethnic urban rebellion of 1992.

In addition to its inattention to the details of local political cultures, the global cities discourse has been characterized by a lack of attention to differences in local institutional structures of governance and administration. Peter Ward (1995), for instance, has pointed out that world cities researchers have failed to analyze world cities as cities, setting aside consideration of their local political and social structures, and other local forms of human agency like political management and administrative structures. Ward views cities as "outcomes of conditioning relations with the outside, forged through an articulation and engagement with regional local elites and multiplex social and political structures" (ibid.: 299). This argument is generally well taken.

Nevertheless, there is a danger that those persuaded by the argument advanced thus far will proceed from a kind of neatly nested or highly bounded view of the "local" dimension of urban politics, in which purely "inside" structures and agents interact with purely "outside" actors and processes to produce the historical and contemporary character of global city politics. This view lacks an appreciation of the role of social, political, and economic *networks* in criss-crossing the boundaries between spatial "insides" and "outsides" and thus complexly articulating local with global social processes. (For further development of the political implications of the bounded territorial vs. network view of political processes, see Low, 1997: 240–76.)

A central argument of this book is that attention to the analysis of transnational social networks is one way out of this impasse. The practices of transnational political networks exemplify the ways in which situated actors socially construct historically specific projects that become localized within particular cities throughout the world, thereby shaping their urban politics and social life. This type of urban politics is constituted as people connected across borders in transnational networks interact with more local institutional structures and actors, as well as with such putatively more global actors as multinational corporations and international agencies, to produce urban change. The local and the global are thus mutually constitutive in particular places at particular times.

Ramon Grosfoguel (1995) is a political sociologist who has been particularly sensitive to the importance of this sort of network analysis. By my reading, the contemporary urban development of Miami, as analyzed by Grosfoguel (for the alternative reading see Sassen and Portes, 1993), is an excellent example of the transnational urbanism I seek to describe and inscribe in this book. Since Grosfoguel's analysis is situated squarely within the global cities discourse, I will briefly rehearse his argument here, both to critique the global cities discourse and to illustrate the argument for transnational urbanism advanced in the second half of this book.

By my reading, Grosfoguel's nuanced, historicized analysis of Miami's rising fortune as a center for international trade demonstrates convincingly that Miami's increasing prominence as a nodal point in international trade between the US and Latin America was driven more by Cold War considerations of military strategy and geopolitical symbolism than by any dominant economic logic of globalization. Miami's productive infrastructure as well as its emergent Cuban business community was heavily subsidized economically by US state policies that followed from these considerations. Miami's rise to regional promin- ence in the global economy was politically supported as well by local counter- revolutionary Cuban elite social networks tied to other anti-communist elites in the Caribbean Basin through ties and operations pursued by the US Central Intelligence Agency (Grosfoguel, 1995: 165). Far from being an outcome of an overriding global economic logic, Miami's economic role as a regional center for international trade and safe haven for Latin American capital was politically produced and symbolically inscribed by historically specific political actors and state policies that constituted Miami as a showcase of the US economic model in the hotly contested political spaces of the Caribbean Basin and Central and South America.

The key actors in Grosfoguel's global city story include military organiza- tions, intelligence agencies, foreign policy officials, communication and media enterprises, and transnational political networks, along with transnational cor- porations. His is a story in which global economic logic is downplayed and transnational political alliances are localized and "come together" in Miami to produce the transformation of that city's spatial form, economic functions, and local political life. To the extent that Miami can be called a global city it has achieved that status by virtue of the geopolitical structuring of economic investment, not because of its internal agglomeration of functional economic control capabilities. While Grosfoguel chooses to term Miami a global city on the basis of his analysis, it is not necessary to accept this label to appreciate both the richness of his story and its contribution to the advancement of my approach to transnational urbanism.

Historicizing the Global City

This brings me to the next part of my argument. The global cities literature needs to be situated historically as well as politically and sociospatially. Clearly, attention to the interplay of contemporary local and global dynamics in the area of urban spatial restructuring has been a useful focal point for urban theory. The urban literature by economic geographers and sociologists has placed in wider geographical perspective such issues as competition for capital investment and labor flows among cities and regions, as well as between urban markets and peripheral export-processing zones (e.g. Portes and Walton, 1981; Friedmann and Wolff, 1982; Sassen-Koob, 1984b; Sassen, 1988). However, it is necessary to view this literature in wider historical perspective. When viewed in this light, for example, studies in urban social history by Wolf (1982) and Tilly (1983) stress that contemporary global processes of industrialization, deindustrialization, and urban restructuring are in essence nothing new; they have been an expanding and intensifying feature of the world economy since capitalism's embryonic stages in early modern Europe (see also Chase-Dunn, 1984).

In a trenchant analysis of the unmet promises of contemporary globalization, Peter Beinart (1997) points out that the current tendency to treat economic globalization as a purely techno-economic process of modernization and development operating behind people's backs is nothing new. Prior to World War I, when Great Britain was the world's leading military and economic power, by various measures of international trade and investment such as direct foreign investment, merchandise exports, and cross-market correlations between asset price movements, global financial markets were more fully integrated than they have been before or since (ibid.: 21). British domination of the terms of the relatively open international trade and investment system was secured by geopolitical means and sustained by the British navy. Yet leading British international relations theorists and foreign policy elites at the time viewed this form of economic globalization "not as a fact of politics based on a security system, but as a fact of technology, independent of politics" (ibid.: 21).

Norman Angell, a leading exponent of this view, penned a passage in his 1910 book *The Great Illusion* that is strongly reminiscent of contemporary representations of economic globalization in the global cities discourse. "International finance," Angell wrote, "has become so interwoven with trade and industry that . . . political and military power can in reality do nothing. . . . These little recognized facts, mainly the outcome of purely modern conditions (rapidity of communication creating a greater complexity and delicacy of the credit system) have rendered the problems of modern international politics profoundly and essentially different from the ancient" (quoted in Beinart, 1997: 20). Among the "profound differences" discerned by Angell was his belief that global economic interdependence, achieved and expanded by new technologies of communication, was forcing nation-states to integrate peacefully into the fiscal discipline of the global marketplace, rendering military power irrelevant, balance-of-power diplomacy *vis-à-vis* Germany unnecessary, and globalization inevitable (Wade, 1996; Beinart, 1997). For better or worse, the shock of World War I at that time, like the political crises in Mexico and Indonesia today, vividly underlines the point that globalization is an inherently political process, not a technological or functional mode of development, independent of politics. These crises were produced not by "structural contradictions," but by historically specific social and political actors who rejected the inevitability of the economistic logic of globalization and acted to redefine the terms of global interdependence.

In a series of important writings, including their influential article "Globalization and the Future of the Nation-state" (1995) and their book *Globalization in Question* (1996), Paul Hirst and Grahame Thompson offer a pointed critique of the globalization thesis germane to my analysis. Their historical analysis of changes in international trade, production, and investment from the pre-World War I era until the present demonstrates that these processes continue to occur disproportionately within the context of nation-states and the changing geopolitical system of relations among nation-states. While the Great Powers may no longer exercise the hegemonic geopolitical influence over the terms of international economic relations that they did prior to World War I, they are "still in business" in the form of G-7 efforts to regulate the global financial and trading system (Hirst and Thompson, 1995: 419).

The USA, while no longer enjoying the fruits of the post-World War II Pax Americana, is still the "first among equals" among the G-7; its military power remains unrivaled. It is no accident that recently Russia was selectively incorporated into this political club, now the G-8. Russia's inclusion was largely, if not entirely because of its nuclear capability, and the desire of G-7 political elites to regulate it by political means. President Boris Yeltsin was thus segmentally included in the political but not the economic discussions of this geopolitical regulatory structure. Great Power politics thus still contextualizes and constrains multinational corporations as well as states pursuing globalization strategies and helps set the boundaries within which economic globalization materializes and its locational impacts are played out. The increasing visibility of unfolding efforts by the G-8, the World Trade Organization, the IMF, the World Bank, and the regional trading blocs to regulate global economic relations in the late 1990s, helps explain why "global governance" has become a crucial topic of theoretical reflection, empirical research, and political debate, drawing attention even from previously more economistic urban scholars such as Sassen, who is beginning to contribute importantly to this emergent research field (see, for example, Sassen, 1995, 1998). Ironically, however, the very emergence of these institutional regulatory efforts belies the expectation of the global cities theorists that an ordered urban hierarchy is an already existing structural feature of the evolving capitalist world system.

The "Global Governance" Agenda

In light of the historical legacy of international economic and geopolitical relations just considered, it is important to situate the global cities discourse in the contemporary historical context of the far larger and still ongoing public discourse on the meaning of globalization. Recent work by McMichael (1996), Drainville (1998), and others (e.g. Mander and Goldsmith, 1996) argues that globalization, like its binary "local diversity," needs to be understood as a historical construct rather than a naturalized economic process operating behind our backs. As McMichael (1996: 27) points out, global economic exchanges have predated not only the contemporary period but also capitalism *per se*. Why, then, are these exchanges given the appearance of a ruling logic of the late twentieth century, propelling and legitimating, as they do, such practices as corporate downsizing, state deregulation, and capital mobility, all justified under the icon of "creditworthiness"? Whose historical construct is "globalization" anyway?

Today's grand narrative of economic globalization has been advanced most forcefully not by academics but by an emergent international monetarist regime, a set of institutional actors who have instituted a political offensive against developmental states and institutions. The globally oriented institutions spearheading this offensive were established "under the auspices of the 1980s debt crisis" (ibid.: 25) to advance the monetarist agenda of global efficiency and financial credibility, against the nationally oriented institutions of developing countries. This globalist political project has, in turn, produced a series of struggles over the meaning of "the local," as cities and other localities, via their political, economic, and cultural actors and institutions, seek either to find a niche within the new global public philosophy, or resist pressures to "globalize," i.e. to practice fiscal austerity and conform to monetarist principles and policies.

The origins of the contemporary ideology of globalization are historically specific. They constitute efforts by powerful social forces to replace the developmentalist institutional framework of the 1960s to 1980s, premised on modernization theory, with a new mode of economic integration of cities and states to world market principles. Abandoning the argument that a convergent path of development will follow from the spread of Western-oriented "modernization," it is now argued that locational specialization or "niche formation" is an inevitable by-product of globalization. The principles legitimating economic globalization have been posited by their advocates as inevitable by-products, or ruling logics, of the material condition of globalization "on the ground," rather than, as they are, the social constructs of historically specific social interests, including transnational corporate and financial elites, heads of international agencies, state managers that have embraced neoliberalism, various academic ideologues, and most especially "the managers of newly empowered multilateral institutions like the IMF, the World Bank, and the World Trade Organization" (ibid.: 28; see also Drainville, 1998). This regime seeks to transform the discourse of development to one in which shrinking the state is a social virtue and "structural adjustment" an unavoidable imperative. This neoliberal regime of "global governance" as it has been called (Drainville, 1998), is viewed as an incipient global ruling class whose efforts to achieve global economic management can only be thwarted when globalization itself is recognized as a historically specific and hotly contested project of social actors and agents rather than an inevitable condition of contemporary existence.

McMichael and others clearly overestimate the coherence of this global project and underestimate the potential effectiveness of the oppositional forces they acknowledge. As grassroots social-movement scholars operating from quite different perspectives have shown (e.g. Sikkink, 1993; M. P. Smith, 1994; Smith, Pagnucco and Chatfield, 1997; Castells, 1996), forceful national, local, and transnational political identities have sprung up to resist the hegemonic ideology and austerity policies imposed by the global neoliberal regime. Thus it is not possible to agree entirely with this pessimistic assessment of the global future. It is surprising, nonetheless, that the global cities scholars, whose politics would surely oppose "global governance" based on neoliberal principles, seem not to have given much thought to the question of whether their research agenda and its "objective" findings implicitly naturalize that very project by legitimating the "reality" of global cities as part and parcel of an unstoppable process of economic globalization. Unintentionally, their epistemology thus becomes the ontology of global cities.

Once globalization is unmasked as the most recent historical version of the free-market ideology, once it is recognized, as Polanyi taught us long ago, that "the free market was planned," a more fruitful way forward is suggested by the trenchant critique of the globalization discourse offered by two leading post-Marxist feminist theorists writing under the pen name J. K. Gibson-Graham (1996/1997). Gibson-Graham argue that the globalization thesis, both in terms of the economy of global production and finance and in terms of the culture of global consumerism fueled by the assumed capitalist domination of global telecommunications, suffers from theoretical and empirical overreach, but has telling political consequences. These consequences – a politics of fear and subjection by workers, communities, and other potentially oppositional forces – are most apparent when the two threads of the globalization thesis are combined into a single masculinist grand narrative of the penetration of capitalist social relations not only of production and consumption but also of meaning-making and the constitution of subjectivity. (For examples of the latter see Jameson, 1991; Rouse, 1995.)

The global penetration metaphor may be challenged on theoretical and empirical grounds. Theoretically, Gibson-Graham argue that by relying on the sexual metaphor of penetration to invoke the power of capital, but failing to acknowledge that sexuality is a process of *inter*penetration, not a one-way flow, the globalization discourse refuses a contingent countervision of the capitalist economy "as penetrable by non-capitalist economic forms" and social relations (Gibson-Graham, 1996/1997: 17–18). Relatedly, the very logic of the metaphor of the global reach of capitalist command and control arrangements can be reinterpreted as a project inherently subject to over-extension, a set of tasks often frustrated by global overreach.

Despite the deconstructionist tone of their epistemological argument, Gibson-Graham advance their political argument by empirical means. This usefully challenges globalization theorists to deal with evidence contrary to the expectations of their theories. Thus, for instance, globalization theorists must address the fact that only a small percentage of transnational corporations are truly global in scale of operations, most others being either bi-national or "reaching" only three or four nation-states (see Dicken, 1997). The role of national and regional business cultures discussed above also must be considered as a constraint on capitalism's global reach. More pointedly, global corporate investment has been shown to be vulnerable to such countervailing social and political forces as (a) changes in political leadership or trade policies; (b) loose transnational networks of corporate raiders eager to liquidate the assets of targeted transnational corporations (TNCs); (c) the institutional power of labor-controlled pension funds; (d) cross-border labor organizing campaigns; and (e) transnational grassroots activism (Gibson-Graham, 1996/1997: 8–13).

The potential efficacy of active political resistance to global neoliberalism is insightfully illustrated in Gibson-Graham's narration of a transnational political campaign conducted during the early 1990s against a TNC, the Ravenwood Aluminum Company (RAC). The campaign was led by the United Steelworkers of America (USWA), working through the channels of several international labor organizations. It combined cross-border political lobbying by labor unions in 28 countries, on five continents, with a US-based consumer boycott. By going global, the unions and transnational grassroots activists involved in this campaign succeeded in obtaining a favorable labor contract in the USA and imposed restrictions on the key global trader who had organized the purchase of RAC in a leveraged buyout. Gibson-Graham (ibid.: 9–10) conclude their narrative with a metaphor of dogged determination, noting that "terrier-like, the USWA pursued the company relentlessly around the globe yanking and pulling at it until it capitulated. Using their own globalized networks, workers met internationalism with internationalism and eventually won."

The moral of the story is clear. Far from being the exclusive preserve of global capital, global space is a discursive arena and very much a contested terrain. One key dimension of globalization, the telecommunications revolution, is often assumed to be a straightforward tool of global capital in organizing production, directing financial flows, and orchestrating consumer desire. While it may facilitate these processes to some extent, it also has become a viable channel for spatially extending the contested terrain of globalization, enabling oppositional forces to jump scale and go global. New technologies of communication such as e-mail, fax, and the internet have become viable mechanisms facilitating the transnationalization of culture and politics, enabling cross-border information exchange, transnational political networking, and the sociopolitical organization of a wide variety of new forms of what I have elsewhere termed "transnational grassroots politics" (Smith, 1994). Such modes of transnational political networking include, but are not limited to, transnational labor organizing (Herod, 1997), international human rights campaigns (Sikkink, 1993; Castells, 1996), indigenous peoples' movements (Kearney, 1995), multinational feminist projects (Sturgeon, 1997), and global environmental activism (Princen and Finger, 1994). For better or worse, the transnationalization of communications provides access as well to such transnational networks of social action "from below" as Islamic fundamentalism, neo-Nazism, and the militia movement (see Castells, 1997; Tarrow, 1998), a development that progressive scholars and social activists doubtless find less salutary. The question of the scope and impact of such transnational grassroots movements, and their implications for urban theory, will be revisited in greater detail in chapter 7.

Transnational Urbanism: Beyond Reification

In light of these dynamic political and cultural developments, it is time to move beyond the boundaries of the global cities discourse. Instead of pursuing the quest for a hierarchy of nested cities arranged neatly in terms of their internal functions to do the bidding of international capital, it is more fruitful to assume a less easily ordered urban world of localized articulations, where sociocultural as well as political–economic relations criss-cross and obliterate sharp distinctions between inside and outside, local and global. These partially overlapping and often contested networks of meaning are relations of power that link people, places, and processes to each other transnationally in overlapping and often contested social relations rather than in hierarchical patterns of interaction (see, for example, Appadurai, 1990, 1996; Smith and Guarnizo, 1998).

Numerous examples of these criss-crossing linkages that literally "re-place" the urban, reconfiguring "the city" from a global epiphenomenon to a fluid site of contested social relations of meaning and power, are discussed in Part II of this book. To bring this chapter to a close, however, a historically specific example of what I have in mind may be helpful. I offer the case of the political crisis in Indonesia in which grassroots student protests and urban

unrest in Jakarta and other Indonesian cities brought down the Suharto regime. These street-level forms of political practice have been represented as
"local" responses to a perceived national crisis. Nevertheless, the protests,
occurring in various cities throughout Indonesia, were occasioned by the
transnational IMF austerity policies imposed on Indonesia from a putative
"outside" as a condition for an IMF bailout of the Suharto regime in the face
of the Asian financial crisis. Moreover, global media representations of the
interplay between Suharto and the IMF reinforced the outside–inside duality
by featuring a widely circulated photograph of an IMF official standing behind
Suharto with arms folded as he signed an IMF austerity agreement. While
the bodily gesture was meaningless to the IMF official, it was pregnant with
meaning within Indonesian cultural practice, symbolizing personal domination
of one body by another and creating an impression of Suharto's declining
strength as a symbol of national development and modernization. This impression was reinforced when the austerity policies were at first avoided and then
implemented selectively "on the inside" by Suharto, who imposed sharp price
increases on daily necessities such as food and fuel for ordinary citizens, while
striving to protect his family's vast fortune in the face of a declining currency
market and maintain the collusive business practices with ethnic Chinese
business elites that had been the source of the family fortune.

Prior to Suharto's fall, a keen observer of the Indonesian scene (Farley,
1998) described this collusive arrangement as follows:

> The Chinese elite provides business skills and links to a regional [i.e. transnational]
> financial network. Suharto's ruling circle grants lucrative monopolies and con-
> cessions in key commodities and markets. Economists estimate that more than
> 80 percent of Indonesia's top business groups are controlled by Chinese; of
> those many have ties to the government's inner circles.

Thus, a key target of the popular urban protests that eventually led to
Suharto's ouster were the wealthy Chinese business elites that some scholars
(e.g. Ong, 1999) depict as part of a Chinese diaspora, a transnational entrepreneurial class tied to networks of Chinese business elites operating in other
cities in Asia and throughout the world. This group, comprising less than 3
percent of the Indonesian population, dominates the nation's economy and
has nearly 70 percent of the nation's wealth, but has been absent from the
military and the public political arena. Thus, a "Chinese" ethnic background
became an easy initial target of nationalist and racist discourses and practices
during the early stages of the financial crisis. Indeed, as criticism of Suharto
and his inner circle mounted, the government tried to deflect the blame onto
a more generalized target, the entire ethnic Chinese population (Farley, 1998).

This effort was initially partially successful, but when the student component of the urban protests emerged in Jakarta and other Indonesian university

cities, the various student groups focused like a laser beam on political democratization as well as economic grievances. Their frequent demonstrations
charging corruption and calling for Suharto's ouster captured as much, if not
more, global media attention than the initial round of anti-Chinese violence.
The growing student protests in various cities throughout Indonesia also further emboldened the discontented urban masses, who lashed out in a new
round of urban rioting, looting, and burning directed largely against banks,
shops, supermarkets, electronics stores, and the home of a prominent Chinese
billionaire (Pintak, 1998: A17). These developments, in turn, refocused discontent on the vast wealth of Suharto and his family. In this changed and
highly charged political context, Suharto was unable to defend his interests by
commanding the army to repress the students or the urban masses. Instead the
army largely stood by during the demonstrations and street rioting, as various
military leaders maneuvered behind the scenes to oust Suharto and jockeyed
for position in the new regime.

Suharto's fall from grace and power in Indonesia was accompanied elsewhere in Asia by the emergence of anti-IMF protests in cities like Seoul,
Korea, where in late May 1998 tens of thousands of workers walked off their
jobs and participated in street demonstrations in central Seoul directed against
a state law making it easier to lay off workers. The law was passed by the
South Korean government under pressure from the IMF, which had made
increased "labor flexibility" a condition of granting Korea a $58 billion bailout
package. While the workers railed against their government and the Korean
corporate conglomerates, or *chaebol*, whose elites have escaped the hardships
experienced by ordinary Koreans during the financial crisis, they left little
doubt that they perceived the IMF as responsible for their plight. Standing in
front of Seoul Station, the city's transportation hub, the workers raised their
fists and chanted slogans like: "Let's destroy restructuring! Let's fight to secure
our jobs!" The Korean Confederation of Trade Unions representing over
500,000 members followed up the demonstration by demanding that the state
renegotiate the "labor flexibility" issue with the IMF (Strom, 1998).

In the face of increasingly visible popular opposition against their policies,
both the IMF and the World Bank have been forced to reconsider the rigidity
with which their agents have pursued the neoliberal agenda. For example, in
July 1998 the World Bank resumed aid to Indonesia by granting a $1 billion
loan under far less stringent terms than had previously been expected of the
Suharto regime. The new accord allowed for more social spending than
previous agreements and permitted the state to run a sizable budget deficit, an
item explicitly prohibited in previous agreements (Sanger, 1998).

In the Indonesian case, a complex web of social relations and conflicting
discourses of "globalization" came together and were localized in confrontations
in Jakarta and other Indonesian cities. In the historically specific context of a
general economic crisis in Asia, accompanied by urban protests in Indonesia

and transnationally, a state-centered power structure that had colluded for three decades with a transnational economic network to regulate and appropriate the lion's share of Indonesia's economic wealth and expansion was significantly challenged. This alliance was caught in a collision course. They were squeezed between transnational regulatory bodies such as the IMF and the World Bank seeking to legitimate neoliberalism by ending "crony capitalism," and a series of geographically "local" irruptions of discontent in Indonesian cities by students who were connected to transnational communication circuits by internet information flows, and perceived themselves as central agents of democratization operating on a "global" stage (Kusno, 1998). The student protests were accompanied by other episodes of urban violence by popular classes venting frustration at Chinese ethnic scapegoats or simply seeking survival in the face of austerity-induced economic hardships. These local and global crises of confidence were mediated by national cultural understandings, played out in the global media, and had effects beyond the boundaries of the nation-state. Though differently inflected, a related global–national–local discourse on economic "globalization" was being played out in Seoul. This is the stuff of the new urban politics of transnational urbanism.

The future course of transnational urbanism in Jakarta and Seoul are open-ended. Yet even a brief examination of these cases clearly illustrates the fruitfulness of viewing cities as sites where national and transnational practices become localized; local social actions reverberate transnationally, if not globally; and the networks connecting these social relations and practices intersect in time and space and can be discerned, studied, and understood.

A further advantage of this approach to urban studies is that a wide variety of cities, rather than a handful of sites of producer service functions, or a score of interwoven, mainly Western, centers of global command and control, become appropriate sites for comparative research. Viewing cities as contested meeting grounds of transnational urbanism invites their comparative analysis as sites of (a) the localization of transnational economic, sociocultural, and political flows; (b) the transnationalization of local socioeconomic, political, and cultural forces; and (c) the practices of the networks of social action connecting these flows and forces in time and space. These emergent transnational cities are human creations best understood as sites of multicentered, if not decentered, agency, in all of their overlapping untidiness. This is a project in which studying mediated differences in the patterns of intersecting global, transnational, national, and local flows and practices, in particular cities, becomes more important than cataloging the economic similarities of hierarchically organized financial, economic, or ideological command and control centers viewed as constructions of a single agent – multinational capital.

The "new urban politics" uncovered by this move is a disjointed terrain of global media flows, transnational migrant networks, state-centered actors that side with and oppose global actors, local and global growth machines and green movements, multilocational entrepreneurs, and multilateral political in-stitutions, all colluding and colliding with each other, ad infinitum. The urban future following from this contested process of "place-making" is far less predictable but far more interesting than the grand narrative of global capital steam-rolling and swallowing local political elites and pushing powerless people around that inevitably seems to follow from the global cities model. Rather than viewing global cities as central expressions of the global accumu-lation of capital, all cities can then be viewed in the fullness of their particular linkages with the worlds outside their boundaries. Their "urban" specificity, in short, becomes a matter of discerning at given historical moments "the particularity of the social interactions which intersect at that location, and of what people make of them, in their interpretations and in their lives" (Massey, 1994a: 117).

Reimagining Los Angeles from the Ground Up | 4

Many of the changes in LA's urban landscape – the increasing population density, the appearance of street vending and other informal economic activities like neighborhood garage sales – are seen by elders, mostly Anglo, as symptoms of the erosion of our quality of life. . . . Just what is it that LA fears? The terror of mangos, papayas, neighbors gathering on doorsteps, actually conversing with one another on the street? For too long LA has turned its back on the true nature of the city, which is to seek human warmth, to seek the other through the multiplicity of experiences that is only possible in the city. It is this human contact that creates character and history.

Ruben Martinez, "Meet the Future in the Past"

The focus of the global cities discourse has been on the centrality of global cities to the evolving global political economy, as key command and control centers, as engines driving global economic growth, primarily through the capacity of their political economies to command capital flows. Global cities are depicted metaphorically as magnetic fields attracting global labor migrants as well as capital flows. Global economic restructuring and labor migration are frequently depicted as two sides of a single dynamic: the general reorganization of capitalism orchestrated from the global cities. Research on global cities has evolved into a kind of economistic description of three places: New York, London, and Tokyo, with Los Angeles often thrown in for good measure. How valid is this representation of Los Angeles?

The closest approximation to this conceptualization of Los Angeles as a global city is to be found in the work of Saskia Sassen (1988, 1991) discussed in the previous chapter. Although Sassen's empirical base for generalizations about global cities has been drawn from her analysis of the social organization of financial and business services in New York, London, and Tokyo, she also has treated Los Angeles as an economic contender for designation as a global city (see, for example, Sassen-Koob, 1984b). John Friedmann's work on world cities also treats Los Angeles as a major world city because of its presumed economic place in an emergent global system of cities (see chapter 3).

Sassen and Friedmann are clearly not alone in casting Los Angeles as a global metropole. The work of the postmodern geographer Edward Soja (1986, 1989, 1996) has been most explicit in representing Los Angeles as a global city, in part because of the global cultural reach of its film industry. Nevertheless, for Soja, as for Sassen and Friedmann, it is the "progressive globalization of its political economy" and not its impact on global popular culture that makes Los Angeles "perhaps the epitomizing World City" (Soja, 1986: 256). In the booming 1980s Soja and his LA school colleague Allen Scott attributed this period of growth to the rise of Los Angeles to global city status, characterizing LA as "one of the most significant hubs of contemporary international capitalism" that had "taken on the character of a truly global city, above and beyond its nodal position with respect to the western US and the Pacific Rim" (Scott and Soja, 1986). Other, differently inflected, but nonetheless periodizing and largely economistic grand narratives celebrating Los Angeles have inscribed the Los Angeles region as a paradigm case of late-capitalist postmodern urbanism (Jameson, 1984; Dear, 1991a, 1991b; Dear and Flusty, 1999) and a developmental model of polynucleated regional development (Scott, 1993, 1995). Similar tropes of staged economic development may be found in other writings of what is now called the LA school of urban studies (see the literature critiqued in Curry and Kenney, 1999). These grand narratives of Los Angeles's paradigmatic status tend to take the political out of political economy and treat the cultural as entirely derivative of epochal economic transformations.

My aim in this chapter is not to offer an alternative grand narrative of Los Angeles's political, economic, or sociocultural development to displace the boosterist tropes often found in the discourses on Los Angeles as paradigmatic postmodern global city. Instead I wish to move beyond all of these staged developmental models of Los Angeles's economic and cultural landscape. In my view each of these approaches shares in common a tendency to treat LA as a "thing," a material manifestation of something entirely new in the history of capitalism and urban development. (For a related critique of the LA school see Beauregard and Haila, 1997.) Instead, I offer a political–economic and sociocultural reading of Los Angeles that tries to capture certain features of LA's transnational urbanism from below. My reading highlights past influences of state policies and the practices of transnational sociocultural networks on Los Angeles's current racial and ethnic relations and tries to retell its economic development story in less teleological terms. My purpose is to provide a historical context for interpreting the character of transnational urbanism in contemporary Los Angeles.

This chapter thus culminates in a narrative account of the making and remaking of the Los Angeles neighborhood of Koreatown over the past three decades. My narrative is intended to convey some of the texture and tone of one facet of LA's transnational urbanism. The story of the social construction of Koreatown is a grounded story of transnational business and household formation, struggles over livelihood, place-making sociospatial practices, and grassroots social activism that infuses our understanding of "everyday life" in contemporary Los Angeles not only with a degree of transnationality, but also with a significant measure of agency and dynamism from "in between" and "below" that is noticeably absent from the "LA as global city" discourse, save for an occasional rhetorical call for disruptions from "the margins" of the unidirectional logics of postmodern hyperspace and global city functions. The story I will tell is both hard to conceive and easy to marginalize if we start from a key determinist assumption shared by the global city theorists and the LA school alike, namely that contemporary Los Angeles is a straightforward resultant of the workings of an entity known as "the global capitalist economy," conceived as an external reality "that is revealed rather than constituted by thought" (Arvidson, 1995: 9).

Post-Marxist critic Enid Arvidson (1995) has offered a trenchant critique of this way of viewing cities and urban development. She has shown that the project of those who would apply this logic to Los Angeles has been to map the contours of a postmodern built environment assumed to be largely a product of late capitalist developmental logic. In the case of the LA school Arvidson shows that urban theorists writing in this genre, like Michael Dear and Edward Soja, among others, have followed David Harvey's lead by appropriating Frederic Jameson's theoretical framework. In so doing they have combined in their reasoning (a) a depth model of social relations in which an underlying economic formation structures the cultural forms of particular epochs; (b) a conception of the economy as forming only one set of productive relations; and (c) a conception of capitalism as an independent reality operating entirely outside the processes of thought. Starting from these assumptions it is a short step to the reduction of various cultural processes, such as transnational social network formation and urban place-making practices, to mere epiphenomena whose "surface" appearances conceal an "underlying" economic logic operating "out there" and mask late capitalism's characteristic modes of domination, exploitation, and surplus appropriation. The spatial diversity of Los Angeles is thereby explained not as the result of the crisscrossing of heterogeneous social processes but as a differentiating mask used by multinational capital to conceal the underlying economic unity of the postmodern metropolis.

By reinscribing the capital vs. labor contradiction in postmodern Los Angeles as a grand narrative in which the poor, non-white oppressed struggle against a white, global capitalist elite oppressor (Arvidson, 1995: 15–16), this reading fails to account for a variety of forms of social antagonism and re-source extraction, both capitalist and non-capitalist, e.g. the surplus extractions involved in "shared ethnicity" discussed below, that are unevenly spread across the LA landscape, pitting various non-white groups against each other and even, at times, against themselves. Moreover, by showing little concern for the role of state policies in urban development, save as a globally bypassed relic, a good deal of the history of urban restructuring in Los Angeles is likewise rendered opaque. My own approach to understanding changing socioeconomic and political relations in Los Angeles shares the post-Marxist emphasis on power, underlines the interplay of the macro-politics of the state and the micro-politics of social networks, and views the economy as a socially constructed conceptual category emerging through power struggles rather than an underlying epochal totality that structures a period's cultural and political forms.

If we try to take stock of Los Angeles using the assumptions and criteria underlying the various grand narratives of capitalist globalization just consid-ered, I will argue, LA cannot be viewed as a dynamic center of global capital-ism. Rather, it might more properly be represented as a dependent city, a receiver rather than a sender of transnational commands and controls. In the global city narrative, Los Angeles's political economy is represented as a key engine of Pacific Rim economic dynamism. A close historical reading of the Los Angeles political economy from the early 1970s until the late 1990s, however, reveals the uneven and fluctuating character of global investment flows into the Los Angeles region. Although LA did attract global investment by Japanese and other Asian finance capitalists, largely in a downtown real estate boom that peaked by the late 1980s, the Los Angeles political economy remained excessively dependent on US defense spending as its central engine of growth. It thus experienced rapid economic decline in the early 1990s following the end of the Cold War. While its media-related economic sectors had begun to reverse its decline since the mid 1990s, LA's highly fluctuating economic fortunes over the past three decades render problematic those rep-resentations by some global city devotees characterizing Los Angeles as "the industrial growth pole of the twentieth century" (Soja, 1986). Addressing the "social polarization" assumptions of the global city narrative, I will further show that the diverse racial and ethnic landscape of Los Angeles is the result of the spatial relocalization and temporal convergence of historically particular social networks of transnational migrants and refugees drawn to Los Angeles by contextual factors other than a simple global logic of capital accumulation or a "global control capacity" implemented by its financial and business ser-vice sector.

The articulations of the global and the local in Los Angeles constitute its transnational urbanism. These criss-crossing articulations are both more complex and more fascinating than those expressed within the global cities framework.

There are transnational forces and processes localized in Los Angeles, to be sure, just as there are national, regional, and local ones. Sorting out these forces and processes that have "come together" in Los Angeles is by no means easy, but it is the task at hand. The question of why LA has become a kind of "receiver from below," an obscure object of desire, for so many transnational migrants from so many places across the globe, despite the rapid ups and downs of its economic fortunes, is central to this task.

Mexican Transmigration to Los Angeles

The case of Mexican migration to Los Angeles must be dealt with first, because of its complexity and because it does not fit neatly into the economic globalization motif. The most obvious dimensions of the story of Mexican migration to Los Angeles are its timing and its vast scale. More than two thirds of all Latinos living in Los Angeles are of Mexican origin. Many of these are longtime Angelenos who are Mexican-American US citizens. They are the offspring of earlier generations of Mexican migrants, whose migration pre-ceded the epoch of global economic restructuring and was driven more by the ebbs and flows of US agricultural policy and its permissions and constraints than by global developments. This is an old story, but one that has long fed the endemic local racist stereotyping of Mexican migrants as "uneducated peasants" or "low riders" by middle-class Angelenos. These stereotypes have frequently had substantial material consequences. During the Great Depression, for example, long before California voters passed Proposition 187, but foreshadowing its racist spirit, Los Angeles initiated a voluntary deportation program that led to thousands of unwelcome Mexican transmigrants returning to their native land (Garcia, 1994). During the 1950s many more thousands of Mexican migrants to Los Angeles were forcefully repatriated as part of a US government policy known as Operation Wetback.

A more recent dimension of Mexican migration to Los Angeles is rooted in the operation of another dimension of US state policy, the Immigration Reform and Control Act (IRCA) of 1986. The amnesty provisions of IRCA allowed undocumented Mexican workers who had been living in California for four years preceding the amnesty to obtain green cards. Although not envisaged in the IRCA amnesty, many of the hundreds of thousands of newly legalized male workers who had been living in transnational households then chose to bring their wives and children to live with them in California, thus dramatically altering the gender composition of more recent Mexican migration.

IRCA was passed in part at the behest of California growers to insure a large, and hence cheap, labor supply. In addition to the amnesty, other loop-holes in the law allowed California growers to retain workers who had worked in California agriculture for as little as 90 days in the previous year, and even to replenish their supply of legalized farm workers by replacing those newly legalized workers who chose to move from rural to urban California. The "control" portions of the law, in turn, were intended to tighten border controls against illegal immigration and to impose sanctions on employers in agriculture, manufacturing, and services who continued to hire undocumented workers (Guarnizo, 1998).

The law had several unintended consequences. Low wages in the agricultural sector drove many male farm workers who had brought additional household members from Mexico to California to move to cities like Los Angeles in search of higher-paying urban service and manufacturing jobs, in the state's then still robust metropolitan economies. Both the threat of employer sanctions and the need to protect newly united transnational family members from surveillance by employers and immigration authorities generated a virtual cottage industry in forged documents. Increasing numbers of the children of Mexican migrants entered the public schools, setting the stage for one of the most punitive, exclusionary, and unconstitutional provisions of Proposition 187.

As can be seen from these developments, the IRCA-driven expansion of recent Mexican migration is an interesting phenomenon both within California and transnationally. It has changed the demographics and expanded the transnational social networks operating in Los Angeles as well as many other cities and towns in California. Yet it too may be viewed as a historical extension of long-term bi-national relations of production, labor supply, household survival, and social network formation between California and Mexico, rather than as either a singular manifestation of economic globalization or a proof of Los Angeles's emergence as a "global city."

A third major dimension of the Mexican migration to Los Angeles from the late 1980s through the 1990s does appear to be linked to global economic restructuring, but this has been part of a process of restructuring produced not by commands and controls emanating from a "global control capacity" to be found in the economic infrastructure of Los Angeles, but from three quite different politically interrelated sources of policy initiative: (a) the policies of historically specific transnational institutions pursuing a neoliberal agenda, such as the World Bank, the IMF and, more recently, the World Trade Organization; (b) the US state's consistent support for neoliberalism and for transnational neoliberal policy initiatives like the North American Free Trade Agreement (NAFTA) through political representations of the inevitability of "globalization," issued by the agencies of the US presidency, particularly the US Treasury Department; and (c) the collaborative institutional responses of the Partido Revolucionario Institutional (PRI)-dominated Mexican state, which relentlessly pursued austerity policies domestically while brokering NAFTA transnationally.

This most recent period of Mexican transmigration to Los Angeles thus was neither a simple resultant of an impersonal economic process of "globalization" operating behind people's backs, nor the outcome of the practices of LA's business and financial services sectors deftly articulating the local with the global. It was a politically produced outcome of historically specific policy initiatives. The newest wave of transnationalization of Los Angeles was driven by declining living standards and growing income polarization within Mexico, produced by a combination of the austerity policies of international banks, the Mexican debt crisis, and the conscious decision of Mexico's ruling political elites to meet this crisis by export-oriented neoliberal economic policies favored by the "global governance" policy elites of the IMF, the World Bank, and the US Treasury and foreign policy establishment.

The social base of this latest transmigration between Mexico and Los Angeles has been very broad, including growing numbers of Mexican urban working and middle classes, and even some members of the entrepreneurial strata (see Guarnizo, 1998), who were prompted to move to or invest in LA and other US cities with large Mexican transmigrant populations by sharp changes in the opportunity structure within Mexico. These developments, exacerbated by NAFTA, have made it difficult for many households in Mexico at all but the elite level to survive on the income they could generate within Mexico's borders. This, in turn, led to the formation of ever more transnational households capable of tapping into the income-producing possibilities of cities like Los Angeles and the remittances generated by the transnational social networks they have forged. The destabilization of the peso on global financial markets in the wake of Mexico's political crisis of legitimation accelerated this process, despite tightened border controls by the US Congress and the Immigration and Naturalization Service (INS). By passing a "dual nationality" law for Mexican transnational migrants in the wake of California's Proposition 187 initiative, the PRI-dominated Mexican state appears to be facilitating precisely such an acceleration on terms that would enable the Mexican economy to continue to benefit from the estimated $5–7 billion in remittances sent to Mexican households and communities annually by the transnational migrants to the US that PRI likes to call "Mexican communities abroad," while increasing the heretofore limited political influence of transnational Mexican migrants in US cities (Guarnizo and Smith, 1998).

Ironically, in the case of Los Angeles, despite the flow of remittances, Mexican transnational migration is not the one-way "cash drain" constructed by anti-immigrant groups in the racial discourse surrounding the passage of Proposition 187. Rather, the goods and services consumed by this and other segments of the Mexican-origin population in Los Angeles clearly contributes to demand-driven employment in the city and region. Yet this grassroots dimension of the Los Angeles political economy, its "demand side," is given scant attention in either the popular media or the "LA as global city" literature.

(It is fair to note that Sassen's analysis of global cities is an exception because she has paid attention to this dimension of global city formation. See, for example, Sassen-Koob, 1987.)

The Legacy of Empire

When we turn from the case of Mexican migration to the other leading transnational migrant groups living in Los Angles today, we discover a different sense in which LA has become transnational. Yet this type of transnationalism is different from that envisioned in the global cities scenario. Much of the transnational migration to Los Angeles from the 1970s until the 1990s can be interpreted as a legacy of the Cold War and of the long-standing "global reach" of US foreign policy in the era of bi-polarity. Let us first consider the national origins of the major transnational migrant groups, especially the refugee groups that have settled in LA in the largest numbers, and interrogate their relationship to the failures and successes of US foreign policy during the Cold War. In LA, next to Mexicans, the nationality groups comprising the largest segments of its multi-ethnic population have been Koreans, Filipinos, Southeast Asian refugees, and massive numbers of people who fled Cold War inspired violence in Central America, particularly from El Salvador and Guatemala. Los Angeles is now home to the largest concentrations of Koreans, Guatemalans, and Salvadorans outside their homelands. One-tenth of all Salvadorans in the world now live in Los Angeles (Davis, 1992), drawn there by the promise of sanctuary, peace, and jobs. The largest concentration of Cambodians outside Phnom Penh now lives in the metropolitan LA city of Long Beach (Pastor, 1993; Ong et al., 1989). As these examples make clear, the Cold War foreign policies of the United States over the last 40 years have come home to roost in the transnational migration streams that have reconstituted LA's ethnic landscape. In this respect LA is clearly a cultural crossroads of transnational urbanism. But in strictly economic terms this does not make it a "global city," poised to command and control, let alone take advantage of any new growth dynamic of the putative "Pacific Rim Century" we have just rung in.

Now that we have come to the end of the Cold War, some commentators have characterized our present global geopolitical condition as a new world disorder. (Compare, for example, the quite different representations of "new world order" in Gray, 1998, and Rodriguez, 1995.) In this contested historical and discursive context, the "end of empire" strikes me as an appropriate way to characterize the current state of "globalization" in Los Angeles and the "legacy of imperialism" an apt metaphor for the current state of its racial and ethnic relations. The next portions of this chapter will further examine the transformation of the social structure and economic life of Los Angeles over the past two decades, and the ways in which its major racial and ethnic groups have taken up antagonistic economic, residential, and community roles and identities that are at the heart of much social unrest, including the urban rebellion of 1992.

The case of Korean-American small business owners in Los Angeles and their antagonistic relationship to African-Americans and political refugees from Central America is an especially intriguing case in point (see Smith and Feagin, 1995; Cho, 1993; Hazen, 1993). Following the stalemate produced by the Korean War, the US-allied South Korean state exhibited an authoritarian political posture and a domination of political life by its military that has only recently changed. South Korean political and economic elites also pursued an export-oriented economic development strategy that produced rapid economic growth and urbanization of its population. By the late 1970s Korea was producing more upwardly mobile urban professionals than its society was capable of absorbing or its political system was willing to incorporate. Many highly educated urban Koreans whose social mobility was blocked in their homeland chose to migrate to the United States during the 1970s and 1980s (Lee, 1995). This migration was facilitated by a major liberalization of US immigration law embodied in the Immigration Reform Act of 1965, which removed national origin restrictions against Asian migrants and encouraged the migration of skilled workers. However, the occupational niches open to the Korean migrants in the US political economy were limited, since they often faced anti-Asian discrimination, lacked English language skills, or possessed professional credentials that were not easily transferable to the US context. Using household capital or loans from transnational ethnic associations, many of the Korean migrants thus became small business owners in large US cities. This was especially true in Los Angeles, which is home to the largest concentration of recent Korean transmigrants and Korean-Americans in the United States.

The economic niches that ethnic Koreans occupied in LA placed them in potentially antagonistic relationships with other minorities, e.g. as convenience store and liquor store owners in mixed black and recent low-income Mexican migrant neighborhoods like South Central LA, as sweatshop owners employing undocumented Salvadoran and Guatemalan workers in Koreatown, as landlords for the Central American residents of MacArthur Park, Koreatown (now predominantly Latino residentially), Pico Union, and even Hollywood, a transitional neighborhood locally, despite its metaphorical connection to the global media "dream machine." Not surprisingly, the landlord–tenant, employer–worker, and merchant–customer conflict in the micro-relations of power between Koreans and Latinos was played out with special vehemence in the targeted destruction of Korean business property in Koreatown, Hollywood, and other neighborhoods that were part of the LA uprising. This dimension of the LA rebellion was an expression of outrage by multiply marginalized

Central American refugees and recent low-income Mexican migrants, whose exclusion from mainstream economic and political institutions has been so pronounced in LA that these "Latinos" have even been excluded by local Mexican-American politicians who, following the uprising, were quick to downplay Latino-Korean antagonism, pointing out that no one in the long-established Mexican-American neighborhood of East LA had looted or rioted.

As these examples illustrate, the movement of Cold War-related migrants from former US "colonies" to Los Angeles and their assumption of antagonistic economic, residential, and commercial roles in LA's sprawling post-urban landscape, widened and deepened the black vs. white urban unrest unleashed by the Rodney King verdict. The result was hardly congruent with the expectations of the Cold War foreign and defense policy-making elites who had benefited most from the state restructuring from welfare to warfare spending throughout the 1980s under Reaganomics. What "came together" in LA was not a Pacific Rim multicultural melting pot ushered in by a geopolitical Pax Americana, but a transnationalized multi-ethnic class warfare.

From the standpoint of cultural globalization, in the aftermath of the LA rebellion it has become clear that unfavorable US media representations of minority Americans are both a local and a global phenomenon. Even before LA's Cold War-related migrants came to US shores, these hostilities were fueled by the endemic racialization of US culture and its global transmission abroad. As a result of US military interventions over the past 40 years, Hollywood films along with US videos and television shows distributed overseas provided racist stereotypes of black Americans in advance to migrants from other former US colonies. As Sumi Cho (1993: 199) has argued in the case of South Korea, as a result of this global transmission of the dominant US racial hierarchy, "when Koreans immigrate . . . internationalized stereotypes are reinforced by negative depictions of African-Americans in US films, television shows and other popular forms of cultural production." Thus, the absorption of anti-black attitudes into their conceptual repertoires by Korean and other Cold War migrants often preceded actual local experiences with African-Americans. In the Korean case, the global deployment of these media images played a role in the social construction of a local Korean vs. black cultural antagonism that hardened the antagonistic social roles these two groups came to occupy in the Los Angeles political economy as Korean small business entrepreneurs moved into economic niches opened to them, such as liquor and convenience store operations in black neighborhoods.

It is important to realize that the social recomposition of the ethnic landscape of LA I have been describing, while produced in large part by migration networks formed in the context of Cold War-inspired international relations, was also in part fueled by the lure of the cultural imaginary contained in the phantasmagoric images of daily life in LA that form the backdrop of many films and television shows exported abroad from Southern California as popular cultural products. Such products now constitute the nation's and LA's second biggest export item after aircraft. Throughout the 1980s LA's self-projected international image as "global city" was further crafted by globally transmitted media extravaganzas like the 1984 Olympics, which, together with the junk bond shenanigans of Michael Milken and the speculative building frenzy unleashed by the deregulated savings and loan industry, co-produced the spectacle of Los Angeles as the quintessential site of Pacific Rim *nouveau riche* dynamism. Stoking the illusions fostered by LA's commercial and residential "real" estate boom, the prevailing media hype fostered by local real estate capitalists depicted LA as the world's premier multicultural melting pot, a land of opportunity where it never rained and every day ended with a sunnier tomorrow (Garcia, 1992). Small wonder, then, that not only surplus Japanese capital but also transnational small business entrepreneurs, along with many of the world's economically and politically dispossessed, were drawn to this place, all dreaming of a better future.

The experiences of daily life encountered by these dreamers were far different from the media images. Precisely when transnational migration to Los Angeles was accelerating, its economic vitality was undermined by two waves of economic restructuring. The first was driven by global corporate relocations in the primary industrial sector; the second by a downsizing of the defense industry since the end of the Cold War. The 1970s and 1980s saw a very sharp reduction in high-wage manufacturing jobs as a possible avenue for upward economic mobility for the transnational migrants and refugees who were moving into Los Angeles at that time, and at an accelerated pace in the 1980s. Whereas the city of Los Angeles was once the second largest auto assembly city in the United States, the last auto plant in the Los Angeles region closed its doors in 1992. GM and Chrysler moved to Mexico, encouraged by the welcoming arms of the neoliberal policies of the Mexican state. The same was true in other previously unionized, high-wage manufacturing sectors. For example, Uniroyal went to Brazil and Turkey; Motorola and Litton Industries joined the move to Mexico (Ong, 1993).

Thus, the deindustrialization of primary manufacturing in Los Angeles and its reindustrialization in a different form into non-unionized, low-wage, sweatshop labor, blocked one of the avenues for transnational migrants that earlier decades of foreign-born immigrants had used in order to move up in the American opportunity structure. It also moved substantial numbers of working-class black males into the ranks of either low-paid service work or permanent unemployment. Reliable estimates place the direct high-wage manufacturing job loss in the Los Angeles economy at 200,000 from 1978 to 1989. These jobs were concentrated largely in the black and Latino South Central area of Los Angeles which exploded in 1992 (Johnson, Farrell, and Oliver, 1993; Johnson, Jones, Farrell, and Oliver, 1992). An indirect negative multiplier effect of these job reductions and plant closures was to put the local

suppliers and small businesses that were connected to these industrial complexes out of business, adding further to the employment crisis in Los Angeles.

A second wave of plant closures then faced Los Angeles as a result of the
end of the Cold War. Major defense- and aerospace-related plant and base
closures in the first half of the 1990s added to the employment crisis because
of the Los Angeles region's dependency on the military budget as a central
engine of economic growth. This is an important consideration when reflecting upon what is meant by a "global city." What are the engines driving a
regional economy? How do they change over time? How are they affected by
global economic restructuring as well as national patterns of public policy? To
the extent that we look at the transformation of the international political
economy produced by state and corporate practices, LA's current economic
plight can be viewed as an adverse impact of the global capital flight legitimated by the globalization discourse. To the extent that we also look at LA's
most recent round of decline as a direct result of shifts in US foreign and
defense policy following the end of the Cold War, LA's plight can be seen to
be driven by policies designed to reduce defense expenditures as the US state
apparatus moves from a mode of global military domination to a mode of
global economic hegemony. In either case, however, Los Angeles has been on
the receiving rather than the sending end of "global commands and controls."

Between 1989 and 1993, an additional 240,000 jobs disappeared in Los
Angeles County (Johnson, Farrell, and Oliver, 1993). As the Cold War ended,
the once seemingly recession-proof aerospace and electronics industries, and
with them the construction and real estate sectors, abruptly reversed course,
contracting with alarming speed. LA's rapid economic decline between 1990
and 1995 suggests that far from being a central cotter pin of Pacific Rim
economic vitality, Los Angeles had become a kind of declining colonial out-
post of national defense and procurement policy shifts over the past 40 years.
Instead of gaining in autonomy in the epoch of "globalization" as the nation-
state weakened, the city found itself on the receiving end of national policies
that detrimentally affected its future.

In the first half of the 1990s the defense-related job transformation of Los
Angeles was precipitous. In 1993 alone, 110,000 defense-related jobs were lost
from the LA economy. LA's official unemployment rate was 10.4 percent.
This high-wage job decline continued throughout the first half of the 1990s,
as defense cutbacks continued despite President Bill Clinton's symbolic efforts
to compensate for the cuts by a federally subsidized high-tech development
initiative focused on the state he relied upon to gain re-election. These job
losses were addressed by local political elites by an "enterprise zone" policy
that passed for a public effort to stimulate "local economic development." By
early 1993, after five years in operation, the tax breaks offered to lure investment into LA's inner-city areas had produced a grand total of 837 jobs. Only
159 of these were in Watts, another 157 in East LA, and 220 in the central

city zone. Worse still, not all of this handful even amounted to new jobs, as many of these "enterprise zone" jobs were simply already existing jobs in LA, moved around by employers seeking to take advantage of tax breaks (Mann, 1993). Thus, the city's net effect was to become worse off. Because the tax breaks added to the billion dollar shortfall in the LA budget, the city had fewer tax dollars and very few new jobs.

The Social Construction of "Local Economic Development"

The story of economic change in Los Angeles that I am telling is not simply one of economic dependency and decline, but a more complex tale of uneven development. As already noted, LA's growing "global culture" industry is now one of the city's leading export sectors as well as one of the sources of its attraction to global migrants. By some estimates (e.g. Storper, 1999) new jobs added in the film, entertainment, and multimedia sectors in the second half of the 1990s have more than replaced the number of jobs lost by economic restructuring and the defense downsizing recession of the mid-1990s. Nevertheless the pay structure in these sectors is more uneven than was the case for high-wage unionized manufacturing (Curry and Kenney, 1999).

Two other sectors of LA's political economy have also shown signs of growth. The first of these growth sectors, particularly before the defense collapse, is advanced business services, a sector whose jobs have gone to yuppies and downtown business elites. In the 1980s the downtown investment nexus was driven by a combination of Mayor Tom Bradley's urban development strategy, and the availability of surplus capital Japanese industrial corporations and financial investors were willing to move into global real estate speculation (and which they are no longer willing nor able to do, given the current crisis conditions of the Japanese economy, to say nothing of the political crisis in Japan). LA's downtown boom thus has not continued under Mayor Richard Riordan.

The mythology of Los Angeles cultivated by its leading civic boosters in the late 1980s mirrored the tropes of the global cities literature. LA was depicted as a dynamic city poised to take advantage of the capital accumulation possibilities offered by its "locational advantage" as a Pacific Rim megapole in the emergent "Pacific Rim Century." As noted earlier, the media images of LA as the land of opportunity for entrepreneurs, multicultural melting pot, and last US frontier for the globally adventurous, added further to the image of LA as a global city. The net result of the conjunction of global media and capital flows and local boosterism in the 1980s was a shining new downtown and LA's limited – and heavily state subsidized – new subway system. These new "postmodern" urban architectural forms were consciously designed by urban planners, as Mike Davis (1990) and others have shown, to exclude most ordinary people – particularly people of color – in yet another reenactment of the nineteenth-century psychodrama of the dangerous classes being excluded from the Central Business District (CBD) by a combination of robo-cops, twenty-first century surveillance technology, high prices, limited non-business or tourist hotel services, and an exclusionary street design, thus making downtown LA a truly walled city, a closed city at the core.

As it rose from the ashes of older urban spatial uses, a messianic social imaginary, dripping with modernist nostalgia, was deployed by developers portraying this exclusionary business and tourist zone as a crowning achievement of the "recentering" of Los Angeles, an achievement in which all Angelenos could rightfully take pride. It is quite remarkable how rapidly the dominant social construction of the "real" LA changed, even in these circles, as Los Angeles faced the decline of global real estate investment and the end of the Cold War. Such hyperbole all but disappeared from the political discourse on urban development in Los Angeles in the face of downtown overbuilding, falling commercial and residential real estate values, the widening employment crisis, and a sharp decline of Japanese overseas investment in real estate ventures as rates of profit among Japanese industries declined. As the economy declined, the usual civic boosterist rhetoric began to ring hollow. Even the most rampant civic boosters fell silent in the aftermath of the LA rebellion.

The assault on jobs in the defense sector and the meager results of the "Rebuild LA" campaign, punctuated by the resignation of four successive chairpersons of the reinvestment campaign, was only the tip of the iceberg of an observable loss of nerve among LA's corporate and real estate elites comprising the local "growth machine." Ironically, in the face of the disappearance of 240,000 private sector jobs in LA County from 1989 to 1992, the LA Chamber of Commerce responded to the employment crisis by laying off eight of its sixty staff, including its entire economic development department (Mann, 1993; see also Sims, 1994). It thus had moved from unbridled civic boosterism to despair and defeatism in four short years. This is not merely ironic but symbolic. It suggests that the move from a utopian to a dystopian image of Los Angeles was internalized even by its sectors most actively responsible for LA's economic development.

It is now clear that the local growth machine in LA poorly mediated Los Angeles's global investments in real estate. National banking deregulation, unregulated growth, commercial overbuilding in LA, and the Savings and Loan (S & L) scandal were closely intertwined. In LA, downtown office space, fueled by the availability of Japanese and S & L capital, rose from 6.3 million to 33 million square feet in the 1980s. Overbuilding produced a 19 percent vacancy rate by 1992. Developers could not fill their buildings in order to pay back their real estate loans. Foreclosures on office buildings rose from $1.1 billion to $4.1 billion between 1988 and 1991. Subsequently, the region's

Savings and Loan industry collapsed as desperate S & Ls tried to dump fore-closed properties at deep discounts. For example, the former headquarters of the now defunct Columbia Savings in Beverly Hills, built in 1989 at a cost of $40 million, was sold for $2.8 million in 1992 (Garcia, 1992; Sims, 1994).

Real estate was further depressed in greater Los Angeles as the relocation of displaced aerospace and electronics engineers shrank demand for upper-middle income housing. Defense downsizing also had a multiplier effect on the law firms, insurers, and financial institutions servicing defense contractors, whose own staff cuts produced higher vacancy rates for downtown office space and further dampened housing demand. By 1993 the LA real estate bubble had burst and with it the confidence of LA's local growth machine.

Transnational Urbanism and the "Ethnic Economy"

Transnational urbanism, however, was itself the catalyst of a third significant growth sector in Los Angeles in the 1980s and 1990s that is still actively generating jobs. The new modes of employment in this sector are concen-trated largely within and across the social spaces of transnational ethnic com-munities. Work in these transnational communities is concentrated in the low-wage service and manufacturing sector (e.g. the restaurant, hotel, and domestic service workers) and the light manufacturing "sweatshops," whose plant openings have been in poorly paid, non-unionized, highly competitive segments like garment manufacturing and micro-electronics assembly. In so-cial science discourse this new urban employment sector has been termed variously the "ethnic enclave" (Portes, 1987), the "ethnic economy" (Light and Karageorgis, 1994), or the "immigrant economy" (Light, Bernard and Kim, 1999), depending, respectively, on whether or not the economic activity engaged in is spatially concentrated in particular ethnic neighborhoods; is more spatially dispersed but nonetheless brings together co-ethnic owners and workers; or cuts across ethnic divides, but nonetheless involves social relations between "new immigrant" employers and workers. For purposes of simpli-fication I will refer to these alternative arrangements as three types of ethnic economy.

Some of those who have written about the ethnic economy have romant-icized the entrepreneurial element in this kind of economic activity and its putatively beneficent consequences for co-ethnic workers (see, for example, Portes and Manning, 1986). The entrepreneurial image of the ethnic economy has fostered two quite distinct social constructions: one assimilationist, the other transnationalist. Both of these representations tend to be celebratory in tone. In the assimilationist variant transnational migrants, particularly those from Asian countries, are represented as creating co-ethnic economic opportunity structures and contributing dynamically to the urban economy. In the next generation it is envisaged that workers in this sector will be easily absorbed, like earlier waves of immigrants, into the mainstream US economy. In this variant the ethnic economy is thus envisaged as a kind of temporary stepping stone, an opportunity for workers to learn skills and to acquire social capital and develop human potential.

In the context of a perceived decline in the political influence of nationally organized working-class movements in the face of global economic restructuring, a second image of ethnic entrepreneurship, which might be termed transnationalist, has entered into social science discourse on urban development. All sorts of "new social actors" on the transnational stage, including "ethnic entrepreneurs," are currently being invested with transformational possibilities, despite the fact that their practices are neither self-consciously resistant nor even loosely political in character. For example, Alejandro Portes' recent work on the rise of "transnational communities" (Portes, 1996a, 1996b) inscribes the activities of transnational migrant entrepreneurs with a series of attributes, which taken together, socially construct small transnational capitalists as "common people," "working-class segments," and "grassroots" actors, whose entrepreneurial practices amount to an expression of "popular resistance" to multinational corporate capitalism. In this curious social construction of "transnationalism from below" the meaning of "from below" is derived from the putative *effects* rather than the *intentions* of transnational entrepreneurs. In my view, transnational ethnic entrepreneurs clearly intend to make money by employing co-ethnics or other transmigrants. In so doing they may alter the prevailing business practices of multinational capitalists, for example, by encouraging major clothing chains and fashion designers to subcontract work to the factories the entrepreneurs own. But this hardly seems a justification for conflating this effect with grassroots popular resistance.

What sense are we to make of the global–local interplay in LA's ethnic economy? Whether the ethnic economy is viewed as something separate from the mainstream economy, or as intimately tied to it through subcontracting arrangements, one thing is certain: it does not pay its workers very well. It also tends to be heavily dependent on a transnational urban workforce. Hence it has not absorbed very many of those workers in Los Angeles displaced from other sectors, such as the downwardly mobile white-collar defense and aerospace engineers, portrayed so chillingly by Michael Douglas in the film *Falling Down*. Nor have LA's various modes of ethnic economy employed many blacks.

What have been the observed local impacts of this particular form of transnational urbanism in Los Angeles? A detailed case study by Paul Ong, an urban planner at the University of California at Los Angeles, precisely addresses this question. Ong's study offers a thorough discussion of the costs as well as the benefits of LA's ethnic economy. Ong's study, *Beyond Asian-American Poverty* (1993), reveals that in 1993 over 124,000 Asians lived in poverty in Los

Angeles County. While this only represents a 13 percent rate of poverty for
Asians as a whole, several Asian nationality groups, particularly those that are
part of the Cold War legacy, such as recently arrived Southeast Asian refugees
from Cambodia and Laos, had rates of poverty of 45 percent. Vietnamese
had a 25 percent poverty rate; Pacific Islanders 24 percent. Even the touted
"entrepreneurial" Korean population had a 16 percent poverty rate. The
people who work in the new industries being created by those who happened
to own and manage "ethnic enterprises" (e.g. in textile manufacturing) receive
marginal wages. Many new Asian workers get permanently ensconced in
dead-end jobs in monolingual workplaces that impede them from learning
English. This calls into question celebratory assimilationist expectations.

By comparison, at the time of this study the poverty rate in Los Angeles
was 21 percent for African-Americans. Thus, when taken as a whole the
poverty rate for Koreans was only slightly less than the poverty rate for
African-Americans. Southeast Asian migrants to Los Angeles had twice the
rate of poverty of African-Americans. As a further comparison, the poverty
rate in Los Angeles was 23 percent for Latinos, which is actually slightly
higher than the African-American rate. Many of the poor Asians working in
the new sweatshops in the ethnic economy are part of the "working poor."
The poor Southeast Asian refugee families who remain eligible for declining
forms of public assistance are part of what has been labeled the "new welfare
poor." Taken together these two segments of the new Asian population in
Los Angeles belie the stereotype of "Asian-Americans" as a new "model
minority," indeed as an answer to the economic development agenda of Los
Angeles. In light of such stereotypes it is well to remember that the INS data
for 1983–6 show that while 43 per cent of legal Asian transnational migrants
to LA came from managerial, technical, and professional backgrounds, 36
percent had previously occupied menial, labor-intensive jobs.

Many of the latter are living a marginal existence under virtually Dickensian
conditions. Consider the following qualitative findings from Ong's study: "In
conducting our survey, we found low income Asian families living in horrid
conditions; small deteriorating back lot units, possible illegally converted
garages and apartment buildings with trash lining dimly lit hallways" (Ong,
1993: 32). In Koreatown, the study found that "attractive exterior facades
often hid desolate courtyards and corridors." It also found that 1 in 4 Koreans
and Chinese in inner-city Los Angeles live in poverty despite media constructed images of both groups' collective entrepreneurial status and economic
success. These celebratory images, in turn, stereotype the groups as a whole,
ignoring class, social, regional, gender, and other internal divisions such as
transmigrant vs. immigrant identities, within each of the "new minorities" in
Los Angeles's multicultural mosaic.

In many cases, moreover, the degree of poverty is severe; it is not just
that people are slightly below the poverty level. In 1993, 10 percent of

Vietnamese, 12 percent of Pacific Islanders, and 16 percent of all Cambodians and Laotians in Los Angeles lived on an annual income of $6,307, which was less than 50 percent of the poverty threshold. The irony here is that fiscal austerity policies, and the urban fiscal crisis of Los Angeles, have reduced public spending for English as a Second Language (ESL) programs and other English language acquisition opportunities in California. Such measures discourage "immigrant incorporation" into US citizenship and encourage the continuation of enclave workplaces and neighborhoods where transnational networks and identities are reproduced.

Some might argue that because "ethnic enterprise" does not require English language skills, this is not a "real" problem. The ethnic economy is depicted as a resource that puts one generation, that lost generation I am now discussing, in a holding pattern so that the next generation can move up. The reality is more double-edged. Firms in the ethnic economy do offer paid employment, cultural continuity, and a protected internal labor market in the face of exclusion and discrimination in the mainstream economy. Nonetheless, such firms still give little room for self-affirmation within the US social formation. Instead, they tend to offer workers low wages, limited or no benefits, and sometimes inter- or intra-ethnic exploitation by marginal entrepreneurs who themselves have been excluded from other employment venues. The example of educated Korean professionals whose professional mobility has been blocked in the US and who instead have turned to running liquor stores and mom and pop grocery stores in poor neighborhoods, or owning sweatshops that employ transnational migrant workers, comes readily to mind. In Los Angeles this new interplay of class and ethnic relations has not played out very well, to say the least.

The phrase "the exploited of the excluded" aptly designates the workers employed by those ethnic entrepreneurs who have been blocked from entering into mainstream economic roles in US cities because they are reserved for others or because they are excluded from lending institutions and cannot get sufficient credit outside their own co-national group to move up. Many of LA's businesses owned and run by transmigrant entrepreneurs exclusively employ co-ethnics. In these instances, the appeal by the entrepreneurs to "shared ethnicity" has been used in the past as a political resource to culturally depoliticize the resistance of the workforce. The irony is that the people working in these types of "enclave" businesses are often worse off because they end up being doubly marginalized, exploited in conventional economic terms and culturally manipulated into passivity. From an assimilationist standpoint they have little room for mobility except to acquire English language proficiency, no easy task in the face of the fiscal austerity policies of the city and the state, punctuated by the anti-immigrant backlash in California in the mid 1990s that supported a referendum that would deny even basic schooling to the children of undocumented immigrants.

From a transnationalist perspective the picture of co-ethnic workplaces is more complex. Ethnic entrepreneurs are certainly not exemplars of grassroots resistance to multinational capital. Many of their co-ethnic workers locally continue to engage in transnational practices like sending "home" family remittances from their meager incomes to their translocalities of origin. Their local enclaves still constitute transnational cultural spaces. Nevertheless, the widespread reaction to Proposition 187 and the desire to avoid the punitive aspects of recent federal anti-immigrant legislation has increased the rate of both Latinos and Asians seeking naturalization among California's transmigrant minorities. In due course this may well translate into local electoral power to accompany the interesting forms of community mobilization that have already emerged in Los Angeles's urban political landscape. The urban issues that fuel such mobilizations are not difficult to discern.

Among some segments of the "exploited of the excluded" interesting new forms of labor organization in the LA ethnic economy have emerged. For instance, Latino dry wallers have successfully organized against Korean and other Asian entrepreneurs in that sector to improve pay and working conditions (Clements, 1992). This type of collective action suggests that when there are ethnic differences between new transnational workers and new transnational owners, the possibility of grassroots mobilization is increased. In hyperethnic LA, such mobilizations tend to ethnicize class conflict. This is not the sort of grassroots activity "from below" envisaged in the transnationalist celebration of the ethnic economy. In these instances of grassroots mobilization the transmigrant entrepreneurs have been the targets rather than the originators of grass-roots social practices. As we shall see below in the case of my discussion of the complexly interwoven intra-ethnic politics that have been part of the social construction of LA's Koreatown, new modes of class conflict have begun to emerge *within* as well as between Los Angeles's transnational migrant communities.

Before turning to the story of the place-making sociospatial practices that have gone into the making and remaking of Koreatown, however, it is important to point out that, whether inter-ethnic or intra-ethnic, the very emergence of grassroots resistance "from below" to labor exploitation and other forms of domination among LA's transnational minorities belies the cursory dismissals of LA's "Third World workforce" as passive subjects frequently found in the LA-as-global-city discourse. Edward Soja, for example, in one of his seminal articles on the globalization of Los Angeles provides an extensive and impressively detailed synoptic guided tour of the "silvery web of financial and commercial transactions" that have gone into the making of LA's postmodern architectural and sociospatial landscape, but devotes only three paragraphs to the view of LA "from below." Soja prefaces his brief discussion with the following dismissive comment: "There is too little time now to tour the sites contained in the compartmentalized corona of the inner city." In his discourse the new Asian and Latino immigrant enclaves of Los Angeles are constructed as sites of cheap labor which house a "subject population" – more precisely, in his words: "above all, the largest concentration of cheap, culturally splintered, occupationally manipulable Third World immigrant labor to be found so tangibly available in any First World urban region" (Soja, 1986: 266). His representation of the manipulability of new immigrant labor is reminiscent of the trope frequently used by postmodern geographer Michael Dear which marks Los Angeles as a First World city resting "atop" a Third World city (Dear, 1991b; Dear and Flusty, 1998). How valid are such binary representations of the transnational communities that now occupy large swaths of the urban landscape of contemporary Los Angeles? Considering the complex discourses and practices that have shaped the social construction and reconstruction of LA's Koreatown during the past two decades is an instructive way to address this question.

Constructing and Reconstructing Koreatown

Unlike many ethnic areas in US cities, the historical construction of Koreatown in Los Angeles dates back less than three decades (Kim, 1993: 2). Roughly bounded by Hoover Street, Pico Boulevard, Wilshire Boulevard, and Western Avenue, and including the downtown area of Los Angeles along Olympic Boulevard, Koreatown is a largely retail and commercial zone created since the early 1970s (Lee, 1995: 46). The initial driving forces for the spatial concentration of a Korean commercial, residential, and retail district in Los Angeles were the social networks and business associations of Korean transnational entrepreneurs who began establishing businesses in Los Angeles at that time. Koreatown may thus be viewed initially as a social construction of transnational migrant networks whose place-making sociospatial practices in LA began by the opening up of a cluster of small businesses including ethnic restaurants, retailing, and small manufacturing. The labor force for these initial businesses was largely drawn from within the transnational Korean migrant community; the capital was supplied by self-organized rotating credit associations, known as *kye,* a kind of informal underground banking system, which provided credit to fellow Korean transnational entrepreneurs to set up operations in Los Angeles. These social actors relied upon ethnic media – Korean radio, newspapers, and eventually television – to give cultural identity to their place-making project. Local political lobbying by the Koreatown Development Association secured the official identity marker "Koreatown" from Los Angeles city hall in 1980 (Pearlstone, 1990: 88). Once this was accomplished the entrepreneurial networks of small-scale developers, manufacturing contractors, and commercial business owners used their associational resources (e.g. the Korean-American garment contractors' and grocers' associations) and their continuing ties to their homeland to attract major Korean-based financial and corporate capital investment into Koreatown. Korean-owned banks, office buildings, shopping centers, and professional service firms thus sprang up there during the boom years of the 1980s (Lee, 1995). A prime example was Koreatown Plaza, a $25 million tri-level indoor mall.

Throughout the 1980s economic connections between Korean transnational entrepreneurs and Korean-based multinational capital investors were not the only transnational ties linking Koreatown to South Korea. Many of the entrepreneurs continued to live in transnational households, maintaining ties with spouses and children that remained in Korea. In 1988, for example, the US embassy joined with a Korean transnational newspaper to organize a reunion between transnational entrepreneurs operating in Los Angeles on temporary visas and their spouses still in Korea. According to Pearlstone (1990: 90), "Some of these couples had not seen each other for six years. The wives (or in one case the husband) stayed for a month and then most returned to Korea to await the time when their spouses would have permanent visas."

By 1990 this transnational social construction known as Koreatown had become the location of over one third of all Korean-owned firms in the United States (ibid.: 89). Once constructed, Koreatown became a key center for entrepreneurial activities, providing a "protected market for the supply of labor, financing and reliable customers through the establishment of community networks" (Lee, 1995: 47). This in turn led to further growth in Korean-owned and operated service firms in entertainment, finance, insurance, real estate, communications, law, and medicine. Koreatown became a self-contained ethnic economy with the attendant persistence of monolingualism among Korean proprietors, workers, and residents of the transnational ethnic enclave. This enclavement also facilitated the formation of an ever wider variety of ethnic associations in business, commerce, trade, and communications.

It is important to realize that despite the key role of transnational business ties in the making of Koreatown, the Korean transnational entrepreneurial class did not view Koreatown merely as a localized social space of commodity relations from which resources could be extracted to sustain transnationalized social relations. Transnational and local social relations are not mutually exclusive. Instead, it is more fruitful to imagine the "transnational" and the "local" as interlocked and mutually constitutive in processes where power and meaning come together and are localized. In the instance at hand, as Lee (ibid.) has pointed out in his study of business experience in Koreatown,

> The Korean shopowners' relations to Koreatown convey sociocultural meanings beyond the material manifestation of ethnic relations. Although many tended to move out to suburban residences as they accumulated wealth, a large number often returned to Korean restaurants and bookstores with their families during weekends and holidays. This attachment to ethnic identity is embedded in the

built environment of Koreatown, and it is continuously being recreated by spatial practices of social networking. It is the focus of ethnic history, collective experience, and intentions onto particular settings. Thus Koreatown achieves significance beyond commodity relations.

Despite the power of this ethnically based social imaginary, during the final decade of the twentieth century the solidaristic "Korean community" constructed by the discursive and material practices of Korean immigrant entrepreneurs to give meaning to the particular setting of Koreatown, became unsettled by other social practices, relations, and imaginings that came together in Koreatown. These unsettling developments included the ethnic recomposition of the labor force in Korean-owned businesses, the residential transformation of Koreatown itself, and the rising tide of class awareness among Koreatown's Korean-American working class.

In building up their businesses in Koreatown and elsewhere in Los Angeles the Korean small business sector had originally relied upon labor supplied by family members or other Korean-based social networks. According to Pearlstone (1990: 88), by 1990 80 percent of Koreans working in Los Angeles worked for Korean-owned firms in Koreatown and other clusters of Korean-owned businesses established in run-down areas like South Central Los Angeles. At the same time, the rapid expansion of Korean-owned small businesses throughout the 1980s was accompanied by an equally rapid transnational flow of migrants from Latin America. The largest components of this transnational influx of labor to Los Angeles were driven by the economic crisis in Mexico and civil wars in Central America occasioned by US interventions there. Many of these transnational migrants were undocumented Mexicans or refugees from El Salvador and Guatemala who had been driven from their homelands by IMF-driven austerity policies, Cold War counterinsurgency strategies driving US foreign and military policies, and growing regional and income inequality promoted by the export-oriented development strategies of the World Bank. These contextual factors made it difficult for many households in Mexico and Central America to maintain nationally based survival strategies and set the stage for the formation of transnational households capable of tapping into the income-producing capacities of labor demand in US cities like Los Angeles (Smith and Feagin, 1995; Rodriguez, 1995, 1996).

Since a good deal of the "labor demand" in Los Angeles was being created by the Korean transmigrant entrepreneurship I have just described, many members of transnational Latino households became workers in Korean-owned businesses, whose labor recruitment strategies eventually extended out of the Korean-origin community to encompass other groups of affordable transnational migrant workers, among the most affordable of which were undocumented Latino transnational migrants. A key case in point is the garment contracting sector, where Korean-owned garment sweatshops relied increasingly on Central American and Mexican undocumented workers, largely female, throughout the 1980s and early 1990s (Kwong, 1992). It is important to realize, as Light and Bonacich (1988) have shown, that the Korean owners in this garment contracting sector are linked not only to the low-income transnational workforce that they directly employ, but also to the large transnational textile manufacturing corporations which subcontract large orders on a piece-work basis to the Korean contracting entrepreneurs. It is these sorts of transnationalized social relations that came together so explosively in the Los Angeles unrest of 1992.

In the 1980s and early 1990s, criss-crossing transnational connections also came together in Los Angeles in the realms of household reproduction and residential resettlement. Not surprisingly, many low-wage undocumented Latino households chose to move into affordable rental housing located near their workplaces. This, in turn, contributed to the gradual residential transformation of Koreatown into a multi-ethnic neighborhood which is now home to more Latinos than Koreans. The emergent inter-ethnic relations between Koreans and Latinos that came together in Koreatown and Los Angeles at the confluence of these transnational flows were also class relations – owner–worker and landlord–tenant antagonisms – that boiled over as a key dimension of the urban violence now condensed under the rubric "LA rebellion." As we have seen earlier, in addition to the Latino–Korean articulation, this dimension of the LA unrest also included the fallout from the abrasive merchant–customer relations that had emerged between Korean merchants and black customers in other parts of Los Angeles. This latter antagonism is vividly symbolized by the killing of a young black woman, LaTasha Harlins, by a Korean merchant in a dispute over a bottle of orange juice, an event now widely regarded as one of the key precipitating events of the LA unrest. The black–Korean antagonism was particularly vehement, since approximately 47 percent of the heavily damaged buildings in the wake of the Los Angeles uprisings were occupied by Korean merchants (Reinhold, 1993: A1).

Many of the Korean entrepreneurs whose self-image had included an ethos of hard work, minding one's business, and taking care of one's own, were rudely awakened by the violence directed against them by blacks and Latinos as well as by the failure of the Los Angeles Police Department (LAPD) to protect Koreatown and other transnational migrant-owned business property from looting and arson (the LAPD marshaled scarce resources to protect more privileged white enclaves on the West side of LA). In the wake of the unrest, the once politically quiescent Korean merchants in Los Angeles quickly mobilized both locally and transnationally. Locally, they organized protest demonstrations to object to an ordinance passed by the LA city council at the urging of black neighborhood organizations in South Central Los Angeles to limit the rebuilding of liquor stores, an estimated 70 percent of which were Korean owned (Mydans, 1992: 1). The entrepreneurs stood in front of city hall for two weeks, engaging in confrontational political rituals drawn from the experience of urban protests in South Korea, such as beating drums to gain political attention and to obtain a meeting with the mayor about removing the limits on business location. In this instance the middle-class Korean protesters got their meeting but the ordinance stood (Smith and Feagin, 1995).

Transnationally, the Korean entrepreneurial class mobilized to establish relief organizations designed to tap into the networks of social and financial support linking Koreans in Korea with Korean diaspora enclaves throughout the world. A few of the organizations they formed, like the Koreatown Emergency Relief Fund Distribution Committee (KERFDC), distributed small checks not only to displaced business owners but also to Korean and other workers who had been employed by Korean businesses that had fallen victim to arson. For the most part, however, other organizations created by the Korean entrepreneurial class followed the pattern of the Korean American Relief Fund (KARF), whose organizers distributed relief checks only to fellow Korean business owners (Lee, 1996: 51–2).

Interestingly, the class-based dimensions of both of these forms of intra-ethnic political mobilization tend to be masked by their highly visible ethno-cultural dimension. In the case of the Korean liquor store owners, both the class composition of the owners and the class relations between merchants and customers in South Central are masked by the ethnic homogeneity of the protesters and the cultural style of protest they imported from Korea to express their interests. In the case of the transnational mobilization of the entrepreneurial strata to obtain relief support, the worldwide appeal to help fellow Korean brothers and sisters in Los Angeles relied upon nationalistic appeals to "Koreanness" to promote a transnational ethnic solidarity that tended to mask the largely class-specific benefits flowing to the Korean small business and commercial classes.

When the lens of class difference is added to the lens of ethnic difference and criss-crossing transnational connections are kept in mind, our reading of the politics of difference in Los Angeles takes on more complex and ironic turns. For example, despite what I have just said about Latino–Korean relations in general, Latino transnational migrant merchants also were looted and burned in the LA uprisings, in neighborhoods such as Pico Union, MacArthur Park, and South Central. In an ironic twist, these Latino merchants, many of whom had fled violence and political instability in their homelands, staged a protest demonstration following the LA unrest. They demonstrated against urban violence in Los Angeles at the second trial of the LAPD police officers who were subsequently convicted of violating Rodney King's civil rights. These urban protests by Latino merchants were not directed against the violence of police brutality. Rather, they expressed concern that another acquittal might trigger more unrest in the streets and thereby threaten their livelihoods because they doubted that the LAPD would protect them from any ensuing violence (*Los Angeles Times,* March 18, 1993).

Another interesting twist, particularly germane to the story of Koreatown, is revealed when the lens of class difference is foregrounded in our story of the politics of transnational urbanism in Los Angeles. In the year following the riots, the lion's share of the transnational relief money raised to help "fellow Koreans" in Koreatown who had suffered losses in the unrest was pocketed by members of the Los Angeles Korean merchants and business owners associations (Lee, 1996). This provided the impetus for a class-based mobilization by displaced Korean workers who felt shortchanged by the process of relief gathering and distribution. From 1993 until early 1995 hundreds of Korean displaced workers fought strenuously to reverse the claim on these funds made by the business associations who had argued that both the local and transnational monies raised in the relief efforts should be "invested" rather than used to satisfy immediate needs (ibid.: 47). These workers joined a political coalition led by a grassroots organization, the Korean Immigrant Workers Advocates (KIWA), in a protracted campaign to force the Korean entrepreneurial class to share the relief funds. The workers viewed themselves as challenging an internal establishment that had constructed an ethnic economy in LA that benefited unduly from appeals to ethnic nationalism at the expense of working-class co-nationals (ibid.: 50).

KIWA eventually won this fight. Its research revealed that over one third of the Korean workers displaced by the unrest worked for Korean-owned businesses and spoke virtually no English (ibid.: 54). This gave them a fairness issue on which to build political support.

Not insignificantly, KIWA's political organizing efforts also effectively mobilized transnational informational resources of their own. These proved quite useful in the struggle. As an example, to call attention to the plight of immigrant workers in Los Angeles, KIWA joined in a campaign with Local 11 of the Hotel Employees and Restaurant Employees International Union (HERE) to deal with the union-busting tactics of the new Korean owners of the Plaza Hotel, who had fired a unionized and mostly Latino staff and began hiring cheaper non-unionized transnational migrant workers (Kim, 1999: 6; Lee, 1996). As Lee (1996: 55) has shown, KIWA successfully researched the history of the Korean firm by using transnational connections of its own because KIWA had "access to information sources in Korea not available to the union."

In the local political arena KIWA further organized petition drives, protest rallies, and publicity campaigns designed to gain coverage in the Korean ethnic media in LA and to gain community support among Koreans who were neither business owners nor directly affected workers. Ultimately, KIWA won its fight in January 1995 when KARF, the principal Korean business association targeted by KIWA, decided to avoid further unfavorable publicity by transferring the balance of its relief account to KIWA (Lee, 1996: 59).

Since this victory KIWA's brand of political activism has become a highly visible force in the urban politics of Los Angeles's Koreatown. In the past two years KIWA has engaged in a bitter struggle against hundreds of Korean-owned restaurants in Koreatown to improve wages, overtime pay, and working conditions for the restaurants' nearly 2,000 workers. Significantly, while over two thirds of these workers are Korean, the remainder are largely Latino. Thus, while KIWA has retained its name, "Korean Immigrant Workers Advocates," it has begun to advocate the interests of all workers it regards as exploited by Korean owners, not merely those of Korean origin.

This ongoing political struggle has clearly split the Korean transnational migrant community in Koreatown along class, generational, cultural, and ideological lines. KIWA's eight full-time staff activists are mostly Korean transnational migrants in their twenties and thirties, born in Korea but reared in the United States. Migration scholars refer to such migrants as the "one and a half" generation. These activists accuse the largely first-generation Koreatown restaurant owners, who were born and raised in Korea, of exploiting their employees by violating US minimum wage, safety, and overtime laws. One of KIWA's co-founders, Danny Park, has said that his organization's goal is to transform a Korean transnational migrant mindset "that tends to view the people at the bottom of the economic ladder as inferior because of the Korean emphasis on education and hierarchy" (Kang, 1998b). The restaurant owners in turn have responded by accusing activists like Park of trying to destroy their parents' generation; of being too political, radical, and disrespectful; and of seeking political support "outside the community." They warn of dire consequences for Koreatown businesses already "adversely affected by the financial crisis in South Korea" (ibid.). Attitudes such as these hardened when KIWA scored a major legal and political victory in April, 1998 when a popular Korean-owned barbecued beef restaurant was forced to reinstate a fired cook with full back pay (ibid.).

Whatever the outcomes of the various organizing campaigns now being waged in the restaurant sector of Koreatown's ethnic economy, the very intensity of these ongoing struggles indicates that the social construction of Koreatown is very much an unfinished project. It thus is instructive to view Los Angeles's Koreatown as a social construction being reconstituted by a local politics of place-making and struggles over livelihood in which diverse transnational flows and connections, such as those detailed in this narrative, are likely to continue to play important roles.

Beyond Victimization

Cities and their race, class, gender, and ethnic relations are culturally constructed, politically mediated, and historically modifiable human creations, for better or worse. The optic of transnational urbanism profoundly complicates my reimagining of Los Angeles from the ground up, but also renders it understandable and hence changeable by human agency. This is its principal advantage over discourses such as the global cities, time-space compression, and postmodern urbanism narratives considered in Part I of this book. Such narratives elide the question of human agency in transnational times and project a role of "victim" onto women, minorities, and migrants, that overlooks what labor and community organizer Peter Olney (1993: 13) has termed the "subjective social dynamite" ignited by the nearly one million largely Mexican and Central American migrant service and light industrial workers that have mobilized, often successfully, to resist unjust working and living conditions in the Los Angeles basin in the past decade. The prevailing master narratives of urban restructuring have entirely overlooked these emergent political practices, in both their local and transnational dimensions. They have also failed to notice the local and transnational political interplay revealed in our story of Koreatown. In large measure this is because the proponents of these discourses resolutely maintain a synoptic gaze that reifies the "global economy" as a thing operating transhistorically and driven by its own laws of motion. In my view it is preferable to envision the global economy as a thoroughly historicized set of political, economic, and cultural practices that can best be understood by a social imaginary capable of "locating" globalization in the discursive and practical intersections of social relations that become localized in specific places at particular times.

Having established that globalization must be located on the ground if it is to have any practical meaning, we now turn to the four chapters comprising Part II of this book. They build upon my critique of the globalization discourse deployed in urban theory to develop a more grounded epistemic optic capable of discerning the main contours of what I have termed transnational urbanism. The central assumption underlying this quest is that paying close attention to the localized practices of transnational social and political networks can help us to make sense of urban politics in these spatially fluid times.

PART II

Reconstructing Urban Theory

Re-presenting the Local: Beyond Communitarian Metaphors

5

Localities . . . are not just about . . . capital momentarily imprisoned; they are about the intersections of social activities and social relations . . . which are necessarily, by definition, dynamic, changing. There is no stable moment, in the sense of stasis, if we define our world, or our localities, ad infinito in terms of change. . . . It is an accepted argument that capital is not a thing, it is a process. Maybe it ought to be more clearly established that places can be conceptualized as processes too.

Doreen Massey, "The Political Place of Locality Studies"

To a certain extent it seems obvious that urban studies is a domain whose object of study is "local" social, economic, political, and cultural processes. But in the past two decades the growing interest in globalization in general and the global–local interplay in particular has significantly disrupted this relatively straightforward equation of the urban with the local. Many urban theorists have cast their net widely to encompass processes of transnational and even global sociospatial scale, insisting that the urban cannot be clearly understood unless it is considered as an element in a wider sociospatial matrix. Yet even the most global of these urban theories remain committed to conceptualizations of the "local" as an empirically and even ontologically discernible space that exists as a purified "inside," understood as clearly distinct from the transnational flows of ideas, information, financial transactions, religious and cultural movements, media images, and people, that cut across and penetrate localities "from the outside," disrupting preexisting local modes of culture and social organization.

Two themes in particular have informed this construction of the "local" in the discourse on the global–local interplay in urban studies. The local has been frequently represented as the cultural space of embedded communities and, inversely, as a naturalized space of collective resistance to disruptive processes of globalization. In this chapter I will discuss the limits of this two-sided understanding of the local as a preface to my effort to frame a more dynamic conception of the local, one more likely to capture the connections linking people and places to the complex and spatially dispersed transnational communication circuits now intimately affecting the ways in which everyday urban life is experienced and lived.

The first aim of this chapter is to move urban studies beyond naturalistic constructions of locality. I begin this analysis by showing that the schema used by leading urban theorists to conceptualize the global–local connection has tended to reify the terms in this dialectic. In so doing they have reproduced a totalizing binary framework, which privileges the local as a space of "authenticity" and "community," and thus inverts the value of the terms. Second, I try to show how this binary way of thinking overlooks the extent to which transnational networks are constituted by their interrelations with, and thus their groundedness *inside* the local. My third aim in this chapter is to illustrate the conjunctures in contemporary urban politics where the politics of place-making within bounded political jurisdictions overlaps with a delocalized, network-based conception of political life. I think it is important to locate such overlapping political intersections, since without such overlap, in a pure "space of flows," the local and national state begin to disappear from view, as does their important role in mediating economic, political, and cultural flows that cut across territorial jurisdictions. The fourth and final aim of this chapter is to begin to identify some methods of urban research capable of capturing the socially constructed character of urban political life under conditions of contemporary transnationalism.

Localities as Defensive Community Formations

In writings ranging from the traditional anthropology of villages, tribes, and urban ethnic communities to emergent discourses on globalization, the "locality" has been used to signify an embedded community. "Community" in turn is represented as a static, bounded cultural space of "being," where personal meanings are produced, a cohesive set of cultural values is articulated, and traditional ways of life are enunciated and lived. One way or another, this view of the local as the site of "authentic community" has been treated as the binary opposite of the capitalist marketplace. In classical urban sociological thought the "urban" served as a surrogate for the rational instrumentalism of the capitalist market and the bureaucratization of the life-world: the transformation of *Gemeinschaft*-like social relations into the mediated impersonal ties of a *Gesellschaft*-like urban society. In the contemporary period the "urban" has been replaced by the "global" as a metaphor for the central "outside" threat to the primary social ties binding local communities. "Globalization" in turn is represented as a process inherently antagonistic to the sustainability of local forms of social organization and meaning-making.

This representation of the local as a once-firmly situated cultural space of community-based social organization now rendered unstable by the global dynamism of capitalist modernity is well captured in the following excerpt from David Harvey's *Condition of Postmodernity* (1989: 238–9, emphasis added):

> Movements of opposition to the disruptions of home, community, territory, and nation by the restless flow of capital are legion. . . . Yet all such movements, no matter how well articulated their aims, run up against a seemingly immovable paradox. . . . The movements have to confront the question of value and its expression as well as the necessary organization of space and time appropriate to their own reproduction. In so doing, they necessarily open themselves to the dissolving power of money as well as to the shifting definitions of space and time arrived at through the dynamics of capital circulation. Capital, in short, continues to dominate, and it does so in part through superior command over space and time. The "othernesses" and "regional resistances" that postmodernist politics emphasize can flourish in a particular place. But they are all too often subject to the power of capital over the coordination of universal fragmented space, and the march of capitalism's global historical time *that lies outside the purview of any particular one of them*. . . . Part of the insecurity which bedevils capitalism as a social formation arises out of this instability in the spatial and temporal principles around which social life might be organized (let alone ritualized in the manner of traditional societies). During phases of maximal change, the spatial and temporal bases for reproduction of the social order are subject to the severest disruption.

This narration of the waning power of local cultural formations in the face of capitalist globalization takes many complex turns, but Harvey's central argument is clear enough. Capital is the author of social change. Its superior global command over resources to reorganize time and space is opposed to the disorientation of defensive "local" social movements representing the interests of home, community, place, region, and even nation. The latter are represented as static forms of social organization, efforts to organize social life around "being" rather than "becoming." Defensive place-based movements are represented as cultural totalities expressing entirely place-bound identities in a world in which the dynamic flows of globalization exist entirely outside their purview. Oppositional movements representing "locality" may win some battles in what Harvey terms "postmodern politics." But they confront a restless adversary, whose processes of accumulation thrive on constantly disrupting the spatial and temporal arrangements upon which stable forms of local social organization might be constructed. Thus, in this grand narrative, in the final analysis, "capital" is the only agent of social change. Capitalist economic dynamics continue to dominate localities whose specific histories are relegated to the dustbin, rendering them fit only for periodic bouts of reactionary nostalgia.

Manuel Castells is another major urban theorist who has represented the local as a political space of social movements defending threatened cultural and political meanings placed under siege by global economic and technological restructuring. At first glance his view of locality appears to be quite different from Harvey's theorization. In Castells' work, late modernity is represented as an informational mode of development, a "space of flows" which accelerates global financial and informational linkages, converts places into spaces, and threatens to dominate local processes of cultural meaning. While the space of flows is a global space of economic and technological power, the space of cultural meaning and experience remains local (Castells, 1984). The global networks of wealth and power accumulate and exchange information instantaneously as a central source of institutional power. This boundary-penetrating process disrupts the sovereignty of the nation-state and threatens to marginalize the life-worlds of local cultural "tribes." As Castells (1984: 236) expresses the argument succinctly :

> On the one hand the space of power is being transformed into flows. On the other hand, the space of meaning is being reduced to microterritories of new tribal communities. In between cities and societies disappear. Information tends to be dissociated from communication. Power is being separated from political representation. And production is increasingly separated from consumption, with both processes being piecemealed in a series of spatially distinct operations whose unity is only recomposed by a hidden abstract logic. The horizon of such a historical tendency is the destruction of human experience, therefore of communication, and therefore of society.

Following from this logic is a kind of structural dialectic of domination and resistance. Global domination produces local resistance. Resistance to globalization is tied not to the agency of specific actors confronting unique historical conjunctures, but to the very structural dynamic of the technological revolution which threatens to render the local "tribes" irrelevant to the new informational world that has come into being.

Castells argues that in the new network society, localities, as communal forms of identity formation, are actually growing in significance precisely because "the subject" in the informational age is no longer constructed on the basis of the representational power of coherent national civil societies. In his view the nation-state is disintegrating as a space of internalized identity formation. Rather, for Castells two modes of identity formation now give rise to different types of communal resistance to globalization. Taken together these sources of cultural meaning give rise to the primacy of identity politics in the network society (Castells, 1997: 11). He terms these two modes of subject formation "project identities" and "resistance identities." Castells views "project-based" communal identities as encompassing such bases of social identity as religious fundamentalism and ethnic nationalism. It is the structural connection of vastly different cultural formations as "bypassed" cultural spaces, forged in the context of disintegrating national civil societies, that allows Castells (ibid.) to lump together social movements as diverse as the Zapatistas in Mexico, the militia and patriot movements in the USA, and the Aum Shinrikyo cult in Japan, treating them as functionally equivalent "social movements against the new global order," despite their historical differences in goals, ideologies, national and local contexts, and specific histories.

Castells distinguishes these project-based modes of identity formation from the purely local and micro-territorial defensive community formations that he terms "resistance identities." His analysis of this latter type of "local" social movement is also framed by using a structural logic that leaves little room for local processes of identity formation which might emerge out of social practices of appropriation and accommodation as well as resistance to various aspects of globalization or transnationalism. Nor does he consider the possibility that a multiplicity of local identities might be selectively internalized by variously positioned local social actors operating in the context of historically variable local and national civil societies experiencing processes of globalization or transnationalism. Instead, he inscribes the "local" dimension of urban social movements as precisely something that produces meaning *entirely against* the dynamics of global processes. This is well captured in Castells' *The Power of Identity* (1997: 61). According to Castells, urban social movements in the 1980s were becoming

> critical sources of resistance to the one sided logic of capitalism, statism, and informationalism. This was . . . because the failure of proactive movements [e.g. political parties and organized labor] . . . to counter economic exploitation, cultural domination, and political oppression had left people with no other choice than either to surrender or to react on the basis of the most immediate source of self-recognition and autonomous organization: their locality. Thus, so emerged the paradox of increasingly local politics in a world structured by increasingly global processes. There was production of meaning and identity: my neighborhood, my community, my city, my school, my tree, my river, my beach, my chapel, my peace, my environment. . . . Suddenly defenseless against a global whirlwind, people stuck to themselves: whatever they had, and whatever they were, became their identity.

In the 1990s, Castells (ibid.: 62–3) credits such defensive place-based movements, conceived as coherent totalities, with helping to revitalize the local state as a source of political control and social meaning; nurturing grassroots environmentalism, particularly in middle-class neighborhoods; and promoting the collective survival of squatter settlements, US inner-city areas, and working-class neighborhoods in Asia.

The passage just quoted from *The Power of Identity* is radically different in tone from the passage by David Harvey quoted earlier. Where Harvey sees social disorganization emerging from economic and technological globalization, Castells sees communal resistance; while Harvey rejects identity politics *a priori*, Castells judges identity politics by its consequences; while Harvey sees localism as a dead-end, Castells thinks local identities still constitute a viable space of resistance to global capitalist hegemony. Yet in one fundamental respect Harvey and Castells converge: namely, both represent the local as a cultural space of communal understandings, a space where meaning is pro-duced entirely outside the global flows of money, power, and information. People in these narrow social worlds make sense of their world and form their political identities in a culturally bounded micro-territory, the locality. These local cultural meanings, in turn, are represented as generating identities inher-ently oppositional to the global restructuring of society and space. For both, then, "place" is understood as the site of cohesive community formations existing outside the logic of globalization. While Harvey and Castells differ in their assessments of whether globalization will annihilate or defensively ener-gize these community formations, they both maintain a systemic disjunction between local and global social processes.

In this chapter I will argue that the operation of social networks is central to the social construction of the politics of place and identity. However, in today's world of accelerated transnational economic, migratory, and cultural connections, we must move beyond views of local associational life that fail to fully account for the transnational networks of meaning and power that now regularly cut across the territorial boundaries of local and national political space. These transnational networks do not operate in a pure space of flows. They locate on the ground in particular localities at particular times. When they do so, they intersect with more purely local networks of meaning and power, significantly shaping the character of the local politics of place-making. How can we best make sense of this criss-crossing of scales of social practice?

Rethinking the Boundaries of Locality

In an effort to unbind the conceptualization of "place" from the conflation of locality and community, critical urban geographer Doreen Massey has ad-vanced an imaginative response to the question of the interplay of the global and the local. Massey's view of place is decisively fluid. On the one hand, her critique of David Harvey's conception of time-space compression warns against the tendency to view the implosion of time and space that Harvey terms the condition of postmodernity as equally accessible to all. In her view different individuals and social groups are differently positioned *vis-à-vis* the flows and interconnections that constitute the "globalization" of capital and culture (Massey, 1993: 61). On the other hand, these flows and interconnections intersect in particular places at particular times, giving each place its own unique dynamism and making it possible for us to envision a "global" or "progressive" sense of place.

Theoretically, Massey depicts localities as acquiring their particularity not from some long-internalized history or sedimented character, but from the specific interactions and articulations of contemporary "social relations, social processes, experiences, and understandings" that come together in situations of co-presence, "but where a large portion of those relations . . . are constructed on a far larger scale than what we happen to define for that moment as the place itself" (ibid.: 66). When understood as articulated moments among criss-crossing networks of social relations and understandings (ibid.: 67), places do not possess singular but multiple and contested identities. Place-making is shaped by conflict, difference, and social negotiation among differently situated and at times antagonistically related social actors, some of whose networks are locally bound, others whose social relations and understandings span entire regions and transcend national boundaries. Massey, in short, provides key theoretical ingredients for conceptualizing the transnational urbanism I am seeking to inscribe in this book.

In two of her essays, Massey (1991a, 1993) gives specific resonance to this theoretical formulation by taking a brief walk down Kilburn High Road, her local shopping center, and describing in detail the criss-crossing social worlds that she sees. In addition to the many signs of an Irish presence and IRA political activity, she gazes upon saris on Indian models in shop windows, chats with a Muslim about the Gulf War, watches airplanes pass overhead, and confronts a traffic jam of cars leaving London. This simple exercise in participant-observation ethnography is a useful way to "map" places without drawing fixed boundaries around them.

Massey's approach would trace the trajectories of both residents' and non-residents' routes through a place, as well as identifying "their favorite haunts within it, the connections they make (physically, or by phone or post, or in memory and imagination) between here and the rest of the world." This is a good way to grasp the fluidity, diversity, and multiplicity of any place and the ways in which social relations affecting that place are stretched out over space and memory (i.e. time). It is also a good way to avoid an essentialist construction of localities as closed communities, as ontological "insides" constructed against a societal or global "outside," by tracing connections between the locality and what Arjun Appadurai (1991) has called the "global ethnoscape."

It is the same mode of ethnographic practice that cultural anthropologist Ulf Hannerz (1996: 150–1) has used imaginatively to trace the connections entailed in the Turkish and Finnish newspapers, Vietnamese and Middle Eastern baby walkers, and the billboards for an Argentinian play that he encounters in a walk around his own creolized city of Stockholm. It is the same mode of field observation I recently used on a trip to Copenhagen where, within the space of a single hour, I walked past small groups of Turkish, African, and Middle Eastern transmigrants, observed several veiled and unveiled Arab women, read signs in various non-European languages, and had an interesting conversation with an Irish bartender, in a English pub, across from Tivoli Garden. The bartender had once lived in Balboa Beach, California and worked as a stockbroker in New York City. While maintaining relations with people in both of these places, he now preferred to live in Copenhagen, which he characterized as a place less prone to violence. These field experiences were to prove helpful following a talk on transnational connections I gave in Copenhagen later in the week, when a questioner insisted that transnationalism was a phenomenon that might apply to "global cities" like New York or London, but had little relevance to more insular places like Copenhagen.

It should be obvious at this point that I am indebted to Doreen Massey's (1991a, 1991c, 1993, 1994a, 1994b) theory of locality in framing my conceptualization of transnational urbanism and developing research methods suitable for investigating transnational connections. In one respect, however, my approach differs sharply from Massey's. By my reading there is a tendency in her work to essentialize social actors "from below" in these transnational spaces by portraying them as disconnected victims of global processes, entirely lacking in the dynamic connections to transnational flows that she assigns to place. Thus, for example, in making her case that people have differential access to processes of globalization, Massey distinguishes between those who have the power to initiate global flows and be "in charge of" time-space compression and other actors she sees as altogether excluded from this compression, including poor migrants, immobile receivers of the consequences of globalization, and those "imprisoned" in time-space compression, like people in the favelas of Rio (Massey, 1993: 62). Her own global gaze depicts those connected to mobile networks by satellites, airplanes, faxes, e-mail, films, and other cultural and financial flows, only to contrast them with a woman on foot somewhere in sub-Saharan Africa, "who spends all of her day collecting water" (ibid.: 61).

This way of representing reality assumes that those at the bottom of national systems of social regulation and control will automatically reside at the bottom of hierarchically structured systems of transnational mobility. To give two counter-examples, however, it is precisely to escape from national constraints on upward social mobility that many transnational migrants have entered transmigrant streams and constructed translocal social relations; and it is precisely to resist unjust national systems of socioeconomic and political stratification that relatively marginal indigenous people's organizations have coalesced to engage in collective action on a transnational scale. Jumping scales may be an economic, political, or cultural strategy for transforming local or national power relations. Access to transnational flows cannot be read off directly from people's "original" economic class or social status position. Remote villages in Mexico and Central America now have satellite dishes (Kearney, 1995) and an African woman who gathers water from a remote well may be tied to an African street vendor in New York City in a transnational household engaged in active social practices.

Indeed it is precisely Massey's anecdote about the sub-Saharan African woman that serves as a counterpoint to Coombe and Stoller's (1994) recent ethnography of the social relations and cultural productions of transnational African street traders in reconfiguring a "black public sphere" in New York City. Coombe and Stoller introduce their study of the strained interactions between West African street vendors in New York City and their African-American customers by advancing a pointed critique of Massey's agency-less view of the prototypical African peasant woman. They state:

> There are other ways to imagine the African woman drawing water, recognizing her unique positioning without romanticizing her purported isolation or deny-ing her agency. This woman might be receiving remittances from her husband who sells hats on the streets in New York City. This in turn might enable her to hire others to draw her water and engage in her own marketing of dry goods. Early this year, due to World Bank and IMF structural adjustment policies, the value of the African franc was cut in half overnight. Abruptly, the woman's cost of doing business doubled. Compared to her neighbors, whose incomes are generated solely from local livelihoods, the woman is still relatively well-to-do. . . . West African vendors in New York tell us that migration is the most viable form of accommodation to devaluation: more and more women are left to cope with the needs of children and relatives alone.

My point is not that Coombe and Stoller's way of imagining a particular woman in Africa is necessarily empirically true in this instance, but merely that it captures more effectively than does Massey the possibilities for new forms of agency "from below" that transnational migration, investment, communica-tion, exchange, and travel have made possible in these times, for better or worse. Their narration resonates well with the transnational connections and interdependencies now being actively maintained with people in their places of origin by transnational Nigerian taxi drivers at the San Francisco Airport, transnational Mexican flower sellers in New York City (R. Smith, 1996), and transnational remittance senders from various localities of origin now working in cities as diverse as Berkeley in California, Milan, Italy, and Chicago (Guarnizo, 1999).

Perhaps more to the point, Coombe and Stoller's narration resonates well with the highly effective ongoing civil disobedience campaign against police brutality in New York City triggered by the killing of Amadou Diallo, an unarmed transnational migrant street peddler from West Africa who was gunned down in his doorway on the streets of New York by the Street Crime Unit of the New York Police Department. In New York a wide variety of new political subjects have been drawn into a broad political coalition supporting daily acts of civil disobedience. The new subjects, mobilized against arbitrary police practices, have included both local and transnational actors – radical and moderate black and white citizens, Jewish rabbis, media celebrities, local, state, and national political figures, and hundreds of ordinary people who have submitted themselves to arrest for their acts of civil disobedience. They have included such strange bedfellows as former mayors (and long-time adversaries) David Dinkins and Edward Koch; the incumbent Republican Governor George Pataki, who has criticized fellow Republican New York City Mayor Rudy Giuliani's and, not insignificantly, Amadou Diallo's West African mother, who rebuffed Giuliani's belated effort to express regret and participated in a protest rally organized by the Reverend Al Sharpton while accompanying her son's coffin to the airport so that he might be buried in his home village in Africa. Just before taking her son back to Africa to be buried, Diallo's mother turned to the assembled reporters present at the rally and forcefully declared "I'll be back." Since then she has done just this, returning to the United States to participate in a multi–city civil rights campaign designed to end police brutality.

The emergence of a new political coalition such as this is no mere epi-phenomenon of "globalization." Political coalitions in urban politics operate in and through "local" conditions of cultural production. Yet, in considerable measure, as this case illustrates, the "local" itself has become transnationalized as transnational modes of communication, streams of migration, and forms of economic and social intercourse continuously displace and relocate the spaces of cultural production. The social imaginary necessary to discern the signifi-cance of these social relations requires a kind of recombinant and historicized political economy and transnational ethnography that can make coherent sense of these transnational connections and give concrete meaning to the notion of "global interdependence."

Localities and the Politics of Difference

Anthropologists Akhil Gupta and James Ferguson (1997a, 1997c) have offered another clear-headed critique of the scholarly conflation of place and culture germane to my effort to contextualize emergent transnational social relations and to situate them in the field of urban studies. Gupta and Ferguson point out that representations of localities as cohesive community formations fail to recognize and deal with a variety of boundary-penetrating social actors and processes now very much a part of the transnational world in which we live.

Left out of such localized communitarian narratives are the border-dwellers who live along border zones separating localities, regions, and nation-states. These social actors engage with actors and networks based on the other side of juridical borders in processes of intercultural borrowing and lending which anthropologists now call "transculturation." (For useful studies of this process see Herzog, 1990; Martinez, 1994.) The "locality as community" problematic is equally inattentive to the sociocultural and political implications of the growing number of border-crossers, i.e. migrants, exiles, refugees, and diasporas, who now orchestrate their lives by creating situations of co-presence that link social networks across vast geographical distances around the globe (see chapter 8). Such border-penetrating processes go a long way toward helping explain, though they by no means exhaust, the difference-generating relations of power that constitute cultural and political identity and difference *within* localities defined as both political jurisdictions and as sociocultural spaces.

Gupta and Ferguson have identified three dimensions of cultural production that complicate efforts to view localities in communitarian terms and thus to ground ethnographic practice and urban research locally in a transnational world. The first of these is the growing interdependence (economic, socio-cultural, and informational) across linked spaces that belies notions of discrete, autonomous local cultures. Second, the emergence of wider discourses and practices of postcolonial politics (abetted, in my view, by the globalization of mass media) is producing a variety of hybrid cultures, even in geographically remote localities and nations, that problematize the very notion of "authentic cultural traditions" even as social analysts seek to inscribe and preserve them. Third, the boundary-penetrating processes now characterizing our transnational world have facilitated the social construction of "communities in the making" as imagined spaces, often occupying the same geographical locale. These imaginings of communal identity necessarily entail processes of inclusion and exclusion, i.e. processes which create "otherness." For example, the social construction of the constitutive outside, or "other," is very much part of the ethnic and racial relations that have erupted antagonistically throughout the 1990s in transnational cities around the world (see, for example, Smith and Tarallo, 1995).

The culturally and politically constructed character of such racial antagonisms and their relation to power and place has been well captured by Gupta and Ferguson (1997c: 17). Identity and alterity, they explain, are produced

> simultaneously as the formation of "locality" and "community." "Community"
> . . . is premised on various forms of exclusion and construction of otherness. . . .
> With respect to locality as well, at issue is not simply that one is located in a
> certain place, but that the particular place is set apart from and opposed to other
> places. The "global" relations that we have argued are constitutive of localities
> are therefore centrally involved in the production of "local" identities too.

Viewing locality (like ethnicity and nationality) as complex, contingent, and contested outcomes of political and historical processes, rather than as timeless essences, also challenges the theoretical framing of locality as an inexorable space of resistance to globalization. Instead of opposing autonomous local cultures, be they tribes, militias, urban formations, or regions (à la Castells or Benjamin Barber, 1995), to the economic domination of global capital, the homogenizing movement of cultural globalization, or the hegemonizing seductions of global consumerism, Gupta and Ferguson recommend paying close attention to the ways in which dominant global cultural forms may be appropriated and used, or even significantly transformed, "in the midst of the field of power relations that links localities to a wider world" (Gupta and Ferguson, 1997c: 5).

Germane to this larger question are several more particular ones: How are perceptions of locality and community discursively constructed in different time-space configurations? How are the understandings which spring from these perceptions internalized and lived? What role in producing politically salient differences within localities is played by the cultural, political, and economic connections localities have with worlds "outside" their borders that configure their interdependence? What roles do the global and local mass media play in framing the understandings and practices within socially constructed communities and their constitutive fields of otherness? (On the latter two questions see Smith and Feagin, 1995; Thompson, 1995; Cvetkovich and Kellner, 1997; Gupta and Ferguson, 1997c; Kellner, 1997.)

Having raised these questions I would further suggest that we leave open to ethnographic and historical investigation the character of the contextualizing sociospatial interdependence in which particular localities are enmeshed at particular times. Specifically, I agree with Gupta and Ferguson that it is possible for local interventions to "significantly transform" dominant cultural forms. I would therefore leave open the question of whether or not the criss-crossing relations of power that come together on the ground in localities must necessarily be understood hierarchically. Gupta and Ferguson appear to assume that they must be so understood when they state that in studying the forms of interdependence linking places and spaces in our transnational world we must move our gaze from the local sites of community formation to the wider issue of "the spatial distribution of hierarchical power relations" (Gupta and Ferguson, 1997a: 40).

If Gupta and Ferguson are here envisioning a hierarchy of larger to smaller spatial scales (e.g. from localities, to regions, to nations, to the world) in which the larger scales necessarily dominate and constrain the smaller, then they are negating their insight about local to global transformations and simply reproducing the metaphor of nested hierarchies of scale thoroughly critiqued in my earlier discussion of the limits of the global city metaphor. If, however, Gupta and Ferguson mean to suggest that social relations between global-level actors and local-level actors are necessarily hierarchical, a different problem is raised. At the level of social action, hierarchical power relations are only one among many different sociospatial patterns of power that a transnational gaze can discern. The agency-based power relations implicated in what some have called "global localization" are often indeed asymmetrical and hierarchical, as when multinational corporations locate an export processing zone in a poor Third World city, or when migrant groups in a new local and national milieu seek to renegotiate slowly changing urban racial hierarchies. Transnational power relations may, however, be more competitively structured, as when transnational small business enterprises forge relations to their landlords and clientele. This may be so even as the relations between transnational entrepreneurs and their (often co-ethnic "new immigrant") workers are hierarchically structured (though often contestedly so). When thus viewed contextually and relationally, transnational power relations may even be relatively egalitarian, as when local environmental activists coalesce across national boundaries to object to locally specific environmentally degrading projects such as rainforest logging or a large-scale urban development project. The point I am trying to make is not to deny that power relations are often hierarchically structured, but to maintain that all power relations must be viewed contextually as contingent outcomes of political struggles. Historically, these struggles have produced a multiplicity of power relations ranging from more to less to non-hierarchical, depending on the historically specific circumstances and understandings that make and remake particular structures of power.

The Social Construction of Space as Place

When Gupta and Ferguson turn from the question of the patterning of power relations across space to the issue of the social construction of space as place, they acknowledge this contingency. The open-ended questions they raise in response to this issue are, in my view, as germane to questions of the spatial distribution of power as they are to issues of identity and place-making. These questions are: "With meaning-making understood as a practice, how are spatial meanings established? Who has the power to make places of spaces? Who contests this? What is at stake?" (Gupta and Ferguson, 1997a: 40).

It is precisely questions such as these that can move urban researchers interested in the social construction of locality beyond essentialist assumptions about the equivalence of locality and culture. For example, research on the politics of urban heritage has produced a spate of studies on "the making of place" by a wide variety of political actors, including local neighborhood groups, government officials, and business interests, as well as wider networks of social practice such as architectural activists, historic preservationists, and global developers. In particular places these actors collude and collide in contests over the cultural meanings of place (see, for example, Bird, 1993; Watson, 1991). Historically and ethnographically grounded case studies bring into focus the issue of the politics of representation, thereby modifying a discourse on global-ization and community that has been dominated by agency-less narratives of urban and regional change that tend to exclude from consideration non-capitalist actors and their representations of space and place.

In two such grand-narrative interventions in the "heritage debate," Harvey (1989) and Zukin (1991) have essentialized local cultures as vernacular tradi-tions about to be erased by the march of capitalist modernization. In their capital vs. community motif, global capital, as a unitary actor, is framed against a multiplicity of separate, internally coherent, and "authentic" local cultures. The former is seen as penetrating the latter by a one-way flow of mystification and power. Abstract "capital" is denounced for having appropriated and mar-keted various dimensions of authentic cultural heritage, as in the case of the appropriation and use of local vernacular architecture by real estate capitalists in shaping the built environment of theme parks, luxury apartment com-plexes, and shopping arcades. Viewed in this light, the appropriation of local cultural forms, in this instance architectural artifacts, becomes yet another leit-motif of a grand narrative that invests capital with unidirectional, omnipotent dynamism, while relegating local residents to passive roles as bearers of a dying cultural heritage. The social construction of the local as a static, sedimented community roots non-capitalist social actors in place and freezes them in time. It also suggests that the fixed place to which they are "bound" is about to be replaced by a phantom simulacrum scripted by global capital.

In an insightful essay, Peter Jackson (1991) considers the complex politics of place-making found in a series of detailed case studies of historic preservation. Jackson's study (ibid.: 225) nicely illustrates how the turn to the analysis of culture by leading urban political economists like Harvey and Zukin has been partial, naively modernist, and even essentialist. It is a projection of "authent-icity" onto a putatively disappearing historical past for the purpose of de-nouncing the role of capitalism in the historical present. Jackson suggests that the heritage debate is better understood as raising questions about the politics of representation rather than posing a stark choice between "genuine pre-servation" and "misappropriation" of an actually existing "authentic" urban past. "Rather than simply showing how capital 'uses' culture in an instrumen-tal way," he concludes, abundant case study evidence demonstrates that

> such a crude argument has to be modified in light of the contingencies of each
> particular situation. Which groups were involved and how were their interests
> articulated? How did the changing legislative and fiscal environment make cer-
> tain forms of investment more attractive than others? What coalitions between
> different interest groups were sought and achieved, and with what effects? Clearly,
> one cannot divorce the "cultural" aspects of reinvestment or preservation from

the apparently "political" and "economic" dimensions . . . but neither can the
political economy of urban and regional change be understood without a more
fully developed understanding of its cultural politics.

In short, economic processes like investment, disinvestment, and reinvestment in "place" are unavoidably culturally coded. Likewise the cultural processes of representation take place in and change their material contexts,
including the built environment of cities. We, as analysts, are thus unavoidably
involved in interpretive reconstructions of who produces and who consumes
particular images of place and space, and with what effects. The study of these
processes from the vantage point of the politics of representation in cultural
studies enables urban researchers to move beyond a reified and unitary view of
"actors" like "capital" to a historicized analysis of precisely "whose past is
being perceived, how it is being represented, and whose interests are being
served by such unavoidably selective readings" (ibid.: 220; see also Jackson,
1992). In sum, any local community's historical past is a historically contested
rather than a timelessly embedded social phenomenon.

Moreover, the contested politics of representation applies not only to any
locality's historical past, but also to the shaping of its present and the formation
of its alternative future(s). This brings to the forefront the vexing question of
just what makes a place a place like no other place. Phrased differently, what
about a place persists and what changes over time? And this is precisely what
power struggles over "place-making" are all about; namely, who changes
what in alternative representations of any place's present and future and how
do these changes selectively appropriate or reject particular elements of any
place's historical past ?

A good example of empirical urban research influenced by these sorts of
questions is Jon Bird's (1993) study of local resistance by grassroots artists and
activists to the development of the London Docklands by Olympia and York,
the now bankrupt global development corporation. Bird describes the efforts
by local activists in London to use a poster campaign and other street tactics to
offer oppositional versions of the official discourse of Docklands planning
deployed by Olympia and York and their allies within the local state. Bird
characterizes this campaign as an emergent "postmodern culture of resistance,"
a local cultural politics of alternative historical memory which avoids a melan-
cholic politics of loss and regret by recording the "voices of challenge and
resistance encoded in the rhythms of subcultural street life . . . and the presence of alternative traditions of representation" (ibid.: 134).

One advantage of this approach to the representation of locality, when
compared to the conflation of the local with the communal considered above,
is that it allows for the construction of alternative representations of local
traditions in the same place, thus making room for a conceptualization of the
local as a site of contestations over meaning and power rather than a reservoir

of unitary local subjectivity. A limit of Bird's approach, however, from the perspective of a network-based imaginary, is that it conflates the politics of everyday life with a purely local politics of consciousness. Thus, for example, in Bird's narrative the resistance practiced by the artists and activists opposed to global restructuring of London's docklands derives entirely from a narrow subculture of street life that has recovered an equally local "alternative tradition of representation." Given that the activists involved in this grassroots action were also likely to be engaged in alternative discourses of the worlds of the London and international art and architecture scenes, it is at least reasonable to argue that the "local" protest may have emerged from the extra-local networks of communication that may have informed these social actors and inflected their political practices. This criss-crossing of discursive domains is a key dimension of the transnational urbanism I seek to make comprehensible in this book.

Rethinking the Politics of Everyday Life

It is not surprising, however, that Bird readily equates everyday life with the local spatial scale. In so doing, he is simply following in the footsteps of the leading French urban theorists of "everyday life," such as Henri Lefebvre (1971, 1991) and Michel de Certeau (1984). Urban researchers interested in the ethnographic inscription of the practices of everyday life have often conflated the local level of analysis with the politics of everyday life. In so doing they often engage in a process of legitimating local spaces of resistance to modernity in its various forms: capitalism, statism, and technological development. For Lefebvre and de Certeau, for example, ordinary people in their everyday life activities appropriate and use urban space in ways that challenge the abstract urban spaces constituted by capital and the state. Lefebvre (1971, 1991) uses this motif in situationist fashion to legitimate a transformational politics of direct action to secure for all urban residents a "right to the city." De Certeau's (1984) imaginary is more limited. He uses the rhetoric of everyday life to paint a picture of the evasive childlike spatial practices by which people escape the synoptic gaze of urban planners and "inhabit the street" in ways that slip through the disciplinary boundaries of the urban spatial plans enacted by central planners. Despite their differences, these urban theorists of the everyday, like Harvey and Castells, tend to equate "the local" with an oppositional space of individual and collective resistance to more global structures of domination.

To his credit, de Certeau (1984) identifies some of the myriad ways that social space is produced and maintained by discursive practices. In his view, the very meaning of "the city" is intimately tied to the politics of representation. Discursive practices, accessible to ethnographic observation, construct alternative images and boundaries of urban space by weaving alternative tapestries out of any city's "isolatable and interconnected properties" (ibid.: 94). However, one of the foremost critical problems facing ethnographic accounts of everyday life in these transnational times is that "everyday life" is not a fixed object of investigation, a readily discernible set of practices that can be easily located and subjected to empirical observation and cognitive mapping. In my view, at the current transnational moment, "the politics of everyday life" needs to be opened up more widely as a social and political imaginary. The "everyday" needs to be freed from its association with purely local phenomena. In transnational cities people's everyday urban experiences are affected by a wide variety of phenomena, practices, and criss-crossing networks which defy easy boundary-setting. Multiple levels of analysis and social practice now inform the urban politics of everyday life throughout the world.

In his discussion of what he terms the "transversal" politics of everyday life, David Campbell (1996) has clearly expressed this multiplicity:

> Likewise, neither is "everyday life" a synonym for the local level, for in it global interconnections, local resistances, transterritorial flows, state politics, regional dilemmas, identity formations and so on are always already present. Everyday life is thus a transversal site of contestations rather than a fixed level of analysis. It is transversal . . . because the conflicts manifested there not only transverse all boundaries: *they are about these boundaries,* their erasure or inscription, and the identity formations to which they give rise.

Consider the following emergent transnational urban identities. Sociologist Martin Albrow and his associates (Albrow, Eade, Dürrschmidt, and Washbourne, 1997) have written insightfully on the social construction of the boundaries of imagined community in British Muslim neighborhoods in cities throughout the United Kingdom. Rather than viewing religious fundamentalism as a local expression of belonging and identity framed against economic globalization, as in the work of Barber (1995) and Castells (1997), these scholars connect the rhetorics of belonging found in various local British Muslim enclaves to a wider social construction of Islamic community (*umma*) transmitted by transnational religious and cultural networks. Everyday life in the Muslim neighborhoods is infused with knowledge and meanings produced in these transnational networks and encountered in the local neighborhoods on a daily basis. The social construction of belonging to a transnational Islamic community is produced and transmitted through a transnational network of social and technological linkages, including religious ceremonies, telephone conversations, television and radio programs, newspaper accounts, videos, and music. In everyday visits to relatives and friends, in interactions at work, and in other neighborhood forms of community involvement, local Muslims employ this transnational network, which is physically absent but hardly spiritually distant, to socially construct their "locality." In this construction, Islam is viewed not as a purely local or "tribal" reaction to the globalization of capitalism but as a transnational cultural formation, as much involved in the transnationalization of information, cultural exchange, and network formation, as are the networks of financial transactions that comprise what we now regard as the globalization of capital.

In short, everyday life is neither a fixed spatial scale nor a guaranteed site of local resistance to more global modes of domination, whether capitalist or otherwise. Rather, under conditions of transnational urbanism our everyday life-world is one in which "competing discourses and interpretations of reality are already folded into the reality we are seeking to grasp" (Campbell, 1996: 23). Grasping this sort of reality now requires us to develop a transnational imaginary and to fashion perceptual tools capable of making sense of the new identities emerging from this politics of representation and boundary-setting.

In the late 1980s, in the context of the locality-studies debate in British urban geography, Andrew Sayer (1989) wrote an important, and to my mind under-considered essay, which helps move this search for a new urban re-search imaginary forward. Sayer advanced the argument that social structures are context-dependent and are thus produced and reproduced within specific historical and geographical (time-space) contexts. Sayer made a strong case for a narrative approach to urban studies that situates agency, that is, the social actor, in historically particular time-space settings, particularly the setting of the locality, and recognizes these settings "as constitutive rather than as passive" (ibid.: 255). Contextualizing his own move, Sayer explained that the so called "empirical turn" from structural Marxist social theory in urban studies was driven by the widening gap between class-based theories of consciousness and the resurgence of neo-conservative and neoliberal thinking among ordinary citizens and workers in the 1980s. It was fueled as well by growing socio-spatial unevenness in conditions of everyday urban life.

Sayer praised the turn to locality studies for seeking to grasp the everyday life experiences of ordinary people in terms of concrete social practices rather than abstractly. To his credit, Sayer was one of the first urban theorists to call for a close articulation of the then-dominant political-economy approach to urban studies with emergent debates in anthropology on postmodern ethnography. He advocated a methodological marriage of political economy and ethnography because, in his view, ethnography was capable of shedding light on "preexisting cognitive and cultural materials" (ibid.: 256) not available through political–economic analysis. This move produced a convergence of one stream of radical urban geography with an emerging trend among anthropologists toward a contextualized ethnographic practice premised on a desired unification of ethnography and political economy. (For a coherent defense of this approach in anthropology see Marcus and Fischer, 1986; for an excellent recent example of one such successful marriage see Gregory, 1998.)

In my view this marriage of methodological approaches is desirable for reasons other than those suggested by Sayer. It is simplistic to assume that ethnography is a sure-footed, transparent empirical tool for mapping "pre-existing cognitive and cultural materials" onto an otherwise abstract political–economic terrain. Cultural materials, like political–economic arrangements, are constantly being produced, reproduced, or transformed by human practice, rather than standing outside the realm of practical life as pregiven generators of meaning and social action. Accordingly, it is necessary to historicize *both* political economy and ethnography. Once this is accomplished the two approaches to urban studies can be used in tandem to help make sense of highly fluid social processes affecting particular places at particular times. This combination of historicized methods of social inquiry forces to our attention contingent questions of agency and meaning-making. It can help us to sort out the trajectories of the criss-crossing networks of spatially dispersed social relations of co-presence through which social action in a transnational context is now filtered and informed.

Jan Lin's (1998) book-length case study is an excellent example of a carefully historicized, contextually situated ethnographic research project that captures the transversal character of the politics of everyday urban life in transnational cities. Lin tells the story of the historical transformations of New York's Chinatown as an urban "place." The book was written as an antidote to long-standing negative symbolic representations of various Chinatowns and, by implication, of Chinese transnational migrants, as timeless sites of clannishness, insularity, concentrated social problems, and resistance to change. Lin depicts New York City's Chinatown as a site of criss-crossing transnational social and organizational networks of meaning and power that infuse the neighborhood with its dynamism and account for its "internal" political conflicts.

The subject of Lin's *Reconstructing Chinatown* is community change in a global context. Community change is constantly being produced by the intersections and social relations formed among actors representing local and transnational labor and capital, old and new community-based ethnic organizations, local power structures and their opponents, and agencies of the national and local state. Lin's ethnographic and historical research traces the connections between the everyday means of livelihood and social life in this ethnic enclave and the political uncertainties, capital surpluses, and economic transitions in other cities and societies in East Asia in the 1980s and 1990s that accelerated trans-Pacific flows of transnational migrants and capital investment to New York's Chinatown. He also pays close attention to the public policies mediating these flows of capital, people, and culture, including US immigration, trade, economic, and monetary policies, as well as the land use, law enforcement, banking deregulation, and other urban policies of New York City government.

Especially compelling is Lin's portrayal of the considerable factionalism of the Chinatown local polity stemming from a conflictual politics of place where the meaning of "Chinatown" is continually contested. Some of these "internal" political struggles expose cultural and ideological fault lines stemming from still-evolving geopolitical relations among and between the Chinese mainland, its various regions, Hong Kong, and Taiwan – the places originating the flows of people, money, ideas, and transnational connections into and out of New York's Chinatown. The historical, cultural, and political heterogeneity of these connections is often masked by the apparent ethnic homogeneity of the category "Chineseness" (and even "Asian-American") in US political discourse. Lin brings the connections and their political consequences to life by discussing, for example, the political struggles for local influence of a once-ascendant mercantile elite from Guangdong province challenged by new Fujianese merchant associations. He pays close attention as well to other internal conflicts over place-making which pit new immigrant-based labor and community organizations against both of these capital factions, as well as against the urban redevelopment and law enforcement policies of the local state. He also finds instances where these factional disputes are overcome by practices that produce a temporary political unity, formed in opposition to discursively constructed "outside" political interventions into the neighborhood by particular urban redevelopment schemes initiated by transnational Japanese and other Asian real estate capitalists, in alliance with redevelopment agencies of New York City government. Lin's historicized political–economic and ethnographic analysis demonstrates that political identities in a neighborhood defending its preservation are not pregiven features of an ontology of locality, but rather emerge as a result of specific political struggles and collective actions.

Reconstructing Chinatown recognizes that community, ethnicity, and place are all social constructions of contingent solidarities. These socially produced and "temporarily sutured" (Mouffe, 1988) solidarities, as Lin (1998: 204) cogently puts it, "have the power to mobilize and reinforce networks of association and influence, confer human roles and identities, and grant an affective meaning to physical space in the way that 'home' and 'turf' imply an emotive or defensive association with territory." The point worth making here is not that a sense of community has been shown to emerge in defense of a neighborhood's physical space, but *why* it has come into existence; namely because it has been socially and politically constructed by politicized actors and networks that form temporary coalitions at particular times in response to particular efforts to redefine the meaning of "locality."

How was Jan Lin able to capture so well the interplay of these local and cross-border dynamics in the contemporary reconstruction of New York's Chinatown? His recombinant research approach is worth close consideration. Under the rubric of a qualitative community study conducted "in global perspective," Lin combined participant observation over an extended period in several community-based organizations; ethnographic encounters (including both "neutral" observation and active engagement in some of the disputes he studied); an extended case method (see Buroway, 1991; Feagin, Sjoberg, and Orum, 1991) designed to trace connections between micro-community level social situations and "external" contexts such as transnational investment and migration flows; formal interviews with representatives of Chinatown's economic, community, labor, and political organizations, and with urban planners and public officials; and a contextualized semiotic analysis of the political representations of Chinatown and Chinese immigrants found in films, novels, television serials, and journalistic stories. These latter methods, which nicely contrasted media-generated with historicized ethnographic representations of ethnic enclave formation, were, in my view, especially helpful in inflecting Lin's historicized political economy perspective with a nuanced cultural understanding of the social construction of place, ethnicity, and community. This makes his approach to urban studies a fruitful model to consider in studying transnational urbanism. Taken together, his recombinant methods of social research and analysis take a useful step along the path to a truly historicized and transnationalized approach to urban studies.

Transnational Place-making

Recall that at the beginning of this chapter I set out to offer a reconsideration of localized communitarian metaphors in urban theory that had four aims. The first was to move urban studies beyond naturalistic constructions of "locality" which view the local as an inherently defensive community formation. While "race" and "gender" are now widely regarded as socially constructed categories, "locality" is still often assumed to be a space of nature springing from human sociability. In this chapter I have tried to show that even the most material elements of any locality are subject to diverse readings and given different symbolic significance by differently situated social groups and their corresponding discursive networks. The result is a highly politicized social space where representations of place are constructed and contested.

Second, I have tried to show that the schema used to conceptualize the global–local connection by leading urban theorists such as Harvey, Castells, and others has tended to reify the terms in this dialectic. In so doing they have reproduced a totalizing binary framework, which privileges the local as a space of "authenticity" and "community," and thus inverts the value of the terms. (For a related critique of representations of "urbanity" see Goss, 1997.) In this schema the global is equated with the abstract, universal, and dynamic, i.e. "capital," while the local is invested with concreteness, particularity, and threatened stability, i.e. "community." Such a discourse of capital versus community treats the global *a priori* as an oppressive social force while constructing localities in more positive, albeit more static, terms (see Cvetkovich and Kellner, 1997). This binary formulation overlooks the ways in which global and transnational networks are constituted by their interrelations with, and thus their groundedness *inside*, the local. They thus ignore the considerable interplay of spatial scales and discursive practices to be found in any locality and underestimate the intricacy involved in sorting out the social interactions and processes at multiple spatial scales that constitute the complex politics of place-making under conditions of transnational urbanism.

My third aim in this chapter was to illustrate some of the conjunctures in contemporary urban politics, where the politics of place-making within bounded political jurisdictions overlaps with a delocalized, network-based conception of political life. This overlap was illustrated concretely by my rereading of Jan Lin's study of the making and remaking of New York City's Chinatown. It bears repeating that if we fail to locate such overlapping political intersections between local, national, and transnational processes, we are left with a formulation of the transnational and the global as a pure space of flows. In this mode of analysis the local and national state begin to disappear from view, as does their important role in mediating economic, political, and cultural flows that cut across territorial jurisdictions.

It has been the project of some critical international relations theorists writing about globalization and democracy to argue for a reconsideration of the centrality of bounded political communities in political and social thought, because this privileges a politics of place over a network-based view of politics (see Low, 1997). My goal has not been to reverse this privileging but to insist that we open up the politics of place to encompass the articulation of local and transnational networks in the production of power, meaning, and identities.

The final aim of my critical re-examination of the role of locality in urban theory at the dawn of the new millennium has been to begin thinking through some of the methods of urban research capable of capturing the socially constructed character of urban political life under conditions of contemporary transnationalism. This effort to discern the meanings that people give to their social locations in the world – and the consequences that follow from these understandings – forms the basis of my ongoing work. The next three chapters of this book will move beyond my critical reassessment of dominant urban theories of globalization to pursue an epistemological inquiry intended to fashion perceptual tools and to develop an optic capable of making sense of the new identities emerging from the politics of representation and boundary-setting in the multiple and criss-crossing world(s) in which we now find ourselves.

Beyond the Postmodern City: Rethinking Ethnography for Transnational Times

6

What has emerged . . . is a sense of the increasing vulnerability to criticism of things, institutions, practices, discourses. . . . But together with this sense of instability and this amazing efficacy of discontinuous, particular, and local criticism, one in fact also discovers something that perhaps was not initially foreseen, something one might describe as precisely the inhibiting effect of global, totalitarian *theories*. It is not that these global theories have not provided nor continue to provide . . . useful tools for local research . . . Marxism and psychoanalysis are proofs of this. But I believe these tools have only been provided on the condition that the theoretical unity of these discourses was in some sense put in abeyance, or at least curtailed, divided, overthrown, caricatured, theatricalized. . . . In each case the attempt to think in terms of a totality has in fact provided a hindrance to research. . . . I believe that what this essentially local character of criticism indicates . . . is an autonomous, non-centralized kind of theoretical production, one . . . whose validity is not dependent on the approval of the established regimes of thought.

Michel Foucault, Power/Knowledge

During the late 1980s and early 1990s the discourse on postmodernism entered the realm of urban theory by way of debates in urban sociology, geography, anthropology, and politics on the interplay of global sociospatial restructuring, the cultural transformation of cities, the rise of identity politics, and the politics of collective action. In an otherwise skeptical article on the applicability of postmodernism to urban analysis, Sharon Zukin (1988: 431) nevertheless pointed out that postmodernism "sounds right" in urban studies because it intuitively resonates "with the fragmentation of geographic loyalties in contemporary economic restructuring and its expression in new urban polarities." Zukin's periodizing reading of postmodernity, along with the structural–Marxist reading of David Harvey discussed in chapter 2, parallel the conceptualization of the postmodern city advanced by Frederic Jameson (1983, 1984, 1989). These social theorists tend to treat questions of culture and personal identity as direct by-products of new political–economic arrangements and their sociospatial impact on the material form and social structure of cities. Thanks to Harvey, the term "postmodern" is now often equated with the late capitalist or "post-Fordist" historical period and its putatively hegemonic regime of flexible accumulation.

In this chapter I will draw upon the poststructuralist writings of Ernesto Laclau, Chantal Mouffe, Michael Shapiro, and others to critique this grand narrative of postmodern urbanism and to rethink the project of postmodern ethnography. My aim is to continue the discussion begun in chapter 5: how we might develop a workable mode of transnational ethnographic practice that, when combined with a truly historicized political economy, can move urban studies along useful paths under conditions of contemporary transnationalism. The chapter begins by questioning those readings of the paradigmatic postmodern city (such as those discussed in chapter 4 in the case of Los Angeles) that envision an entirely new kind of city, a postmodern metropolis, as a prototypical mode of urban development following from contemporary developments in late capitalist political economy. It then tries to show that despite the overgeneralizations of the postmodern discourse in urban studies, some of the poststructuralist epistemological innovations in the social and human sciences, also sometimes termed "postmodern," offer us an opportunity to open up urban theory to new ways of envisioning cities as crossroads of human practice. The chapter then addresses the uses as well as the limits of the postmodern turn in ethnographic practice. It ends by providing concrete illustrations of how ethnographic research is being reconfigured as a multi-sited, transnational mode of research practice that takes into account the shifting boundaries of place under conditions of transnational urbanism.

The readings of the "postmodern city" by David Harvey (see chapter 2, p. 28), Sharon Zukin (1988, 1991), Frederic Jameson (1984, 1989), and Edward Soja (1989, 1996) differ from each other in many respects. They nonetheless share a common narrative theme that envisages the emergence of something quite new: a postmodern city in which images of urban spectacle created by multinational capital replace "authentic" local cultures. In this reading, mystifications of consumer society are assumed to penetrate the subconscious life-worlds of urban residents and negate the cultural practices of local communities. Viewed politically, a disorienting built environment of "hyperspaces" is said to fragment the social and political consciousness of ordinary people, reducing their capacity to cognitively conceive their environment, let alone to mount any effective resistance to capitalist hegemony.

In this grand narrative of postmodern urban development scant attention is given to the impact upon cities of the spatial practices of ordinary people or the politics of urban difference, save to marginalize them as part of the spectacle. These representations of the postmodern city ignore the myriad ways in which the everyday practices of ordinary people, their feelings and understandings of their conditions of existence, mediate the impact of global capitalism on urban culture, and in the process often modify the very structural conditions of everyday urban life. (For examples of ethnographic studies illustrating these practices see Smith, Tarallo, and Kagiwada, 1991; Smith and Tarallo, 1995; the ethnographic studies in Nonini and Ong, 1997, and Smith and Guarnizo, 1998, as well as those discussed throughout this book.)

Harvey, Jameson, and others in the debate on the postmodern city tend to subordinate cultural processes to the master discourse of Marxist political economy. In so doing they underestimate the ontological, epistemological, and methodological challenge which poststructuralist philosophy in general and social constructionism in particular pose, not only for the Marxist tradition, but for all forms of essentialism. "Post-Fordist" forms of economic organization and the global restructuring of capital and labor may be related in complex ways to certain postmodern aesthetic and cultural practices, but they are certainly not unidirectional determinants of urban culture. Increased flexibility in labor markets and business practices, the emergence of new cultural practices in everyday urban life, and the movement of poststructuralist and deconstructive methods from philosophy to the social sciences, may all share the label "postmodern," but the relationship between these developments must be carefully considered and precisely specified rather than assumed as parts of a pregiven, harmonious epochal totality.

The development of a social constructionist urban social theory which is a key aim of this book counters the current tendency to deploy postmodernism as a totalizing device which conflates and thus obscures the differences among the various postmodernisms now on the scene. Therefore, it is important to specify the boundaries of the postmodern deployed in this chapter. Two urban planning theorists, Kirsten Simonsen (1990) and Michael Dear (1986, 1991b), have assessed the implications of various "postmodern conditions" for the theory and practice of urban planning. In so doing they have usefully differentiated between postmodernism as a parodic and imitative *style*, most prominently displayed in architecture, art, and literary studies; postmodernism as an *epoch*, as in David Harvey's periodization; and postmodernism as a *method*, as in the case of poststructuralist and deconstructive critique or postmodern ethnography. I have already thoroughly critiqued postmodernism as a periodizing device in my earlier discussion in chapters 2 and 4. Setting aside for the sake of clarity the question of postmodernism as an aesthetic style, this chapter will try to sort out those dimensions of postmodernism as a method of social inquiry which can advance our understanding of transnational urbanism and those aspects which are of little help in this respect.

Social Constructionism and Postmodern Social Inquiry

In the social sciences, those receptive to postmodern and social constructionist methods for the conduct of urban research have actively engaged in debates with positivists, neo-Marxists, traditional ethnographers, and virtually all social researchers who seek solely to uncover general patterns in history or human behavior, rather than recognizing the diversity of individual, group, and cultural difference, and hence the unavoidable mediation of general patterns by historically specific understandings. (For a sense of the flavor of these debates see Clifford and Marcus, 1986; Mascia-Lees, Sharpe, and Ballerino Cohen, 1989; Deutsche, 1991; and Massey, 1994b.) The belief in the autonomization of the cultural imaginary from the realm of economic necessity is reflected in this trend in social inquiry. This is a belief that postmodernism shares with social constructionism.

More problematical, however, is that postmodernism as a method of social analysis has been credited with refocusing attention from the macro-structural context of urban life to the realm of the everyday, i.e. to micro-political relations of power, domination, resistance, and struggle, particularly as these articulate with issues of race, ethnicity, gender, ecology, and locality. The metaphorical and empirical return to the "local" in postmodern urban studies has been depicted by David Harvey as a sign of its weakness, namely, its abandonment of the Enlightenment project of rationality, the use of rules of thought to achieve propositions of "global" validity. In renouncing the Enlightenment quest for foundationally grounded thought, which Lyotard terms "master-narratives," postmodern discourse stands in opposition to both liberal and Marxist political–economic reductionism. It calls into question the idea that there can be any firmly grounded master discourse of economic development, political liberation, or social change. Totality theories, including those rooted in neoclassical economics and historical materialism, are reductionist in that they ignore elements of cultural life that they cannot explain or marginalize them as exceptions, often in the "soft" or "epiphenomenal" areas of culture, feelings, or desire. Marginalizing or excluding everyday cultural practices tends to deny their importance as historical modes of urban agency.

Having said this, I have tried to show in the previous chapter that the politics of everyday life under conditions of transnational urbanism cannot be reduced to a simple return to the "local." In seeking to displace the reliance of social theory on grand narratives of macro-social development, by turning to what Foucault terms the "essentially local character of criticism," some social theorists embracing the label "postmodern" have posited an equally "grand" theory of local knowledge which privileges the ethnographic conversation as the only reliable route to personal knowledge, and personal knowledge as the only reliable measure of the "partial truths" about the workings of the world. This is the case, for instance, when postmodern anthropologist Stephen Tyler (1987: 171) asserts, with totalistic rhetorical flourish, that "discourse is the maker of this world, not its mirror."

From a social constructionist perspective, an intellectual focus on the analysis of discursive practices, on discourse itself as space of the "self-production of society," should not simply shift our attention from macro-politics to micro-politics, and then valorize the latter, as if the two were distinct and irreducible binary opposites. Rather, such a focus can be used to shift our attention to the processes whereby *networks of power*, subsisting at every point from the most "local" to the most "global," are formed, related to each other, and transformed. Since human agency operates at many spatial scales, and is not restricted to "local" territorial or sociocultural formations, the very concept of the "urban" thus requires reconceptualization as a social space that is a crossroads or meeting ground for the interplay of diverse *localizing* practices of national, transnational, and even global-scale actors, as these wider networks of meaning, power, and social practice come into contact with more locally configured networks, practices, and identities.

This way of envisioning contemporary transnationalism "locates" globalization and situates the global–local interplay in historically specific milieux. It extends the meaning of the global–local nexus to encompass not just the social actions of "global capitalists" interacting with "local communities," but the far more complex interplay of cultural, political, and economic networks which operate at local, translocal, and transnational social scales and that intersect in particular places at particular times. Closer study of this interplay will, in my view, enable urban researchers to explain the formation of new "subject positions," grasp emergent counterlogics to prevailing modes of domination, and give due attention to the multiple patterns of accommodation and resistance to dominant power relations, particularly the patterns of dominance entailed in the current discourse on globalization itself.

Thus the view of "culture" developed in this book is not restricted to the understandings developed in closed and self-contained local communities. The circuits of communication in which people are implicated are resources as well as limits. People's everyday lives are sites of criss-crossing communication circuits, many of which transcend the boundaries of local social and political life. They constitute sometimes separate, sometimes overlapping, and sometimes competing terrains for the contestation, as well as the reproduction, of cultural meanings, for resistance as well as accommodation to dominant modes of power and ideology. This emphasis on the cultural construction of social agency through individual and group acts of accommodation and resistance to prevalent modes of domination has significant implications for urban research. This book calls for a new way of conceptualizing the *locality* as the place where localized struggles, and alternative discourses on the meanings of "global conditions" are played out. This effort brings to the forefront of urban research the fact that "globalization" is a historical construct, not an inevitable economic force, a realm of necessity "out there." It requires examining at close range but in rich contextual detail the specific historical and contemporary conditions by which "global conditions" are made meaningful in particular places at particular times. Cities thus may be usefully conceptualized as local sites of cultural appropriation, accommodation, and resistance to "global conditions" as experienced, interpreted, and understood in the everyday lives of ordinary men and women.

Given this conceptualization, ethnography is clearly an indispensable approach to urban theory because it is a method designed to grasp processes of meaning-making and yield knowledge of the ways in which consciousness is actually formed, social networks forged, and individual and collective agency connected. As stated by Andrew Sayer (1989: 256), "Even where locality studies do seem quite successful in rendering political and other behavior intelligible, political economy without ethnography leaves the reasons for that intelligibility implicit: the behavior seems intelligible only to the extent that it resonates, not because we have articulated the constitutive structure of understanding or feeling." Yet the turn to ethnography does not offer a transparent grounding for understanding the sense that people make of themselves, their cities, or their world. When ethnographic inquiry starts from social constructionist assumptions, the question of human agency is immensely complicated.

Questioning the Knower and the Known

What I am calling "postmodernism as method" calls into question the possibility that any of us can know an "out there," a real object of investigation existing apart from the systems of signification through which the world is described and understood. In poststructuralist epistemology *discursive practices* unavoidably structure the flow of the "out there." No ahistorical, universalist, or essentialist entity, like "homo faber" or "homo economicus," can give unifying meaning to either history or urban development.

This does not mean that the terrain of knowledge and meaning in the social and human sciences is reduced to pure subjectivity. Rather, discursive practices are always embedded in social relations of power and ideology which readily privilege some representations of the "out there" while impeding others. For this reason, postmodern epistemology problematizes the knower as much as the known. Rejecting both the romantic notion of the transcendentally creative artist and the modernist notion of an intellectual avant-garde capable of pursuing universal reason, poststructuralist social science fundamentally historicizes the process of "writing culture," questioning Enlightenment notions of authorial objectivity, originality, and authority. This move treats knowledge as a social product, emanating from and limited by historically specific and culturally mediated representational practices.

Nevertheless, it is true that the postmodern analysis of the "death of the author" is a curious move which tends to undercut that which it inscribes. In order to debunk the autonomy and originality of the individual "author," as well as to challenge the positivist notion of social scientific verifiability, postmodern critiques in cultural studies have used parody, meta-fiction, experimental writings of ethnographic "findings," and even what is termed "intertextual appropriation" (or direct copying, as in the case of critical photographer Cindy Sherman's and David Prince's appropriated images, and Terry Gilliam's filmmaking in *Brazil*). Yet, in thereby producing quite novel forms of creative expression, their challenge to authorial originality is undercut even as the challenge to scientific verifiability is reinforced.

Despite this apparent contradiction, from a social constructionist perspective, there is an important lesson to be derived from the postmodern discussion of the constitutive structure of understanding. In historical, as in literary discourse, even presumably descriptive language *constitutes* that which it describes. The film *Brazil*, for example, selectively appropriates elements of earlier films like *1984* and *A Clockwork Orange* in constituting something new; it does not merely copy, and hence objectively *describe* that which it appropriates, but creates new meanings by its juxtaposition of images and signs. Likewise, the "travel writing" of colonial discourse relied upon "description" to fix, construct, and hence master the colonized object. It vividly detailed the habits, customs, speech acts, and bodily practices of conquered peoples in order to comprehensively "know," and hence implicitly control, the colonial subject, thereby "enabling itself to transform the descriptively verifiable multiplicity and difference into an ideologically felt hierarchy of value" (Ahmad, 1987: 6). Ironically, the opposite may also be true, as in the case of postcolonial discourses that rely on "thick description" to romanticize "the postcolonial subject" as embodied in the everyday practices of urban taggers, street gangs, or insurgent social movements like the FMLN.

Interpretation, in short, is an unavoidable dimension of descriptive narrative. In postmodern epistemology, even the apparently most direct medium of knowing, the camera's documentation of the "out there," is not a depiction of unmediated reality; rather, photographs, like all other forms of perception, are filtered by "the discursive and aesthetic assumptions of the camera holder" (Hutcheon, 1988: 230). Photographers clearly construct their images by framing, cropping, selectively focusing, and by darkroom manipulations that make image into reality by processes of inclusion and exclusion that are part of any photographic narrative. Likewise, the meaning of a story told by a sociological narrative of city life is produced by the frame of reference, often implicit, assigning patterned regularity to everyday existence. In this same way, contemporary social historians selectively "presence the past" in writing a historical text; cultural anthropologists selectively edit the tapes which give voice to their ethnographic subjects; and contemporary urban theorists foreground or background selected attributes of "globalization" and "locality" in offering representations of modern or postmodern urban life.

It is also useful to keep in mind a second epistemological move first heralded by postmodern theorists, namely that knowledge and meaning are not individual inventions but social products. Thus, in the normal course of writing social science, an author's choices are not made arbitrarily or *in vacuo*, but with some reasonably well-defined audience in mind. This audience is clearly the *reader* of the text, and the *receiver* of the communications imparted in it. Yet because the reader is at least implicitly, if not complicitly, present before-the-fact in the mind's eye of the writer, the text is at least implicitly a collaborative production. Social constructionist epistemology seeks to make this implicit social production of knowledge explicit. This has been done, for instance, in the postmodern discursive style of irony, collage, pastiche, and intertextual appropriation often critiqued by modernist theorists. The purpose of these moves is to make explicit to the reader the *cultural structuring* of narrative reality. The often all too obvious self-reflexive intrusions of the writer into the story being told are designed to let the reader know that we can only know "reality" as it is produced by cultural representations of it (ibid.: 7).

The more careful of the postmodern analysts of the social production of knowledge, like literary theorist Linda Hutcheon, are quick to back away from the poststructuralist position attributed to Derrida, that there is no material or social reality outside the text. Rather, in social scientific discourse as in literature, it is necessary to recognize that "all we ever have to work with is a system of signs, and . . . to call attention to this is not to deny the real, but to remember that we only *give meaning to* the real within these signifying systems" (Hutcheon, 1988: 230). If symbolic systems thus necessarily mediate our world and constitute its historical context, how are we to interpret the semiotic mediation between contextuality and social action? What can urban theory learn from this?

Constructing the Subject

There has been much talk in the debate on postmodernity about the problem of the "decentered subject." Just what is meant by decentering, and who is the subject? How is subjectivity related to human agency? How, in turn, are acting human subjects empowered and constrained by their historical contexts? What can be learned from this debate about the social construction of identities and the role of identity politics in our contemporary historical context, in which urban life in some ways has become transnationalized while in other respects it remains embedded in decidedly local meanings, practices, and power relations?

In postmodern discourse, the subject is decentered precisely because there are no clear-cut roles waiting for subjects to occupy in pursuit of their historical mission. Rather, there are a multiplicity of roles that people come to play in history. These produce a "self" experienced not as a single, completed identity, but as multiple, incomplete, and partial identities, formed in historically specific relation to the different social spaces people encounter, move through, and inhabit over time (see Hall, 1988). Viewed in this light, the constitution of subjectivity is best understood as necessarily contextualizing and historicizing the subject in all his or her spatial particularities and temporal contradictions.

Postmodern subjectivity is thus inextricably implicated in *sociality*. The social production of subjectivity is embedded in symbolic processes of signification that give meaning to "subject positions" emergent within specific "language games," and their discursive practices (Laclau and Mouffe, 1985; Lyotard, 1984; Boggs, 1986). Accordingly, "the subject" is neither natural nor universal, but always already in process of being formed, displaced, and re-formed through communication and the semiotic exchange of signs. How else can we explain the virtual explosion of nationalism and new state formation in the short time since the imperial constraints of bi-polarity have been removed from the global order?

Chantal Mouffe has been especially clear in positing the connections between the cultural mediation of subject positions, the "decentered" subject, the formation of personal identity, and the constitution of human agency. Personal identity, Mouffe insists, emerges out of sociality in highly differentiated contexts which now render its formation fluid and, in her view, radically open. In our contemporary context, often constructed under the rubric "globalization" or "postnationalism," neither liberalism nor Marxism offers an adequate theory of the subject, particularly as these theories fail to develop adequate explanations for the coalescence of subject positions into political action. In their place, Mouffe (1988: 35) argues:

> It is indispensable to develop a theory of the subject as a decentered, detotalized agent, a subject *constructed* at the point of intersection of a multiplicity of subject positions between which there exists no *a priori* or necessary relation. Consequently no identity is ever definitively established, there always being a certain degree of openness and ambiguity in the way the different subject positions are articulated. What emerges are entirely new perspectives on political action,

which neither liberalism – with its ideal of the individual who only pursues his or her own interest – nor Marxism – with its reduction of all subject positions to that of class – can sanction, let alone imagine.

Just as class and individualist theories of subjectivity and collective action are rejected by poststructuralist theorists, so too are radically decentralist urban theories which valorize "locality" by giving unproblematized historical and ontological priority to "the community" as the ultimate source of coherent identity and social action. As Mouffe (ibid.: 44) once again clearly states:

> Many communitarians seem to believe that we belong to only one community, defined empirically and even geographically. . . . But we are in fact always *multiple and contradictory subjects*, inhabitants of a diversity of communities (as many . . . as the social relations in which we participate and the subject positions they define), constructed by a variety of discourses and precariously and temporarily sutured at the intersection of these subject positions.

While I am generally sympathetic to this view of the contradictory character of subject formation, I am less convinced than Mouffe seems to be that the "we" to which she refers can be used so universally, to refer to all people, regardless of their current geographic and social locations, as inhabitants of diverse communities of social relations, and hence as multipositional subjects. For example, the female rural inhabitants of some villages in "developing" countries may belong to only one, fairly self-contained and highly patriarchal local social structure. Other "women in development" may live in villages with more porous communal boundaries or less rigid local social structures. As in the case of the African woman drawing water discussed in the previous chapter, these women may be connected to, and thus may "inhabit," a variety of other networks operating outside their local social structure, such as transnational kinship, household, and/or remittance networks. These ties may form the basis of new positionalities they may come to occupy in transnational cities like New York, as well as in rural African localities or as wage laborers in one place rather than household care-givers in another. The former inhabitants' identities may be more locally bound, while the latter may be more multiple, contradictory, and fluid. I use this example to underline, as I have elsewhere in this book, that we cannot neatly compartmentalize the "tightly knit community" as somehow naturally contained within remote rural areas of "developing" countries or in endogenous urban ethnic enclaves in the "developed" world. Nevertheless, it seems clear to me that the kind of social structures of power and control that are most conducive to the multipositional subject formation that Mouffe has in mind, fits more closely the criss-crossing social relations that many people encounter and inhabit in the more complex and heterogeneous urban social structures, in both the developing and the developed world, that I am calling transnational cities.

For this reason, in the version of urban theory recovered in this book, the presumed global cultural homogenization of what Frederic Jameson (1984) calls "consumer society" is strongly challenged. Like my early criticisms of the totalizing tendencies of various versions of modernization and development theory (Smith, 1980; Smith and Tardanico, 1987), my current effort to re-shape urban theory to study the complex politics of transnational urbanism rests upon a recognition of growing cultural differentiation and the multiplication of complexly situated forms of social agency that transnational sociocultural networks have introduced as accompaniments of and potential modes of resistance to the homogenizing logic of global consumer society. In my view the very concept "global consumerism" is itself a social construct of particular theorists and a political project of specific social interests. I take seriously the poststructuralist argument that the construction of any collective identity can only be achieved by a process of excluding a "constitutive outside" from the selfhood included in identity formation (see Derrida, 1978, 1981, 1985; Laclau, 1990). It is therefore worth asking just who the "others" of a global consumerist identity might be and what sorts of counter-identities might they forge against the grain of the seductions of global consumerism.

Viewed in this light, even the much heralded "global context" of urban life is not an objective structure existing "out there," but an intersubjective and contested set of understandings about material, cultural, and historical permissions and constraints. Defining the context of opportunities and constraints upon social action (e.g. defining "global conditions") is itself a continuous process of contest and struggle in which the historical practices of people, acting on the basis of situated knowledges, are actively inserted as *articulations*, which mediate and in turn modify the permissions and constraints. These criss-crossing articulations do not merely voice new social identities. They are crucial elements in the process of forming social networks constituted within and between cities increasingly connected by transnational flows of culture, capital, and power.

As I further read contemporary "global conditions," the social relations and identities constructed at the intersections that currently inform urban politics have become significantly more complicated at the present time. Class formation within state formations has been especially complicated by the combined effects of several transnational processes and practices interacting with and reconfiguring national and urban social relations. These include the transterritorialization of production; the global extension, speed, and simultaneity of new communications technologies; the end of the Cold War and attendant geopolitical restructuring; the rapid acceleration of transnational migration, and the consequent ethnic reconstitution of localities and regions now taking place on a global scale. These dramatic sociospatial changes have affected prevailing structures of work, residence, and social intercourse, in many localities, great and small, throughout the world, significantly impinging on people's everyday experience of place. These changes, and our understandings of them, reconstitute the opportunities for and constraints upon communication. The global–local interplay is thus usefully understood as a profound spatial reconfiguration of cultural practices. The move to integrate cultural analysis into research on the political economy of transnational cities follows from this sociospatial rearticulation of cultural production (see Wilson and Dissanayake, 1996; Cvetkovich and Kellner, 1997).

The complex changes I have just spelled out have created new political–economic and sociocultural conditions conducive to the production of new forms of political voice. In today's transnational cities, modes of identity formation based on articulated differences in race, gender, class, ethnicity, sexuality, locality, region, nation, and transnation are socially contested. These identities are socially constructed rather than natural or pregiven. As such, their complex interplay in discourses where personal and group identities are formed are incipient social bases of new discursive practices and hence of the emergence of new subject positions in urban politics.

This is nowhere more clear than in the case of the recent emergence of the "new subjects" that have been drawn into a broad political coalition supporting daily acts of civil disobedience against perceived racist police practices in New York City. These protests have been given political force by the moral outrage stirred up by the killing of Amadou Diallo, an unarmed transmigrant street peddler from West Africa who was gunned down in his doorway by a hail of 41 bullets fired by the elite Street Crime Unit of the New York Police Department. The new subjects have provided support for black activist Al Sharpton, who has organized the civil disobedience campaign against the New York City Police Department. Recall from our discussion in chapter 5 the strange bedfellows, including local, national, and transnational actors, who have come together and, as Mouffe would have it, are now "temporarily sutured" as new oppositional subjects in this transnational urban social movement. Recall also that this emergent political coalition has been spearheaded by the symbolic presence of Amadou Diallo's West African mother, Kadiatou Diallo,who has become a highly articulate transnational presence in the coalition. The temporarily sutured political identities drawn together in New York City and in wider political venues in the wake of the Diallo killing have already produced some surprising local, national, and transnational results. Locally, the civil disobedience campaign has resulted in calls by the New York City Public Advocate for the resignation of New York City police commissioner Howard Safir, a decline in public support for Mayor Rudolph Giuliani in recent public opinion surveys, and the indictment for murder of the accused police officers. The locally focused narrative of police repression in New York City has reverberated nationally by prompting a formal investigation of the New York City Street Crime Unit by the US Justice Department as well as catalyzing a multi-city civil rights campaign against police brutality in other US cities. Kadiatou Diallo has played a prominent symbolic and tangible role in this wider campaign. Her activism has extended not only nationally but transnationally as well, to her native Guinea. In Guinea she has participated in public ceremonies in which, ironically, her son's fate as a transnational migrant street peddler has been seized upon by leading politicians as a symbol of threatened national identity. Thus, in an ironic double move, Kadiatou Diallo's transnational political involvement has shifted from grieving mother to forceful celebrity, while her new modes of political activism in different venues have been represented as a sign of national revitalization of the US civil rights movement by Jesse Jackson, at the same time that ruling elites in Guinea have appropriated her presence and her son's fate as part of their own nationalistic discourses (see Sachs, 1999a,b).

In my view the case of Kadiatou Diallo speaks pointedly to the originality of Laclau and Mouffe's approach to political identity formation. When compared to the literature on new social movements in general (e.g. Tilly, 1978, and the essays in McAdam, McCarthy, and Zald, 1996), which treats identities as springing from pregiven interests, Laclau and Mouffe see identity and interest not as something pre-political but as something formed in discourse and hence reformed in political struggle. They insightfully comprehend political process, as Rosenthal (1988) notes, as a problematic of "*identities put at risk,* rather than of a contest between actors whose identities (and hence 'interests') are already given." In so doing, Laclau and Mouffe interpret contextual opportunities and constraints from the vantage point of Gramsci's theory of articulation.

Cultural theorist Lawrence Grossberg (1988: 168–9, emphasis added) expresses this problematic relationship between subject, agency, and context thus:

> The problem of interpreting any cultural text, social practice, or historical event must always involve constituting a context around it. . . . But contexts are not entirely empirically available because they are not already completed, stable configurations, passively waiting to receive another element. They are not guaranteed in advance, but are rather the site of contradictions, conflicts, and struggles. . . . In Gramscian terms, any interpretation . . . [or] historical practice is an *articulation*, an active insertion of a practice into a set of contextual relations that determine the identity and effects of both the text and the context. Articulation is the continuous deconstruction and reconstruction of contexts. These articulated connections are sometimes fought over, consciously or unconsciously, but in any case, an articulation is always *accomplished* . . . and will always have political consequences.

By rejecting the notion of "historical necessity," and instead focusing on the arena of cultural politics as a contested terrain, the Gramsci-inspired theory of articulation implies that people are never merely passive instruments of elite domination, class hegemony, or natural instinctual drives. Rather, as social beings, with capacities for interaction, communication, and the insertion of praxis into life, people are social and political actors engaged in struggles with, within, and sometimes against their understood context. In "real life," relations of domination–subordination exist, but they are always complexly constituted and often actively contested.

For this reason, the quest to understand urban culture has turned to the realm of the everyday and produced a lively discourse on the practice of urban ethnography. The goal of this methodological turn is to gain insight into how articulatory practices are actively inserted in the particular locales of everyday life and how these articulations, in turn, empower or disempower their audiences (Grossberg, 1988: 169). Postmodern ethnography is often represented as an experimental project capable of giving voice to these articulations. I now ask whether this is a valid perception. As we shall see, my answer is mixed.

The Uses and Limits of Postmodern Ethnography

When the discourse on postmodern ethnography first emerged in the late 1980s, a variety of new ethnographic practices were valorized as ways of overcoming the white, Western, male, "colonial" positionality of ethnographic research and anthropological writing. Advocates of "postmodern" ethnography sought to develop experimental research methods and writing strategies that would create a narrative space for the "postcolonial" subject. Some working within this genre sought to develop more effective ways to directly involve the cultural subjects of ethnographic research in the process of signification and the production of meaning. The aim of this move was to give "voice" to the postcolonial subject's view of the world. Anthropologist Stephen Tyler (1986), for example, termed postmodern ethnography a form of "cooperative story making," a kind of "vision quest" on the part of the researcher to recover and evocatively communicate to the reader a "local narrative" about the life-world of the subject, a story produced by mutual dialogue rather than imposed by the authorial scripts of anthropologists and other "writers of culture." Tyler's aim was to produce a "cooperatively evolved text in which neither subject, nor author, nor reader, no one, in fact, has the exclusive right of 'synoptic transcendence'" (ibid.: 126, 129).

In these respects, Tyler romanticized the process of "intersubjective dialogue." The "penetrating" ethnographic encounter became a kind of grand narrative in its own right, one which enshrined and mystified the ethnographic conversation as a "deep" discovery of partial truths through an interpsychic process of "transference" and a transcendental process of "polyvocality" (see Tyler, 1987: chs 5–7). This strain of postmodern ethnography thus tried to have it both ways. While making no pretense to objective truth, indeed while denouncing such claims to scientificity as pretentious, the approach suggested by Tyler nonetheless tended to consecrate the postcolonial subject, as adduced by the ethnographer, thereby making this subject's voice into the measure of all things. In so doing this strain of postmodern ethnography displaced old master narratives that denied the agency of ordinary people with a new master narrative in which populist voices "from below" were released from bondage by the skillful ethnographer and became decontextualized kings and queens of the world. In seeking to transcend the intellectual limits of structural–functional meta-narratives, this move unduly romanticized the "local narrative" produced by sensitive field workers "on the ground" as a sure route to the partial truths of postcolonial subjectivity.

Must the ethnographic imagination be reduced to the pursuit of idiosyncratic *petit* narratives which then become ventriloquized voices of postcolonial resistance? This is not necessarily the case. Another strain of postmodern ethnography, first suggested in the 1980s by George Marcus and Michael Fischer (1986), sought to refocus ethnographic inquiry amidst global sociocultural, political, and economic restructuring upon what they called the power–domination–accommodation–resistance motif. This motif, by situating the constitution of subjectivity within the context of rapidly changing sociospatial boundaries, provided an intelligible starting point for understanding the complex dynamics by which new subject positions can be seen to emerge in and through, for and against, such presumably "global" phenomena as urban sociospatial restructuring, transnational migration and grassroots activism, new state formation, and the bubbling cauldron of ethnic and racial conflict currently being stirred up by symbolic politics in transnational cities throughout the world.

Marcus and Fischer (1986) thus early on provided urban theorists with a useful opening for moving beyond the limits of the binary categories of global versus local, structure versus agency, and modern versus postmodern historical epochs in the formation of consciousness and social practice. In their characterization of contemporary "global conditions," they envisioned a world still full of cultural differences, but in which most, if not all, "cultural worlds" had come into contact and communication "on the ground." They argued that what matters then, "is not ideal life elsewhere, or in another time, but the discovery of new *recombinant* possibilities and meanings in the process of daily living anywhere" (ibid.: 122, emphasis added).

Marcus and Fischer called their project "anthropology as cultural critique." They sought to unearth the hybrid or recombinant possibilities of contemporary life by studying the ways that in daily life people in various life situations accommodated to or resisted the cultural worlds colluding and colliding in their own time and place. Their identification of various modes of "local" accommodation or resistance to "global conditions" is one strategy for uncovering new recombinant possibilities for living, as well as for mapping actual cultural change "from below" in a world that seems to some an increasingly homogenized one of global modernity "from above."

Having said this, I hasten to add that there has been over a decade of richly textured transnational ethnographic story-telling undertaken since Marcus and Fischer first issued their call for anthropology as cultural critique. Throughout the 1990s, in the hands of multilocational practitioners of transnational ethnography who have been sensitive to the social construction of contextuality (e.g. Rouse, 1991; Kearney, 1995; Schein, 1998a,b), these new forms of ethnographic inquiry successfully asked quite big questions to little people and obtained very intriguing results. By asking transmigrants involved in circular migration networks to first construct their understanding of the opportunities and constraints they faced in the world(s) in which they lived, and then to talk about the ways in which they appropriated, accommodated to, or resisted the forms of power and domination, opportunity and constraint that they experienced as they traversed political and cultural borders, this mode of ethnography opened up a discursive space for contextually *situated* ethnographic narratives that captured the emergent character of transnational social practices. Much of this work is taken up in subsequent chapters to illustrate and further develop my theoretical argument.

Drawing on this growing body of transnational field research, two anthropological theorists, Akhil Gupta and James Ferguson (1997b: 42–4), have called into question the spatialized understanding of cultural difference informing Marcus and Fischer's early writings of postmodern ethnography. Marcus and Fischer, to be sure, usefully prompt us to inquire into the global contextuality of local ethnographic narratives. Yet their own view of that global context still remains very much a framework in which different and distinct entities called "cultural worlds" now collide with each other more frequently in myriad ways. The main difference wrought by globalization, in the "cultural critique" view, is that "different societies," including "our own" and "other" societies, now provide us with critical tools for generating "critical questions from one society to probe the other" (Marcus and Fischer, 1986: 112–77; see the more extensive critique of this point of view in Gupta and Ferguson, 1997b: 42–3).

As Gupta and Ferguson point out, this view of globalization as necessarily entailing intercultural learning, whether intentionally or not, ends up parsing out cultural difference in spatially quite familiar ways, neatly inscribing a world consisting of unproblematized territorial "homes" and "abroads." Marcus and Fischer fail to problematize the internal coherence of both the here and the there, which the findings of transnational ethnography discussed in subsequent chapters clearly suggests is necessary. Marcus and Fischer's view is one in which contact and communication take place between "societies" and "across cultures," rather than within and between transnationally linked localities, each containing historically specific *difference-generating* relations of power and meaning. Critiquing Marcus and Fischer's construction of "global context," Gupta and Ferguson propose a more fruitful alternative. Their interest lies "less in establishing a dialogical relation between geographically distinct societies than in exploring the process of production of difference in a world of culturally, socially, and economically interconnected and interdependent spaces" (ibid.: 43).

This shortcoming of the anthropology as "cultural critique" perspective suggests that there may well be an unavoidable tendency for even ethnographically sensitive social researchers to read new meanings into the discourse on globalization derived from their own imaginations rather than from the constructions of their subjects. But is the alternative of simply listening closely to and "recording" ordinary people's characterizations of globalization enough to explain the links they may have to a changing structural context? In my view there is also a clear danger inherent in the postmodern ethnographic effort to assume a subject position of tentativeness, if not authorial passivity, in "recording" the pure, authentic voice of the "marginal" and the "different." Cultural voices are historically contingent, not timelessly pure. The temptation to capture the essence of a "local voice," inscribing it as a heroic individual or collective challenge to the oppressive forces of global modernity, precisely mirrors the problem of idealizing the "other culture" as a radically strange entity which characterized colonial discourse. Commenting critically on the efforts of anthropologists (modernist or postmodernist) to evoke the "essence" of "Indian centered" narrative, Susan Hegman (1989) powerfully derides such academic efforts to represent "authentic" cultural voices. In her words (ibid.: 153): "Contemporary Navajos are neither the shadow of a European [i.e. people "just like you and me"] nor . . . radically strange beings [i.e. subject to a totally divergent and incomprehensible worldview], but people working within multiple cultures, value, and belief systems – adapting, inventing, preserving and defending where they see fit."

My version of social constructionist urban analysis is at home with this view of cultural practice as adaptive, inventive, and multivalent. It thus rejects the view that "cultures" are closed systems or singular wholes as much as it questions the view of "the global" as a single modernist/capitalist social space. By my reading it is necessary to question all abstractions that tend to ignore the historically specific conditions of cultural production as these become *localized, interrelated,* and *mutually constitutive* in particular places at particular times. Viewed in this light, the interplay of contested and colluding "voices" in transnational cities, is neither a sign of chaos nor a blueprint for intellectual despair. Making sense of this interplay requires a provisionality premised on a willingness to suspend binary thinking, to consider the cultural improvisations that are part of an urban life characterized by porous borders and boundaries, and in these sites of transcultural production, to critically rework the representations and intellectual constructs through which we have come to know our cities and our world.

In my view the social construction of personal and group identities, and the politics of difference that follows from this, is a socially contested, historically modifiable process. At the present transnational moment, analysis of the social roots of the politics of difference now constituting urban politics has been rendered more difficult by the ineffectuality or incompleteness of the grand narratives of the past in rendering meaningful the shifting boundaries of territory, community, and self. These foundational analytical frameworks reduced social complexity and transcended historical specificity by projecting a theory of consciousness and social action based either upon an ahistorical "individual" subject who is a maximizer of utility, or upon the subject's class position within the social relations of production. At the present time, the partial uncoupling of some cities from national economies, the decomposition of class structures within nation-states, the reconstitution of capital–labor relations as social relations operating on a transnational scale far removed from the immediacy of subjects' lived experience, and the explosion of transnational flows of migrants, media representations, and information, have rendered the conventional grand narrative of class struggle especially problematic as a singular theory of urban consciousness and collective action. Moreover, the rapid sociocultural transformation of localities by the accelerated flows of transnational migration has modified the social relations of "community" that had grounded traditional ethnographies in more or less convergent social spaces of cultural production and place. These growing disjunctures require us to develop new modes of urban research and refine old methods of social inquiry to better fit the new spaces of cultural production and reproduction.

Hybrid Subjects in Patterned Networks

Modernist social actors were often viewed as stable, if not natural subjectivities, rather than socially constituted and hence contestable representations. Renato Rosaldo (1989: ch. 9) uses the metaphor of "border crossings" to challenge this view, envisioning the formation of ethnic identity as one among many processes of cross-border "borrowing and lending." Accordingly, in his view transnational migration is best seen as a dynamic process of cultural improvisation, blending, and creativity, rather than a timeless source of cultural loss. The "border tensions" of postmodernism as method have blurred boundaries between a host of binary oppositions – center–periphery, global–local, assimilation–ethnic purity – that authorize restrictive cultural images of social actors, inscribing them in terms of fixed being rather than fluid becoming (see Anzaldúa, 1987; Rosaldo, 1989; Elizondo, 1989). Calling attention to these border tensions, in turn, has tended to valorize processes of cultural hybridity.

This valorization of cultural hybridity is a recurring theme in the discourse on postmodern cities (see, for instance, the work of Soja, 1996). Its frequent invocation raises an intriguing question concerning another tension between urban social theory and research practice. On the one hand, the postmodern conception of identity formation posits a free-floating, if not voluntaristic, process of individual self-formation, as people criss-cross the array of cultural contents to be borrowed and lent, appropriated or resisted in the multicultural spaces of the postmodern city. On the other hand, the growing field of transnational studies has produced many richly textured ethnographic and historical case studies of transnational families (Hagan, 1994; Rodriguez, 1995, 1996), translocal social networks (R. Smith, 1998; Goldring, 1998), cross-border social movements (Smith, 1994), and international organizational coalitions (Sikkink, 1993; Drainville, 1998). These studies envisage personal and collective identity as embedded in socially structured and politically mediated processes of group formation and collective action. How can personal identity be seen as both hybrid and channeled, multipositional and network-bound, transgressive and affiliative, freely formed yet socially produced? Can this tension be reconciled?

In a fascinating chapter entitled "American Fictions and Political Culture," social theorist Michael Shapiro (1992) offers an insightful way to reconcile this apparent contradiction. Building on the work of Michel Foucault, but moving beyond Foucault's conceptual categories, Shapiro (ibid.: 70–2) calls for a mapping of the "competing situations, local spaces, discourses, media, and genres . . . which affect the building of a person's consciousness of self and others." Among the different venues "through which people move as they form and reform their character and identity over time," he singles out such historicized and socially structured discursive fields as "educational space, military space, metropolitan space, [and] foreign ideational space." Shapiro makes a persuasive case for the poststructuralist view of subjectivity in which the "self" is envisaged as "fragmented and in contention as it is dispersed over a variety of dominant and peripheral discursive practices rather than existing as a homogeneous, centered steering mechanism."

Yet the *discursive fields* through which people travel across space and through life constitute alternative, socially structured networks of social action for negotiating the inner tension and contention over selfhood and identity. Thus the "decentered subject" is not an infinitely plastic subjectivity. Rather, the discourses that occur in the various social spaces with which I am concerned in this book (e.g. translocal migrant networks, transnational urban neighborhoods, transnational working arrangements, cross-border political movements, and globalized neoliberal political circles) can be viewed as affecting the formation of character, identity, and acting subjects in particular venues, at the same time that individual identities can be seen as fluctuating and contingent, as the venues in and between localities through which people move in urban time-space change over time and are appropriated and/or resisted by acting subjects.

The implications of the foregoing for the study of transnational urbanism are intriguing. The discursive spaces through which human subjects, including local, national, and transnational actors, move are socially produced and have shaping effects on character and identity. So also do more general and enduring features of social life, such as patriarchal gender relations, racial hierarchies, and economic inequality. Yet the "localized" spaces of social action through which social actors move and within which they operate are crucial and differentiated, thus making possible considerably wider latitude for identity formation and "made character" than general social inequalities alone would predict.

The loyalties and oppositions forged by transnational migrant networks, the ideological projects of transnational political actors, and the metropolitan cultures in which transnational processes are located, are more often in a state of "becoming" than "arrival." They constitute opportunities as well as constraints. In short, personal identity formation under conditions of transnational urbanism can best be understood as a dialectic of embedding and disembedding which, over time, involves an unavoidable encumbering, disencumbering, and re-encumbering of situated selves. Identity is thus contextual but not radically discontinuous. People seek to be situated, to have a stable mooring, an anchor against the wind, meaning in their lives. I have argued in this chapter that ethnographic practice, particularly if inflected with the domination–accommodation–resistance motif, is a viable means for inscribing and making sense of this meaning-making process.

In the final analysis, subaltern identity formation is a process of constant struggle, a struggle in which discursive communities produce narratives of belonging, resistance, or escape. In these narratives of personal meaning the spaces available for forming non-essentialist identities are *interstitial*, i.e. they open up between such dominant discursive venues as the "nation-state," the "local community," the "ethnoracial formation," and the "new world order." The process of marking differences *within* essentialized identities is no easy task, however necessary and desirable it may be.

The Border Crossings of Transnational Ethnography

Transnational border crossings and the constitution of new urban subjectivities may alter previous power asymmetries, but how they may do so is an open question. The bifocal optic recommended by postmodern anthropologists is a useful starting point but does not go far enough. We must now pay attention to changing social relations on all sides of transgressed borders. This requires both a multifocal imagination and a multi-sited ethnography.

Consider the following example of transnational ethnography. In a study of transmigrants from rural Mexico to New York City, Robert Smith (1998) conducted research on two ends of a translocal migrant circuit. Smith found that these male transmigrants, who worked at occupations ranging from cab-driving to flower-peddling, experienced discrimination from mainstream New Yorkers, who viewed them as a low-status ethnoracial group. To cope with this stereotype, the transmigrants affirmed and recreated an essentialized group identity that *accommodated to* the New York City racial and ethnic hierarchy. In New York they inscribed a localized myth of ethnic origins to position themselves as racially superior to their equally impoverished Puerto Rican and African-American neighbors. In sharp contrast, in their home villages in Mexico, they *resisted* local power relations and widened the public sphere in these localities, to which they regularly returned, by organizing and financing "grass-roots" ceremonial and community development projects. The bifocal imaginary used by Smith, by envisioning the changing power relations across this migrant "translocality," reveals simultaneous patterns of accommodation and resistance to different forms of power at the different end-points of a transmigrant circuit.

Consider, next, a more complicated example. Anthropologists Carole Nagengast and Michael Kearney (1990) have used a multifocal, multi-sited research strategy to study the changing practices and identities of a group of indigenous Mixtec transmigrants from rural Mexican villages to cities and agri-business industrial complexes in the states of California and Washington. They found that the Mixtec transmigrants have used the increased political freedom they enjoyed north of the US–Mexican border to politically mobilize transnational grassroots movements based on shared ethnicity to confront the Mexican state and improve conditions in their home-towns in Oaxaca (Nagengast and Kearney, 1990; see also Smith, 1994). Nevertheless, socially they remain discriminated against and marginalized by their employers and by fellow mestizo Mexicans in US urban and agricultural spaces. In response to the positioning of themselves as "other," the Mixtecs have created their own labor contracting organization to market their labor in California at wages that undercut the mestizo workers who discriminate against them, at the same time gaining a middle-man surplus that can be used for collective self-empowerment (see Zabin, 1995).

How did these new modes of transnational political and economic mobilization come about? This increased politicization of indigenous Mixtecs as both a transnational ethnic group acting for itself and a collective economic actor has involved a transformation of older forms of group identity and difference based on village ties. As the Mixtec migrants moved from the circumscribed discursive spaces of their remote villages, and their attendant rituals of village separateness, to new discursive spaces in US cities and agricultural industrial complexes, their old "positionality" was disrupted. In their

new workplaces and everyday life encounters in the US they were discriminated against as a putatively inferior indigenous ethnic group. They were
more positively inscribed as a discrete ethnic group as well by their encounters
with US-based transnational political activists representing indigenous peoples'
movements, whose discursive practices linked their economic marginality to
their shared "Indian-ness." As they were affected by and appropriated key
elements of the difference-generating mechanisms found in these new discursive spaces, their separate collective identities as members of specific villages in
Oaxaca broadened to encompass a newly acquired ethnic identity as "Mixtecs."
As they further acquired a historicized understanding of the changing political
and economic conditions at both ends of their migration circuit, this new
ethnic identity in turn enabled them to imagine a new transnational political
space of "Oaxacalifornia" (see Kearney, 1995), in which they might pursue a
cross-border political strategy.

This strategy and its implications for urban theory are discussed in greater
detail in the next chapter on the rise of transnational grassroots movements.
For now, suffice it to say that this complex case of multifocal, multi-sited
ethnography illustrates that social inequality and resistance or accommodation
to it are socially constructed by historically specific actors, networks, and
practices in the power–knowledge venues found in specific places at particular
times. Neither is timeless and both are always "in the making." Multifocal,
multi-sited ethnography helps us make sense of this complicated dynamic.

Critics of poststructuralist approaches to social analysis fault poststructuralism
for lacking an explicit theory of agency and an agenda for positive struggle.
This misses the key point that the denaturalized critique of representation at
the core of poststructuralist thinking may well be a necessary precondition for
any type of effective agency. Hence this chapter's focus on the ways in which
politically salient differences are culturally produced is intended to show that
the meaning of such differences is mutable, historical, and socially constructed,
for better or worse. The social constructionist approach to urban theory
advanced in this book treats "culture" as the fluid and dynamic *effect* of
representations, not their source. Viewed in this light, the social construction
of meanings, identities, and places – "place-making" in short – becomes a
humanly produced, and hence modifiable structure of feelings and understandings. In the next chapter we shall focus precisely on the rise of transnational
social networks and their engagement in this politics of representation.

Transnationalizing the Grassroots | 7

The reality in which we live is a cultural construct, and our representations of it serve as filters for our relationship with the world. . . . The world we inhabit today is a global, planetary-scale world, and this is only made possible by information, or the cultural processes with which we represent our world to ourselves. The consequences of this change are enormous. The first is the growing inadequacy of the international system, of relations among sovereign nation-states, to deal with global problems. But the emerging of a transnational dimension to issues and social agents, more than a political question, is a sign of the fact that human action is now capable of culturally creating its own space. . . . Individuals find themselves caught up in a plurality of social systems, membership networks, reference groups. We move in and out of these relationships with much greater ease and speed than in the past, like migrant animals in the labyrinths of the metropolis, planetary travelers, nomads of the present.
Alberto Melucci, "The Global Planet and the Internal Planet"

Conceptualizing the grassroots as a purely urban referent is a localizing move. In today's context of transnational urbanism, this move obscures more than it reveals. In the 1970s and 1980s the "urban" and the "grassroots" were treated as equivalent prefixes for local social movements. Urban social movements were conceptualized largely in two ways. In David Harvey's work they were represented as "localized" forms of class struggle "displaced" from the workplace or productive sphere to "the community," or reproductive sphere (Harvey, 1973, 1978). Other writers on urban social movements viewed them as broad-based forms of social conflict that formed on a multi-class or non-class basis to promote distinctively urban social issues such as defense of place, the promotion of local cultures, or the provision of urban social services (see Castells, 1983; Mollenkopf, 1983; see also, Katznelson, 1981).

Until recently, except as a backdrop, detailed case studies of urban social movements ignored the transnational level of analysis and social practice. The mechanisms mediating the interplay of global political economy, transnational cultural practices, and diverse local cultures, polities, and economies remained unspecified. When the transnational did appear, it was conflated with economic globalization and was generally represented one-dimensionally as an overarching driving force for social transformation that introduced new modes of domination into urban life wherever it became localized (see Sassen, 1991; Harvey, 1989, 1990).

Reacting against this conflation of economic globalization with the cultural (post)modernization of urban life, another group of urban scholars, operating under the rallying cry that "politics matters," developed an approach that has come to be called "urban regime theory." (See Stone, 1989, and Lauria, 1997, for examples of the localist and politically determinist assumptions underlying this approach; see also Cox, 1998.) This approach placed great significance on the actions of urban political elites, who formed electoral coalitions and shaped alternative "regimes" of urban public policy. This genre was a useful antidote to structural determinism. Like the "locality studies" researchers in British urban studies (see, for example, Cooke, 1986; Urry, 1986; Harloe, Pickvance, and Urry, 1990), these urbanists stressed the continuing significance of local variations in the impact of economic restructuring. Yet both approaches tended to confine local politics to the comparative analysis of different adaptive responses to global economic restructuring. They lacked an awareness of transnational processes other than those initiated by capital. When the "global" was introduced into urban analysis it was presented as a binary against which "local" dramas of urban politics continued to "matter" insofar as local responses and resistances played an important role in the dynamics of global economic restructuring (see, for example, Cox, 1997b). The local dramas featured in urban regime theory, however, seldom took into account much more than the activities of local economic and political elites. Pressures "from below" were either not analyzed in great detail or rendered meaningful only if channeled by alternative urban political regimes into winning electoral coalitions.

In conceptualizing the "grassroots," neither urban social movement scholars nor urban regime theorists paid much attention to politics of meaning found in the everyday practices of ordinary people as they came to experience personal troubles at the level of urban households. This is no small omission, since households, though themselves hardly unitary, are among the key social spaces where people acquire practical awareness of the quality and character of urban life. It is out of this practical understanding of the "everyday" that collective action, whatever its roots, and however global or local its inspiration or focus, springs.

One of the leading urban theorists who has considered the household as an important space of meaning and a site of politics, is Manuel Castells. In *The City and the Grassroots* (1983) Castells presented a comprehensive analysis of urban social movements in Europe, the United States, and Latin America. His stated goal was to focus on the role of consciousness, agency, and social action in transforming the conditions of everyday urban life. In the Latin American context, this focus led him to study the activities of grassroots urban social movements in the region's cities that defended territorially based identities and sought "community control" of collective consumption. Castells (1983: 179–85) claimed that these movements were multi-class struggles which should be analyzed in light of how "local sociopolitical arrangements" combined with the "global division of labor" to exclude a growing proportion of the Latin American urban masses from the private housing and services markets.

The underlying theory of urban change developed in *The City and the Grassroots* was informed by several modernist dualisms. The most important of these were binary representations of the city as a space of civil society, feminist politics, and "urban self-management," paired against the state as a key site of patriarchy and centralized administration of everyday life. Castells juxtaposed images of women seeking to overcome "urban contradictions" found in "re-productive relations" in urban households and neighborhoods, with images of working-class movements in which men waged class struggle in "productive relations" at work and *vis-à-vis* the state. Urban social movements were thus conceived as essentially "non-productivist" forms of grassroots politics. They were depicted as capable of producing significant social change if they combined in their practice demands fundamentally divorced from the politics of production; namely, collective consumption, cultural aspirations, and political control of local government.

The nuanced comparative-historical research found in the case studies of urban social protest described in *The City and the Grassroots* did not support Castells' theoretical argument that urban social movements were purely local forms of sociopolitical action that are best viewed as alternatives to a class-based politics of production. Instead, Castells' textured case studies suggest that both the global and the local level of analysis and the processes of production, reproduction, and collective action are inexorably linked (for further elaboration of these linkages see Smith and Tardanico, 1987). In these narrative case studies, the modernist logic of either-or is displaced by a less clearly bounded set of understandings. For example, the case of the Glasgow rent strike of 1917 narrated by Castells, is represented as an example of "urban collective consumption," namely, a mismatch between local industrial growth and housing supply. Clearly this mismatch was a catalyst to the urban social conflict in Glasgow. But as the case study's narrative content reveals, so also was resistance to the proletarianization of skilled craft unions under wartime conditions. The latter pressure on workers, in turn, was a by-product of national production requirements in the context of an ongoing global imperialist war. Accordingly, in this "urban" struggle both national and transnational contextual conditions imploded into the everyday life-worlds of the men and women in Glasgow's urban households, creating conditions that informed their shared understanding of an unacceptable present. Global and local circumstances combined to foster a unification of workplace and community struggles, productive and reproductive politics, expressed in the form of a rent strike.

In Castells' narrative case study of a more recent "urban" mobilization in San Francisco's Mission District in the 1980s, the sociopolitical conditions described as triggering social conflict were local issues of collective consumption and cultural identity, particularly inadequate local housing supply, and urban renewal displacement of Latino households. The narrative details, however, indicate that the wider *context* of these local conditions was clearly transnational: the changing employment opportunity structure in the city and neighborhood because of intensified transnational migration from El Salvador and Guatemala. The transnational migration process, in turn, while a direct outcome of mobility choices made in transnational social networks, was indirectly occasioned by Ronald Reagan's decision to support a global imperialist war in Central America as part of his Cold War foreign policy. Moreover, even when viewed as a purely local political text, the urban protest in the Mission District included demands that went beyond collective consumption issues such as adequate housing, to voice calls for jobs, summer employment for Latino youths, and opposition to ethnic discrimination in the workplace. In sum, in this transnational migrant Latino neighborhood, "grassroots" mobilization encompassed demands for housing, jobs, and cultural respect interpreted as socially and politically interrelated in discourses and debates taking place at the level of urban households (see Castells, 1983: 113ff.). The protesters themselves made no sharp distinction between production and reproduction, economy and culture, despite the effort of Castells' urban theory to mark their protest in this way. Culture and economy, production and reproduction, local and transnational networks, were inexorably linked modes of social experience rather than oppositional categories of urban analysis. Global, transnational, national, and local dynamics imploded simultaneously into the everyday life experiences of the members of the urban households, in a particular place (the Mission District), at a particular time (the 1980s). The protesters' interpretations of this multiply inflected urban "reality" gave meaning, drive, and complexity to their urban social movement.

The Rise of Transnational Grassroots Politics

During the 1990s the study of "transnational grassroots politics" (Smith, 1994) had gained momentum as an intriguing new subject of social research (see, for example, Kearney, 1995; Guarnizo and Smith, 1998; R. Smith, 1998; Goldring, 1998; Mahler, 1998). This turn to the transnational scale of analysis and social practice reconfigured both the "urban" level of analysis and the nation–state bounded discursive practices in which citizenship, civil society, political representation, national and urban politics are ordinarily cast. The spatial extension of households and ethnic communities across national borders, in the current context of changing labor demand and persistent state violence, is producing new patterns of cultural and political appropriation and resistance by transnational migrants, refugees, exiles, guest workers, and diasporas, who in some ways partake of two nation-states, while in other ways move beyond either.

The study of urban social movements is now engaged in a new round of urban theorizing, attempting to invent discursive terms appropriate for adequately representing the agencies and practices that are currently constituting multifocal subjects, translocal social practice, and transnational political space. Manuel Castells' most recent work on grassroots social movements (Castells, 1997), unlike his work in the 1980s, reflects this shift in emphasis. *The Power of Identity*, Castells' second volume in a trilogy on globalization and social change, is particularly conversant with the multilocal, border-crossing political practices made possible by new technological means of communication (e-mail, the internet, etc.) as deployed, for instance, by the Zapatista Movement in Mexico. Beyond technological change, however, both sociocultural and political–economic developments account for a dramatic shift in modes of cultural production. It is this shift in the locus of cultural production from the local to the transnational scale, in turn, that best explains the attempt by social theorists to reshape our ways of reimagining cities at the dawn of the millennium.

Contextually, the accelerated pace, scale, and diversity of transnational migration to what used to be called "core" cities and regions of the global capitalist economy has been driven by several distinct yet overlapping sociocultural, political, and economic processes: the declining capacity of peripheral political economies to absorb the labor that is created within their borders; the austerity policies imposed on developing states and societies by international banks; the production of refugees from Central America and Southeast Asia by Cold War military struggles; the disintegration of state structures ushered in by the Cold War's abrupt end; and the globalization of the media of mass communications, including television, film, videos, and music, which scatter the symbolic ingredients of "imagined lives" and modes of self-empowerment at the "core" to even the remotest of peripheral hinterlands. Taken together, these transnational processes have reconstituted the sociocultural landscape of cities and eroded the boundary-setting capacities of nation-states. They have rendered problematic representations of the interplay between the state and civil society premised on clear distinctions between inside and outside, citizens and aliens, self and other.

The spatial extension of once nationally contained households, social networks, and ethnic formations across national borders is producing new patterns of cultural appropriation and resistance by peoples whose current circumstances render them "borderless" and in this sense, at least, "unbound." The boundaries of the nation-state no longer correspond to the social spaces these borderless people inhabit. The blurring of once taken-for-granted boundaries differentiating states, ethnicities, and civil societies is producing new spaces of daily life, new sources of cultural meaning, and new forms of social and political agency that flow across national borders. The everyday practices of borderless people are currently constituting transnational social spaces of survival, self-affirmation, and political practice.

The remainder of this chapter discusses the emergence of a transnational social space of cultural production which now characterizes the lived experience of transnational migrants, exiles, diasporas, and refugees. It also identifies the ways in which transnational grassroots movements are already practicing modes of thought and action that move our political imaginary beyond the confining limits of the global–local duality in social theory and its practical expression in the political slogan "Think globally, act locally." I will illustrate the much more complexly layered and multiply interwoven scales of thought and action discernible in such movements by reference to four examples: (1) the transnational politics of indigenous Guatemalan refugees led by Rigoberta Menchu; (2) a transnational grassroots movement forged in opposition to US military intervention in Central America; (3) a transnational league of Mixtec associations formed in Mexico, California, and Oregon; and (4) a transnational coalition of immigrant, refugee, and women's rights groups from San Francisco and other transnational cities seeking to change international human rights policies.

Transnationalizing Urban Research

Several key dimensions of the transnationalization of cultural production and reception are useful starting points for the still rudimentary project of mapping the changing contours of what some (e.g. Featherstone, 1990) have called "global culture." My consideration of this question is intended to open up the discourse on the globalization of culture by moving beyond the usual projections of the "global reach" of multinational capitalism and the media of mass communications, to establish a new point of departure for research on the transnationalization of cultural and political practices produced "from below." This effort has been inspired by a close reading of several works in critical anthropology (Appadurai, 1990, 1991; Rouse, 1990, 1991; Nagengast and Kearney, 1990; Kearney, 1991). These studies have moved beyond the theoretical calls of the postmodern anthropologists to develop a bifocal imagination by precisely using such a social imaginary to study the actual production and reception of cultural flows and the emergence of transnational political practices by spatially mobile segments of the world's population such as exiles, transnational migrants, and refugees. For want of a better expression, I regard this chapter as an effort to theorize and illustrate the emerging contours of the "transnationalization of grassroots politics." I hope to show that, far from being oxymoronic, this expression precisely captures the networks and boundaries of sociocultural and political space that some groups of transnational migrants, exiles, and refugees are presently constituting.

As should be clear from what already has been said, not only relations of economic production and exchange, but also modes of cultural production, reproduction, and exchange are becoming more spatially fluid and territorially reconfigured. Nowhere is this more apparent than in the case of transnational migrants, refugees, guest workers, and exiles, who are currently seeking to orchestrate meaningful lives under conditions in which their life-worlds are neither "here" nor "there," but at once *both* "here" and "there." This condition of cultural bifocality, of course, can be the source of much psychic pain, as in the case of many first-wave Vietnamese refugees to the United States, whose opportunities to return "home" or move between "here" and "there" were initially precluded by military defeat and subsequently slowed to a trickle until quite recently by the logic of US foreign policy (see, for example, Freeman, 1989; Smith and Tarallo, 1993b, 1995). Yet for those migrants and refugees less historically constrained, who remain connected to transnational networks of affiliation, symbolic and material interdependence, and mutual support (e.g. circular migrants between the US and Mexico), the social space for cultural reproduction has become delocalized and transnationalized. They are living lives and orchestrating futures "translocally" that transcend the boundaries of the places and nation-states they move between. Put differently, for them, geographical and cultural space are profoundly disconnected.

Appadurai (1991: 191) has cogently expressed the conundrum this poses for ethnography, and indeed for urban research of all kinds: "As groups migrate, regroup in new locations, reconstruct their histories, and reconfigure their ethnic 'projects,' the *ethno* in ethnography takes on a slippery, nonlocalized quality. Groups are no longer tightly territorialized, spatially bounded, historically unselfconscious, or culturally homogeneous." Appadurai has usefully defined these processes of deterritorialization and reconfiguration in terms of the spatial practices of a variety of institutional and collective actors, including (but not limited to) multinational corporations, financial markets, ethnic groups, religious and sociocultural movements, and new political formations. The practices of all of these sectors are being reconstituted in ways that move beyond the confines of given territorial boundaries and identities.

The "deterritorializations" and "reterritorializations" produced by the emergence of what I am calling transnational urbanism poses two special problems for urban research. First, the loosening of the ties between wealth, population, and territory "fundamentally alters the basis for cultural reproduction" (ibid.: 193). Second, ethnographers of deterritorialized peoples are increasingly finding that the "there" or "homeland" of transnational migrants, exiles, and refugees is, in part at least, what Benedict Anderson (1983) would call an "imagined community," invented by deterritorialized people to make present felt absences in their lives.

This raises an intriguing question. Under our present transnational conditions of existence, what kinds of lives are deterritorialized people(s) able to imagine? Appadurai provides rich examples, largely drawn from his own research and personal experience with transnational migrants to the United States from the Indian subcontinent, of a new style of community research suitable to the task of answering this question. He shows that it is possible to investigate social reproduction in the new social space he terms the "global ethnoscape." This global, or at least transnational, ethnography has as its goal an understanding of the impact of deterritorialization on the imaginative resources of transnational migrants and refugees. In the face of deterritorialization, Appadurai (1991: 196) asks, "What is the nature of locality, as a lived experience, in a globalized, deterritorialized world?" To his question I would add the following: What are the boundaries that people draw and redraw for themselves in a world where old state and social structures are in process of unraveling, but new, coherently understood channels of action have not yet been fashioned by new configurations of power and the sign into widely perceived arenas of possibility and constraint? The following discussion explores different responses to these questions discernible in the economic, sociocultural, and political practices of various deterritorialized migrants, refugees, guest workers, and exiles.

Probably the most familiar response to deterritorialization, particularly among exiles and refugees, is the desire to reterritorialize. Reterritorialization is a double-edged phenomenon. The *noire* side of this political imaginary is a "politics of return" that expresses an individual or collective desire to recapture or reterritorialize a "homeland" perceived to be lost. In the United States this response is apparent in the practices of involuntarily deterritorialized groups such as right-wing "South Vietnamese" and Hmong paramilitary organizations in various California cities. It has been most apparent at the global scale in the various political rhetorics invoked to justify the brutal actions of "ethnic cleansing" in the former Yugoslavia.

The more positive side of the "politics of return" is exemplified in the cultural and sociospatial transformation of the Latino and Asian sections of various large US cities into various "Little Havana," "Koreatown," and "Little Saigon" ethnic neighborhoods. In these social spaces, selected elements of the past are recaptured in the place-making spatial practices of new immigrants and refugees. My discussion later in this chapter of the transnational political vision and practice of the indigenous Guatemalan refugee movement led by Rigoberta Menchu is another affirmative form of the politics of return. Vastly different in most respects, these social actions each express the desire to reterritorialize as a collective response to displacement and deterritorialization.

Yet, for a large portion of today's transnational migrants and refugees, "reterritorialization" is far more problematic than a matter of mass recreation of or return to lost homelands by collectively displaced peoples who remain clustered in spatial enclaves outside their former national borders. Substantial numbers of today's transnational migrants actively maintain and are sustained by widely spatially dispersed social networks. While some individual members of such social networks still live in what was once unproblematically termed "sending communities," the migrating members of the networks spend increasing amounts of time away from a (necessarily changing) "there," that might be recaptured or returned to. These social networks are both a medium and an outcome of social practices "from below," by which transnational migrants, individually and collectively, maintain meaningful social relations that cut across territorial boundaries, link several localities in more than one country, and extend meaningful social action across geographical space. As increasing numbers of household, kinship, and formerly village-based social networks extend across national boundaries, becoming bi-national, if not multinational in spatial scale, qualitative urban research becomes literally "displaced" from the local to the transnational scale.

In this changed sociospatial context, three questions for those conducting urban field research in the global ethnoscape emerge as central: (1) "Who do you care about, where?" (2) "What reciprocal obligations are you maintaining, where?" (3) "Why and how are you actively maintaining these spatially extended social relationships?"

One of the best ethnographic studies oriented around these questions is Roger Rouse's (1990, 1991) research on circular migrants who move back and forth between localities in Mexico and the United States, orchestrating lives that are truly bifocal, involved simultaneously in more than one culture while fully living in neither. Rouse's research renders problematic the very concept "immigrant" when dealing with the so called "new immigration." Many of the transnational migrants he has studied have developed a repertoire of strategies for simultaneously managing two distinct ways of life; for example, as proletarian factory or service workers in the urban United States, and as small-scale owners of family-based farms or commercial operations in rural Mexico. These migrants have neither entirely left their country of origin nor fully oriented themselves to their new circumstances. Rather, they reside in what might be termed a state of "betweenness," orchestrating their lives transnationally and bifocally. Rouse dubs this appropriated social space the "transnational migrant circuit." The circuit as a whole, rather than any single locality, is the principal setting in relation to which these circular migrants form understandings of their individual and collective projects. Rouse's study makes clear that when one's significant social relations are spread across several sites on both sides of a putative border, not only do new economic and political arrangements, but new social spaces of identity formation and the production of meaningful social action come into being.

These transnational political–economic and cultural transformations are closely linked. Consider the cash remittances that are now one of the principal strategies by which transnational social networks are actively maintained and reproduced. Historically, key changes in the social organization of global capitalism helped constitute a political–economic context that contributed to the formation of household-based transnational social networks "from below." The austerity policies of international banks and international organizations like the IMF, Cold War counterinsurgency policies, and growing regional and income inequality promoted by the export-oriented development strategies of the World Bank, made it increasingly difficult for households in the countries affected by these policies to maintain nationally based survival strategies. The formation of bi-national and even multinational households capable of tapping into the income-producing capacities of labor demand in high currency exchange rate societies became an alternative survival strategy that extended households and the social networks they formed into global space. Once formed, however, the networks, in turn, have become a distinct social structure in global migration, a cultural medium for the circulation of symbolic and material "capital," i.e. signs, information, and money across national borders.

The scale of cash remittances deployed by social networks "from below" has increased dramatically in recent years. For example, remittances sent to El Salvador by transnational refugees now living in the United States (estimated at nearly 20 percent of its population) constitute nearly one third of the GNP of that "nation's" war-devastated economy, exceeding manufacturing and rivaling agriculture as a delocalized "pillar" (of steel or sand?) of "economic normalization." The network television show *60 Minutes* featured a story in which a Mexican factory worker in a Los Angeles sweatshop, who had been deported four times, had saved $15,000 during his four border crossings. This was enough to make him a "middle-class" homeowner in Mexico. Conservative estimates by official sources like the World Bank and the International Monetary Fund placed the global scale of remittances at $38.4 billion in 1989 (IMF, 1991; World Bank, 1991; Comision Economica para America Latina y el Caribe, 1991). Moreover, the global circulation of signs, information, and remittances "from below" is now facilitated by an institutional infrastructure that includes transnational fast courier companies, money-wiring firms, travel agencies, van and bus businesses, and related multi-purpose agencies that routinely link settlement areas in host countries with communities of origin in the putative "Third World" (see, for example, Rodriguez, 1995).

Whatever else these developments "mean" they suggest that the deployment of remittances is no longer merely a social practice assisting household reproduction in Third World countries. It has become a transnational social force, powerfully affecting the economic base of peripheral nations; altering class relations in sending localities; spreading global and local signs of the possibilities for radical upward mobility to increasing numbers of imagining individuals and households worldwide; channeling material means for additional transnational migration within migratory social networks; and, ultimately, providing stories fueling the rise of perceived "immigration problems" in receiving states confronting a global economic crisis. The perceived "cash drain" and "economic lure" of remittances has become an element of the political discourse on immigration now being shaped by state actors and other sectors of developed societies with large numbers of transnational migrants and refugees and neoliberal political economies. Not surprisingly, this shift in the social construction of "immigration" downplays the fact that national public policies in host countries, enacted in response to employer demands in more Keynesian times, contributed to this process by constituting and legitimating various "guest-worker" labor market niches.

However confined and exclusionary the debate on "immigration problems" has become among the political and economic elites of developed societies, there are two more pertinent questions facing those interested in the emerging contours of the global ethnoscape: (1) "To what events do today's transnational migrants and refugees pay attention?" (2) "How global, national, or local are the sources of information upon which the migrants and refugees base their actions?" Several contributors to the book *Global Culture* (Featherstone, 1990) argue that the images and information circulated by the global mass media are becoming as important as the stories circulated by others in one's immediate network who have renegotiated lives in new places, as sources of personal attention, as transnational migrants forge new life possibilities. The global diffusion of film, television, and video offers powerful images of possible future lives to once geographically isolated and socially bounded peoples. Once again Appadurai offers both theoretical insight and useful illustration. His ethnographic accounts of remote Indian villages vividly describe how dreams, songs, stories, and fantasies derived from these media have become driving forces in geographical mobility and human becoming, both within India and transnationally. Reflecting on this enhancement of the power of imagination in social life, Appadurai concludes that today the ordinary lives of increasing numbers of transnational migrants are powered by possibilities the globalized mass media suggest are available, rather than by the traditional or material givenness of things. As he succinctly puts it (Appadurai, 1991: 198):

> In the last two decades, as the deterritorialization of persons, images, and ideas has taken on new force . . . more persons throughout the world see their lives through the prisms of the possible lives offered by mass media in all their forms. That is, *fantasy is now a social practice*. It enters, in a host of ways, into the fabrication of social lives for many people in many societies.

Appadurai's work focuses largely, though not entirely, on the more positive possibilities of human mobility and becoming embodied in the acting out of these global fantasies. My own research suggests that global fantasies also have their *noire* side. For example, in my recent ethnographic study (Smith and Tarallo, 1995), global fantasies of power, wealth, and violence appropriated from Kung Fu movies were played out disastrously in the "representations of self" and the demands made by four young Vietnamese hostage-takers in a Good Guys electronics store in Sacramento, California. Several hostages were shot and three of the refugee youths were killed by a county Sheriff's Department SWAT team while acting out their global fantasies. One of the demands of these youths, who were small children when Saigon fell in 1975, also brings to mind the power of many exile and refugee communities worldwide to keep alive the myth of "return" as a driving force of meaningful sociospatial practice: they wanted a helicopter so that they could fly to Vietnam to fight the communists.

To the extent that global media representations are being appropriated in the fabrication of local social lives, a series of questions raised by Doreen Massey (1991a) bear important consideration, because they reinscribe the question of migration as a question of power. If, Massey asks, paraphrasing David Harvey (1989), the instantaneity of global mass communications via cable television, film and video distribution networks, faxes, and e-mail, are really "annihilating space by time," the central question remains one of institutional power: "Who is sending and receiving these informational flows? Who is producing their contents?" To these questions I would add: Who consumes these flows, and to what effect? If, as Massey maintains, the differential mobility provided by these new means of communication can weaken the leverage of the already weak, how should ethnographers of transnational migrants, exiles, and refugees interrogate their seemingly quite mobile time-space travelers?

At this stage of my thinking the following questions come to mind: Do transnational migrants, fueled by global images of upward social mobility, pay as close attention to global currency exchange rates of the dollars they are saving as to the contents of cable TV shows depicting daily life in the global metropoles that they live in or dream about? What images of men, women, and gender relations are being deployed in the instantaneous flows of global mass communications? What effect do these forms of imagined lives have on the social relations of gender, particularly upon: (a) differential rates of geographical mobility between men and women in space; and (b) changing gender relations within and among households in different migratory streams? Once women, whether motivated globally or locally, leave their old "place" in the patriarchal domestic sphere to enter the public sphere and pursue new lives as transnational migrants, what special risks do they face as border-crossers who lack a "public space" for acting on the basis of citizen rights? I will return to these questions of gender and migration and give them specific resonance in my subsequent discussion of the multiple scales of thought and action evident in the emergent politics of immigrant and refugee women's rights.

Beyond the Global–Local Duality

The global–local duality in social theory rests on a false opposition that equates the *local* with a cultural space of stasis, ontological meaning, and personal identity (i.e. the "place") and the *global* as the site of dynamic change, the decentering of meaning, and the fragmentation/homogenization of culture (i.e. the "space" of global capitalism). This duality is reflected explicitly in the basic assumptions of modernization theory, as well as the traditional anthropological practice of "salvaging" disappearing exotic local cultures (for critiques see Smith, 1980: ch. 5; Clifford, 1987). It is implicitly present in Frederic Jameson's (1984) notion of the "confusion" wrought by late-capitalist hyperspace. Likewise David Harvey's (1989) conflation of locality, Heideggerian ontology, reactionary nostalgia, and fascism in *The Condition of Postmodernity* rests upon this binary opposition (see chapter 2, this volume; for another critique of this view see Morris, 1992). This sort of binary thinking leaves only two spaces open for practical reason as well as for politics: "Think locally, act locally" or "Think globally, act globally." In conceptualizing transnational migration this sort of binary thinking has set enduring cognitive limits on the way the process of "immigration" is conceived; namely, as a linear process moving from an "old," presumably coherent traditional culture, through a transitional period of delocalization, followed by a period of adaptation and relocalization to the "new" and presumably more "modern" cultural context and way of life.

For the past two decades the slogan "Think globally, act locally" has been treated in both the popular media and in academic circles as a useful antidote to these forms of binary thinking. The slogan has the advantage of allowing the possibility that people operating "on the ground" have some understanding of the wider context in which their lives are embedded and some capacity to resist as well as accommodate to understood global conditions, opportunities, and constraints. Nevertheless, even the kind of politics envisaged by this slogan is one in which the main route used by popular forces and movements is the locality. This way of viewing "grassroots politics" restricts political action to resistance to the actions of a variety of local political and economic elites like mayors, urban service providers, "growth machines," business interests, and the local press.

The type of grassroots political practice that has emerged among transnational migrants and refugees does not fit well into the restrictive boundaries of local politics conventionally used in connecting the local to the global. To open up the discursive space surrounding the global–local duality, reconstitute the notion of the "grassroots" more richly, and to avoid its easy conflation with politics at the neighborhood scale, we turn to narrative means to illustrate three emergent types of "cross-border" grassroots politics being practiced by transnational migrants and refugees. For want of established discursive terms to characterize these dynamic political processes, and recalling Freud's insight that "play" is the opposite of "work" and not of "seriousness," I have coined three sets of terms that play upon and hopefully allow more room for the play of difference in the global–local nexus. They are (1) thinking locally while acting globally; (2) living bifocally, i.e. thinking transnationally while acting multilocally; and (3) thinking and acting simultaneously at multiple scales.

Thinking Locally and Acting Globally

The story of the return in early 1993 of several thousand Guatemalan refugees to their country after more than a decade in self-exile offers a pointed example of a new type of transnational grassroots politics: a form of political practice in which the group's objectives have been largely "localized" around the politics of class, ethnicity, and community in Guatemala, while the political arena in which they have pursued these objectives has been largely "global." In this instance, a self-organized group of indigenous refugees, thinking about orchestrating the terms of their "return" (not properly speaking a "relocalization," but rather a reconstitution of the prevailing relations of domination–subordination in their old "locales"), acted globally to elicit the international mediation of the United Nations, and capitalized on the global visibility and cultural status accorded to their symbolic leader, Nobel Peace Prize winner Rigoberta Menchu, to successfully negotiate their still ongoing and uncertain "return."

Operating largely from a string of isolated border camps in southern Mexico, the self-organized refugees were the first international refugee community ever to overcome the institutionally defined marginality of being "spoken for" by international and refugee relief organizations to directly represent itself during two years of internationally mediated talks aimed at specifying the terms of their own return. During the course of the talks the basically repressive, military-dominated Guatemalan government made several concessions concerning the presence of international observers (e.g. representatives of the International Committee of the Red Cross and the UN High Commissioner for Refugees) to help guarantee the safety of returnees and guard against a renewal of human rights abuses, as well as to allocate land holdings for the refugees upon their return. In commenting on the return a UN diplomat privy to the talks pointed out that by organizing their own representation at the UN-mediated talks, the refugees had created a new political space for the Guatemalan government as well as themselves. By negotiating with the refugees the government avoided negotiating with rebel forces and by making the concessions they did to the refugees they reduced the play of these issues in bargaining with rebel forces. Ironically, prior to the failed self-orchestrated military coup by the dominant right-wing faction of the military, the global institutional and media attention this group of refugees gained by their unprecedented "return" produced a situation in which both the repressive Guatemalan government and the rebel National Revolutionary Unity front embraced the refugees and claimed credit for their political return (Robbertson, 1993). Arguably, the auto-coup failed in part because other parts of Guatemalan civil society were emboldened to resist repression by the global lens focused upon Guatemalan politics and society by the transnational practices of Rigoberta Menchu and her movement.

Bifocal Border-crossers

On August 7, 1992 a multicultural coalition of transnational refugees from Central America and students from the University of California at Berkeley loaded a truck full of clothing, medical supplies, and used office equipment for a journey to El Salvador. This "local" political act was coordinated with the efforts of a "nationally constituted" student organization, Students Against Intervention in Central America (SAICA), which sent an automotive caravan from campus communities in the United States to that war-torn Central American "nation." Although "nationally constituted," SAICA's Caravan for Peace campaign materialized entirely as a result of grassroots efforts by local, but bifocally conscious, coalitions of students, peace activists, refugees, and immigrant and refugee rights organizations in campus communities in the states of Texas and California.

The caravan was clearly intended by its organizers to have political effects in both the United States and El Salvador, as well as elsewhere in Central America. To finance the journey and educate the public in this country to the fallout of United States foreign policy in Central America, the group showed films and sponsored benefit concerts focusing on events in Nicaragua and Guatemala as well as El Salvador. In anticipation of future elections in El Salvador in which the FMLN opposition ran as a legal political party, the caravan's organizers were to leave its cars, trucks, and buses behind to facilitate rural campaigning. A spokesperson for the Berkeley contingent to the caravan explained: "This is not an act of charity. It's more moral and political support for the people of El Salvador." A former soldier for the FMLN, who won political asylum and now lives in Berkeley, added: "The nine bikes we are sending will allow people to get around, since many of the roads leading to smaller towns were blown up" (*Daily Californian*, August 7, 1972: 1).

What are we to make of this story? My interpretation of what was going on is as follows. The student members of this coalition are thinking transnationally and acting multilocally. The political revolutionary who joined this coalition, while constantly aware of the global context of his actions, used his local knowledge of conditions in El Salvador and his local knowledge of the workings of the sanctuary movement in Berkeley, to shape the specific content of the caravan's supplies, with an eye toward the transformation of national politics in El Salvador and the constitution of a civil society there. Contextually, the national legal system of the United States provided the institutional framework for the "constitution" of national legitimacy by the student component of an alliance of local grassroots coalitions whose scale of operations was actually regional, a political expression of transnational grassroots politics emanating from campus communities in California and Texas. Such are the multiple border crossings characterizing one day in the life of the emergent grassroots politics of transnational migrants, refugees, and activists.

Another example of these sorts of multiple border crossings is the emergence of Mixtec ethnicity and the creation of new forms of political practice by indigenous Mixtecs from western Oaxaca, who have taken up jobs in agricultural labor in California and Oregon because of deteriorating economic conditions in rural Mexico (see Nagengast and Kearney, 1990). Evidence of the transnationalization of consciousness and action virtually leaps from the pages of Nagengast and Kearney's description of the political practices of the pan-Mixtec transnational associations that have been established in California and Oregon. These associations operate bi-nationally. One of their objectives is to promote self-help and raise money and other resources for community development projects in various Mixtec villages in Mexico. Since the passage of the 1986 Immigration Reform and Control Act (IRCA), both this objective and the conditions of work in commercial agriculture in the United States have been undermined for substantial numbers of Mixtec farm workers who did not qualify for amnesty under IRCA. The plight of the Mixtecs and other undocumented workers in California and neighboring states has become a salient issue for human and civil rights organizations in both Mexico and the United States, and a priority concern of the self-organized Mixtec associations.

The following passage, drawn from Nagengast and Kearney's (1990: 84–5, emphasis added) description of the Mixteca Asociacion Civica Benito Juarez (ACBJ), based in Fresno and Madera, California and Salem, Oregon, is worth quoting at length because it highlights the self-produced political space that has been created by these multiply marginalized "others," who are both participating in their old and their new civil societies and working to form a wider political space and practice a transnational grassroots politics. The passage underlines the polyfocality of these human agents, the coalitional strategy they are pursuing, and the still-emergent character of their project. It also problematizes the "local" as a timeless site of meaningfulness and social action. Members of the ACBJ, write Nagengast and Kearney,

> promote village development projects in Oaxaca but also increasingly concern themselves with discrimination, exploitation, health, and human rights abuses in Mixtec enclaves in California and Oregon, *regardless of the members' village of origin.* They are now attempting to transform one aspect of their organization into a labor contracting association in which Mixtec farm workers would sell their labor directly to growers, thereby avoiding the usually exploitative labor contractors now depended on by most workers. Concern is also focusing on gathering and publicizing testimonies of human rights abuses through independent human rights organizations. The ACBJ participated in a *transnational conference* in Mexicali on human rights violations suffered by migrants *on both sides of the border* and in a seminar on international human rights law and its applicability to them in Los Angeles. Overall, the ACBJ is working toward forming a *transnational league* of Mixtec associations that will incorporate Mixtec groups on both sides of the border. Mixtecs in the United States say that there is *"more space"* to organize north of the border than in Mexico, meaning that overt political oppression in the United States is less intense.

The Mixtec story is not without its ironies. In response to this effort by Mixtecs to create a transnational political space capable of encompassing the bi-national and multilocal social space in which they are orchestrating their lives, the PRI-dominated Mexican state has taken unusual steps to try to reincorporate the transnational migrants into the more familiar and more politically quiescent rituals and routines of patron–client politics in Mexico. Yet, ironically, to do so, they too have had to cross borders. In April, 1989 Heladio Ramirez Lopez, the self-identified Mixtec governor of Oaxaca, concerned about declining voter support among Mixtecs in Oaxacan and national elections, traveled to Watsonville and Madera, California to meet with Mixtec migrant workers and listen to their grievances and demands *vis-à-vis* the Mexican state. These centered around extortion by government officials and police while traveling north, the appropriation of portions of remittances by corrupt telegraph officials, and poor economic conditions in the Mixteca. Without apparent Foucaultian irony the governor pledged more patronage in the Mixteca and offered his regime's help to insure more effective "policing" of authorities (Nagengast and Kearney, 1990: 85).

Interestingly in the US–Mexican case, this type of border crossing is becoming institutionalized. In the Mexican national elections of 1988 the Cardenas-led opposition to PRI began to make significant inroads on PRI political hegemony by its growing voter support in the border states of Mexico, punctuated by well attended and enthusiastic political rallies in Los Angeles, including a visit from Cardenas. In response to this threat the ever-corporatist PRI pursued a regular state policy of sending PRI governors to political meetings with transnational migrants in various cities in California and Texas and even to Chicago under the aegis of the Mexican state's new Office for Mexican Communities Abroad. Although the objectives of this addition to the Mexican state apparatus are political as well as economic, its creation was justified on cultural grounds as a crossing of borders to "rebuild culture" and "recapture the Mexican identity," not only of Mexican-born transnational migrants but also of those who currently identify themselves as "Mexican-American" and "Chicano."

These examples of Mexican-American cross-border politics parallel the findings of other researchers working on transnational migration, suggesting that the border crossings just described may be less unusual than one might think. For example, Dominican and Puerto Rican circular migrants in New York City also receive regular visits from homeland politicians seeking political support, cultural identification, and a steady stream of remittances to bolster their domestic economies. These efforts, however, have not stemmed the tide of cultural hybridization that is producing bifocal life-worlds, as well illustrated in Luis Guarnizo's (1994) ethnographic study of Dominican migrants to New York. These migrants accentuate their "Dominican cultural traits" in New York as a defense against socioeconomic discrimination and as a niche for exercising political influence there, while appearing "too American" to those who have remained in their homelands when they return to visit or resettle.

The Politics of Simultaneity

On March 8, 1993, International Women's Day, over 150 transnational migrants, refugees, and immigrant and refugee rights activists gathered to participate in a conference at Fort Mason in San Francisco. The conference, organized by a political alliance of 30 women's and immigrants' rights organizations in the Bay Area, was led by the Coalition for Immigrant and Refugee Rights and Services and Mujeres Unidas y Activas, a self-organized group of Latina domestic workers. The conference was designed to gather testimony on human rights abuses suffered by transnational migrant women working in the United States. For seven hours a parade of speakers from Chile, Mexico, Guatemala, China, the Philippines, Haiti, and other countries gave witness to acts of physical and mental torture, rape, workplace servitude, domestic violence, and other denials of human rights they had experienced while crossing the border, living in refugee camps, and working in the United States.

The hearing of Bay Area migrant women was one of many being held by women's and human rights groups in other cities worldwide. The testimony gathered at the various local conferences was presented in June, 1993 to a Vienna meeting of the United Nations Human Rights Commission at its World Conference on Human Rights. This global target of the movement was chosen as part of an effort to raise international political awareness, dispel the myth that human rights abuses do not occur in highly developed societies such as the US, and most importantly, to *genderize* the universalist conception of "human rights" and thus change international policies for stemming abuses. Significantly, after hearing the testimony in Vienna, the UN Commission rejected arguments justifying specific abuses of women on "culturally and ethnically specific" grounds and endorsed the major aims of the women's human rights movement.

In addition to its global objective, other parts of the testimony presented at the San Francisco hearing simultaneously addressed political targets located at various lower levels of state power within the United States. For example, a Chilean woman, facing deportation by the US Immigration and Naturalization Service (INS), testified to the abuses and withholding of pay she had experienced as a legal registered au pair for a professional couple in Rohnert Park, California. She pointed out that, with the assistance of a California Rural Legal Assistance office, she had successfully filed a claim with the State of California to force her employer to pay back wages and overtime. Another speaker, Maria Olea, head of Mujeres Unidas y Activas, called for a nation-wide separation of immigration regulation and local policing, pointing out that many crimes in transnational migrant and refugee neighborhoods go unreported because of widespread fear by crime victims of being reported to the INS (Espinoza, 1993).

Other states, societies, and localities were also implicated in the "hearing's" multilevel mode of political practice. For instance, both to improve her own lot and to focus global attention on domestic and public practices in her country of origin, an Iranian woman testifying at the hearing pointed out that she had filed an application for political asylum in the United States on the basis of the oppression of women in Iran. Testimony concerning the sexual abuse of women at the border and in refugee camps also sought to shed the light of day upon and thereby alter abusive practices of state structures outside the United States regulating the flow of migrating women and "policing" their crossover.

Much more could be said of the multiple texts and subtexts orchestrated by even this single Bay Area component of an emergent global coalition of women's, immigrant, and refugee rights organizations that has now succeeded in rewriting the UN Declaration of Human Rights by genderizing it. Yet enough has been said in this and the previous cases to warrant the conclusion that a good deal of transnational grassroots politics today is a "politics of simultaneity," i.e. a politics in which single political acts can be orchestrated toward multiple targets, operating at a variety of institutional and geographical scales, mediated by the appropriation of the global means of mass communication by transnational grassroots movements, and reflecting the multiple identities of the new social subjects of global grassroots movements.

The Production of Political Space

I would argue, then, that it is easier for ordinary people to think and act simultaneously at multiple scales and to fashion a transnational oppositional politics by their practice, than leading commentators on the "postmodern condition" like Harvey (1989) and Jameson (1984) would have us believe. Their depiction of depoliticization wrought by the supposed "confusion" of late-capitalist "hyperspace" reveals an unwillingness or inability to imagine the new forms of grassroots political agency we have just considered.

Having said this, it is important to realize that the daily practices unleashed by the emergent possibilities for the social construction of new social subjects discussed in this chapter are double-edged. The reprocessing of identity by those who once saw their lives as more or less predictably constrained by the givenness of established orders, may produce new emancipatory social movements with a high degree of political efficacy such as those discussed above. But even in the best of cases, the emergence of new transnational subjects operating outside of the officially constructed categories of identity, calls forth new efforts by established power structures to regularize their behavior, if not recommand their loyalties. Late-modernist receiving states continue to reassert their sensed erosion of sovereignty by finding new means to redefine transnational migrants in terms of a "lack": as "cultural aliens," "undocumented workers," and "illegitimate" political refugees. In the United States recent discursive efforts to marginalize, silence, and exclude undocumented "others" are signs of the failure of the national state and economy to incorporate transmigrants by the means that have proven effective in the past – factory work, trade unions, public schools, and urban politics – all of which themselves are becoming transnationalized and thereby complicated as means of national economic and political incorporation. Less developed states and societies are increasingly resorting to a variety of measures designed to depoliticize grassroots politics and regulate incipient oppositional forces within their borders, while reincorporating transnational migrants into their nationalist discourses and projects. Clearly the new political spaces discussed in this chapter must be actively fought for and maintained if they are to survive as self-organized projects. This is not because they otherwise will wither away, but because existing networks of power seek to erase the new transnational political spaces, and move the scope of politics back to terrains they currently dominate.

From Globalization to Transnational Urbanism

8

I am also somewhat uncomfortable with the rather prodigious use of the term "globalization" to describe just about any process or relationship that somehow crosses state boundaries. In themselves, many such processes and relationships obviously do not at all extend across the world. The term "transnational" is in a way more humble, and often a more adequate label for phenomena which can be of quite variable scale and distribution, even when they do share the characteristic of not being contained within a state. It also makes the point that many of the linkages in question are not "international," in the strict sense of involving nations – actually, states – as corporate actors. In the transnational arena, the actors may now be individuals, groups, movements, business enterprises, and in no small part it is this diversity of organization that we need to consider. At the same time, there is a certain irony in the tendency of the term "transnational" to draw attention to what it negates – that is, to the continued significance of the national.

Ulf Hannerz, Transnational Connections

All representations of cities and urbanization processes are social constructs. Why is the terrain of transnational urbanism a more fruitful optic for guiding urban research than the global cities and time-space compression frameworks? Unlike the latter, which are mired in a structuralist metaphysics and display functionalist proclivities, transnational urbanism directly addresses the interpretive politics of representation that characterizes the current poststructuralist moment in the social sciences. In both the social sciences and cultural studies, a core theme in the growing discourse on transnational connections has been the boundary penetration of national cultures, political systems, and processes of identity formation by transnational circuits of information, exchange, meaning, and power. The nation-state is often represented in this discourse as weakened "from above" by transnational capital, global media, and emergent supranational political institutions (see, for example, Cvetkovich and Kellner, 1997; Drainville, 1998). For others it is envisaged as facing decentering local resistances "from below," such as ethnic nationalism and transnational grass-roots activism (see, for example, Portes, 1996a, 1996b; Mahler, 1998). These developments are sometimes represented in celebratory terms, as harbingers of global market rationality from above, or of liberating practices from below like the cultural hybridity brought to postmodern urban life by transnational migration. In more pessimistic readings, these developments are represented as preludes to a new form of capitalist modernization that is bound to convert the entire planet to global consumerism. In most of these representations, transnationalism from above and below is represented as something profoundly "new."

Yet transnational connections forged by international trade, global migration, cross-border political movements, and cultural interpenetrations are by no means entirely new phenomena. Indeed, each of these flows has a very long history, be they the sojourns of Marco Polo, the economic alliances of city-states, the mass migrations of the early twentieth century, or the political actions leading to the unification of Italy. Nevertheless, at the present historical moment four contemporary processes contributing to the formation of transnational networks of social action do appear to be new. These processes, in turn, appear to be driving both the turn to transnationalism as an urban research focus and the contentious character of the debate on the role of cities in a putatively "postnational" global cultural economy (see Appadurai, 1996). They include:

1   The discursive repositioning of cities in relation to nation-states in the ongoing debate on the meaning of globalization.
2   The emergence of cross-national political and institutional networks that deploy the discourses of decolonization, human rights, and other universalistic tropes to advance the interests of heretofore marginalized others.
3   The facilitation of transnational social ties by new technological developments that have widened access to the means of transnational travel, communication, and ways of being in the world.
4   (Following from these) the spatial reconfiguration of social networks that facilitate the reproduction of migration, business practices, cultural beliefs, and political agency "from below."

Starting from this multidimensional conception of contemporary transnationalism, I wish to explore four themes central to the emergence of transnational urbanism as a research field: (1) the sociospatial agency of transnational social, economic, and political networks; (2) the need to study what has come to be termed the translocality; (3) the continuing significance of the nation-state as a player in the social construction of transnational urbanism; and (4) the need for comparative urban analysis of emergent transnational networks viewed as articulations taking place within, between, and across the local sites that have heretofore been the domains of urban research.

The Agency of Transnational Networks

Transnational sociocultural and political–economic agencies act at multiple spatial scales (see Smith, 1994). The social construction of transnational networks should be treated as the resultant of separate, sometimes parallel, sometimes competing projects at all levels of analysis within the putatively global system: from the global governance agenda of international organizations and multinational corporations, to the most local social practices by which transnational networks are constructed. At the global level of analysis, the specific multilateral collectivities identified earlier by McMichael (1996) and Drainville (1998) seek to construct a global neoliberal contextual space, a "new world order," to regulate transnational flows of capital, trade, people, and culture. In the process, they supplant the disintegrating nationally managed regimes of Keynesianism and Fordism (Drainville, 1998). At the most local level, specific collectivities – local households, kin networks, elite fractions, and other emergent local formations – actively pursue such strategies as transnational migration (see, for example, Goldring, 1998; R. Smith, 1998), transnational social movements (Sikkink, 1993; Smith, 1994; Guarnizo and Smith, 1998; Mahler, 1998), or transnational economic or cultural entrepreneurship (Portes, 1996a, 1996b; Schein, 1998a, 1998b) to sustain or transform resources, including cultural resources, in the face of the neoliberal storm.

Transnational practices connect social networks located in more than one national territory. This does not mean that such practices are inherently transgressive bearers of new social subjectivities. Rather, transnational political, economic, and sociocultural practices are embodied in historically specific, culturally constituted, social relations, i.e. they are networks of meaning, established between particular spatially and temporally situated social actors.

The "local" dimension of transnationalism thus needs to be carefully considered. Although once viewed in social theory as the site of stasis or settlement, one of the main contributions of postmodern ethnography and critical theory has been the redefinition of "the local" as a dynamic source of alternative cosmopolitanisms and contestation (Smith, 1992; Robbins, 1993; Schein, 1998a). In light of this more dynamic view of locality, it is important to consider the shifting boundaries of transnational urbanism as reflected in the enabling or constraining sociocultural networks found in particular sites, very often large cities.

This disruption of the binary of local stasis vs. global dynamism highlights the representation of "the urban" in transnational discourse, and vice versa. In the version of transnational urbanism advanced in this book, cities are not to be viewed as empty containers of transnational articulations. Transnational flows, such as capital investments, migration patterns, or IMF policies, are not simply imposed on cities from the outside. Rather, as we shall see, the local often reconstitutes the meaning of globalization. Thus, for example, because local cultural understandings mediate and thus mutually constitute the meaning of investment, it matters significantly whether Hong Kong capital investment networks are forged *vis-à-vis* Shenzhen or Vancouver (for example, compare Smart and Smart, 1998, with Mitchell, 1996). Likewise, because local cultural practices and political understandings mediate global power relations, it matters whether IMF austerity policies are implemented in San Jose, Costa Rica or Mexico City (for example, compare Tardanico, 1992, with Barkin, Ortiz, and Rosen, 1997). Because local social constructions of "immigrants" may differ from one city to the next, it matters whether migrants from Latin America and the Pacific Rim move to New York or Miami, Los Angeles or San Francisco, respectively, to say nothing of whether they move to Asian or European metropoles (see Smith and Tarallo, 1995; compare Mahler, 1996; Smith and Tarallo, 1993a; and the case studies in Smith and Guarnizo, 1998).

My intention here is not to essentialize local culture. The social production of local cultural practices in New York or Los Angeles is a very heterogeneous enterprise. Because cities, local states, and community formations are not bounded, self-contained, coherent entities but, rather, multiple and even contradictory, and because no necessary correlation exists between any place and the cultural meanings informing the practices that occur there, researchers must leave open the analytical questions of both how and when the "local" mediates the "global." The local, national, and transnational connections that go into the making of transnational urbanism are mutually constitutive.

There is a rapidly growing body of literature on transnational connections (see, for example, the case studies in Hannerz, 1996; Ong and Nonini, 1997; Smith and Guarnizo, 1998). This literature grounds the study of transnationalism in the criss-crossing networks of social practice that collude and collide in particular cities at particular times. The historically specific patterns of politics, culture, and economic life found in particular locales significantly mediate the transnational flows of people, resources, ideas, and information. Any given city receiving particular transnational economic, political, or cultural flows provides a specific configuration of potential opportunities and constraints (e.g. labor market conditions, investment opportunities, popular and official perceptions of a migrant group, the presence or absence of other political activists) into which migrants, investors, or political and cultural brokers enter. Thus, the play of agency operates differently from place to place and even differently within the same place at different times. Because of power differentials among the various networks interacting in particular places at particular times, the local social context of these interactions is in constant flux. Yet at any given moment the confluence of various inward flows and specific urban and regional settings shapes not only the likelihood of generating, maintaining, or forsaking transnational ties, but also the very character of the ties that can be forged. An unraveling of the complexity of transnational urbanism, then, does not stop at calling attention to the continuing significance of cities as grounded sites of meaning-making.

The Rise of Translocalities

Recent research on transnationalism illustrates that the specific social space in which transnational actions take place is not merely local but often "translocal" (i.e. local to local). Translocal relations are constituted within historically and geographically specific points of origin and destination established by transnational migrants, investors, political activists, or sociocultural entrepreneurs. They form a multifaceted connection that links transnational actors, the localities to which they direct flows, and their points of origin. These points of origin implicated in transnational urbanism may be cities like Hong Kong, where investment capitalists direct investments to other locales on the Pacific Rim; rural villages in Mexico, where households send transmigrants to New York or Los Angeles; smaller cities like Oakland, California, where a hotel and restaurant workers' union "local" initiates transnational, multi-ethnic, working-class organizing campaigns; or centers of political ferment like Amsterdam or the San Francisco Bay Area, where activists deploy and reterritorialize various transnational human rights discourses and practices. The social relations forged by transnational networks link such sending locations with receiving cities in complex ways, generating *translocal* discursive and spatial practices that may reconfigure and even transform relations of power.

Consider, as a prime example, a recent study by Alan and Josephine Smart (1998) of the investment practices of entrepreneurial Hong Kong capitalists in the Shenzhen region of mainland China. The Smarts' work investigates the historically particular forging of translocal relations that mediate the pattern of global investment. Their study reveals a particular pattern of "situated ethnicity" as the basis for constructing translocal network solidarity and exclusion that differs markedly from the kinds of translocal ties forged by corporate Chinese capitalists from Hong Kong, who are channeling investment into Vancouver, British Columbia (Mitchell, 1993, 1996). These studies illustrate that in penetrating different cities and regions in the world economy, transnational capitalist segments from Hong Kong are not entirely free agents. Indeed, they have to justify their activities within prevailing local cultural understandings. The entrepreneurial Hong Kong capitalists studied by Smart and Smart foreground their "Chineseness" in Shenzhen, while the corporate capitalists from Hong Kong in Vancouver accommodate to a different setting by downplaying their Chineseness and foregrounding their capitalist economic position within a dominant multicultural public discourse. Far from erasing local identifications and meaning systems, transnationalism actually relies on them to sustain transnational ties.

Several of the contributions to the collection *Ungrounded Empires* (Ong and Nonini, 1997) nicely illustrate the dynamic character of the sorts of local and translocal social ties that go into the making of transnational urbanism. Ong and Nonini have assembled fascinating studies of the forging of translocal social relations that are central to our understanding of both modern Chinese transnationalism and contemporary Pacific Rim urbanization. Following James Clifford's (1992) injunction to consider "travel" as a necessary supplement to "settlement" in conducting ethnographic research at the present urban moment, the contributors lucidly explore the social networks and practices formed by the movements of Taiwanese entrepreneurs into and out of South China (Hsing, 1997), the sojourns of Malaysian ethnic Chinese transnational migrant workers in Japanese cities (Nonini, 1997), and the discourses of national, transnational, and pan-Asian identity, played out among ethnic Chinese minorities living in Bangkok and metropolitan Manila (Blanc, 1997).

These studies of transnational urbanism in Asian cities are complemented by a spate of research in migration studies on the rise of transnational communities that are sustained by social ties forged by transmigrants moving between small villages in Latin America and large US cities (see, for example, Goldring, 1998; Rodriguez, 1995; Mahler, 1998; R. Smith, 1998). By "transnational communities" these researchers mean translocality-based structures of cultural production and social reproduction. Such transnational sociocultural structures are sustained by social networks in migration and their attendant modes of social organization, e.g. organizing translocal "home-town" associations in Los Angeles, New York, and Houston; transmitting economic remittances from income earned in transnational cities to sustain families, promote community development projects, and transform local power and status relations in villages of origin; and reconfiguring local cultural festivals and celebrations in both sites to signify translocality. Such translocal connections are sustained as well by more indirect technological means of transportation and communication – such as jet airplanes, satellite dishes, courier services, telephones, faxes, and e-mail – now available to facilitate the production of transnational social ties.

These processes of constructing translocality cannot be readily reduced to the economistic rubric "household reproduction." Indeed, the everyday practices of transmigrants, including the remittances they control, involve not only household survival but also the reinscription of status positions that enhance the political influence of transmigrants in sending locales (Goldring, 1998; R. Smith, 1998). The resources mobilized by transmigrants have also been shown to reconfigure community power relations (Nagengast and Kearney, 1990; R. Smith, 1998) in sending and receiving locales. Transnational bodily movement is not a movement across a neutral space. Rather, it is an encounter involving an often contentious meeting ground of different urban racial hierarchies and different local social relations of gender. These translocal zones of experience have opened up new spaces for the transgression of local racial and gendered boundaries (see, for example, the case of Dominican urban transmigrant women and blacks in New York and Madrid in Sørensen, 1998). Louisa Schein's (1998a) case study on the invention of Hmong transnational ties with the Miao ethnic minority in China shows that it is even possible to reinvent completely one's ethnic origins by the production, diffusion, and consumption of culturally oriented ethnic videos laden with geographical images and cultural icons. By these means, Hmong refugees from Laos living in small and large cities in California, Minnesota, and elsewhere, are constructing a myth of cultural origins linked not to Laos but to Miao regions of China.

As this example suggests, the social construction of what Benedict Anderson (1983) calls "imagined communities" inextricably links discourses of localism, nationalism, and transnationalism in very complex ways. When the studies by Schein (1998a) and Smart and Smart (1998) are compared, we find that political elites of the local state in different Chinese regions forge links and construct a cultural sense of "we-ness" with US-based Hmong cultural brokers and Hong Kong-based entrepreneurs, respectively, that bypass national party loyalties and the ideology of the Chinese state. Institutional actors representing the Chinese state are eager to attract foreign remittances and investment and thus tolerate these translocal ties within China's borders. Yet they remain watchful, worried about the risks of ethnic separatism and the erosion of the ruling party's control of local politics.

Likewise, when processes of translocality construction that link villages in Mexico to US cities are compared to the translocal Hong Kong–Shenzhen connection, we find quite different translocal social constructions of identity and affiliation. Unlike the Mexican transmigrants who are concerned with using transnational connections to reconfigure power and status relations within their villages of origin and maintain a reconfigured "home-town" identity (Goldring, 1998; R. Smith, 1998), the small capitalists of Hong Kong studied by Smart and Smart (1998) carefully avoid establishing economic ties in their own villages of origin in China, for fear of the "excess" (i.e. non-business related) expectations and demands that might be thrust upon them. Their basis for building transnational economic and social relations is situated ethnicity (i.e. a constructed, thoroughly modern, "transnational Chineseness"), rather than home-town loyalty.

Questioning the Postnational Discourse

Does this way of conceiving transnational connections mean, as some have claimed (e.g. Appadurai, 1996, part 3), that transnational networks "from above" and "from below" are now ushering in a new period of weakened nationalism, a "postnational" global cultural economy? Does it mean, as global cities devotees suggest, that the nation-state faces inexorable decline? There are several reasons to treat these claims with some skepticism.

First, in the present period of heightened transnational migration, many nation-states that have experienced substantial out-migration are entering into a process of actively promoting transnational reincorporation of migrants into their state-centered projects. Why is this so? Global economic restructuring and the repositioning of states, especially less industrialized ones, in the world economy have increased the economic dependency of these countries on foreign investment. Political elites and managerial strata in these societies have found that as emigration to advanced capitalist countries has increased, the monetary transfers provided by transmigrant investors have made crucial contributions to their national and urban economies (Lessinger, 1992). Likewise transnational household remittances have promoted social stability and new forms of local community development (see Kearney, 1991; Smith, 1994; Mahler, 1996). Thus a growing dependence on transmigrants' stable remittances has prompted sending states to try to incorporate their "nationals" abroad into both their national market and their national polity by a variety of measures, including naming "honorary ambassadors" from among transmigrant entrepreneurs in the hope that they will promote "national" interests *vis-à-vis* receiving countries; subsidizing transnational migrant "home-town" and "home-state" associations (Goldring, 1998; Mahler, 1998; R. Smith, 1998); creating formal channels for communicating with these constituencies across national borders (Nagengast and Kearney, 1990; Guarnizo, 1996; Glick Schiller and Fouron, 1998); passing dual citizenship laws; and even, in the bizarre case of the state apparatus in El Salvador, providing free legal assistance to political refugees so that they may obtain asylum in the United States on the grounds that they have been persecuted by the state that is paying their legal expenses. Far from withering away in the "epoch" of postnationalism, sending states once presumed to be peripheral are promoting the reproduction of transnational subjects. In the process, they are reinventing their own role in the "new world order."

Second, the agents of receiving states remain relevant actors. Although weakened by the neoliberal assault in their capacity to promote social welfare policies within their borders, states still monopolize the legitimate means of coercive power to police those borders. It might even be argued that the very uncertainties of national identity posed by transnational penetration of national boundaries from above and below have heightened the symbolic and material consequences of policing borders. The rise of restrictive immigration laws in receiving societies amply speaks to this issue. Thus it is problematic to represent as a "deterritorialization of the state" the expansion of the reach of "states of origin" beyond their own national territorial jurisdictions into other state and urban formations. Rather, when politicians from Mexico, for example, come to campaign and proselytize to Mexican transnational migrants living in Los Angeles or Fresno, California (see Nagengast and Kearney, 1990), or business people from China act in various ways to open or maintain markets in US or European cities, their influence is still exercised in a particular territorial domain, formally controlled by institutional actors of "receiving" states. The juridical construction of transnational social formations by these state-centered actors is often one which denies their "globality" and reterritorializes their meaning as a "boundary penetration," as a "transgression" of the state's own jurisdiction. The recent political controversy in the United States concerning the "penetration of Asian money" into US national political campaigns is a case in point: it suggests that the social actions of political elites ruling nation-states are not merely reactions to, but also are partially constitutive of, the scope and meaning of transnationalism within their territories. State-initiated discourses thus remain important to the reinscription of nationalist ideologies and national subjects in the face of transnationalism, both from above and from below.

There is a third reason for skepticism concerning the postnational character of the cultural and political economy of cities in transnational times. Although cities may welcome the transnational investment flows from above that contribute to their economic development, there is scant evidence that the local context of reception for transnational migrants "from below" has been equally receptive. Rather than being welcomed for their talents, resourcefulness, or hybridity, transmigrants are often stigmatized and stereotyped as signs of poverty, difference, and urban decline. Thus, rather than engendering a public discourse on their contributions to the vitality of urban life in transnational cities, the presence of transmigrants in US cities has reignited nationalist discourses on the "disuniting" of America (Schlesinger, 1992). The same can be said for the racialized anti-immigrant discourses currently shaping the character of urban life throughout Western Europe.

Paradoxically, the expansion of transnational migration has resulted in outbursts of entrenched, essentialist nationalism in both sending and receiving locales. In receiving cities and states, movements aimed at recuperating and reifying a mythical national identity are expanding as a way to eliminate the penetration of alien "others." States of origin, on the other hand, are re-essentializing their national identity and extending it to their nationals abroad as a way to maintain their loyalty and flow of resources "back home." By granting them dual citizenship, these states are encouraging transmigrants' instrumental accommodation to receiving societies, while simultaneously inhibiting their cultural assimilation and thereby promoting the preservation of their own national culture. This, in turn, further fuels nativist sentiments in receiving cities and states.

Undoubtedly, transnational practices cut across the politically instituted boundaries of cities and states. These transnational actions are nonetheless affected by the policies and practices of territorially based local and national states and communities. Yet, in addition to the representations of elites that control national territories and local states, the power–knowledge systems shaping imagined communities at today's urban moment are also shaped by visions of trade, travel, migration, locality, translocality, and diaspora emanating from the meaning-making of transnational networks. Transnational urbanism is thus mutually constituted by the shifting interplay of local, national, and transnational relations of power and meaning.

Towards a Transnational Urban Studies

Clearly, there is a need to expand the study of transnational urbanism to encompass the scope of transnational processes, as well as to focus future urban research upon the local and translocal specificities of various transnational sociospatial practices. Traditional methods for studying people in cities – ethnography, life histories, and historical case studies – are still germane to the task at hand, but their scope and boundaries must be seriously rethought. The challenge is to develop an optic and a language capable of representing the complexity of transnational connections, the dynamics of cross-border networks, and the shifting spatial scales at which agency takes place.

Given this complexity, a fruitful approach for research on transnational urbanism would start with an analysis of sociocultural, political, and economic networks situated in the social space of the city, with an awareness that the social space being analyzed might usefully be understood as a translocality, a fluid cross-border space in which social actors interact with local and extralocal institutions and social processes in the formation of power, meaning, and identities. In contrast, starting from the global level and deducing urban outcomes from global developments, as in the work of Harvey or the global cities devotees, often leads to over-generalization and produces the self-fulfilling "grand theories" that have been the postmodern object of derision. This is particularly problematic when scholars become so wrapped up in the theoretical elegance of their formulations, e.g. late capitalism, or time-space distantiation or compression, that they ignore questions of how the world "out there" is imagined, socially constructed, and lived (see, for example, Jameson, 1984; Giddens, 1991; Harvey, 1990).

An equally problematic pitfall would be to begin and end analysis of transnational urbanism at a purely local level. In privileging local knowledge (Geertz, 1983) or essentializing the local community as a sacred space of ontological meaning, researchers often develop an inward-looking tunnel vision that altogether fails to connect human intentions to social networks, structural contexts, and historical change. Situating the study of transnational urbanism at the level of particular cities viewed as translocalities avoids this pitfall. Specifically, we need to ask how transnational networks operate and how principles of trust and solidarity are constructed across national territories as compared to those which are entirely locally based and maintained. What place-making discourses and practices hold transnational networks together? How are social connectedness and control organized across borders to guarantee commitment and motivate social action? How do transnational networks interact with, accommodate to, or modify, local power structures, including class, gender, and racial hierarchies? With what effects? How does the social formation of a translocality affect the sociocultural bases supporting both local and transnational relations and ties?

The task of reconfiguring urban research for studying translocalities presents serious challenges and offers new opportunities for creative scholarship. Most of the current research on transnational networks has been required by the scope of transnational relations to pursue a multi-locational research strategy that criss-crosses urban, national, cultural, and institutional boundaries (see the studies in Ong and Nonini, 1997; Smith and Guarnizo, 1998). For example, Louisa Schein's (1998a) study of "forged transnationality" explores the social ties linking Hmong refugees from Laos now living in US localities to a fictive community of origin in the Miao "homeland" of China. Her work provides an excellent example of just such a criss-crossing research strategy. Schein inventively deploys unorthodox ethnographic methods which move back and forth between text and context, observation and participation, and localities in the United States and China, acting out her self-described role as an ethnographic nomad. James Clifford (1992) has suggested that the study of "traveling cultures" requires traveling researchers. Yet more than mere travel is required of today's transnational ethnographic nomads. For example, Schein even found herself performing the role of a transnational marriage broker in order to gain effective access to the micro-networks by which Hmong transnational cultural brokers are socially constructing a new Hmong–Miao ethnic identity, by marketing video-tapes of staged "traditional" Miao rituals and ceremonies to Hmong refugees in California and Minnesota. Schein assisted Miao women in rural China to translate faxes and phone calls from prospective suitors among Hmong men in the US, disillusioned by the Americanization of "their" women and seeking more "traditional" marriage partners among their putative co-ethnics in a romanticized Chinese homeland. As increasing numbers of formerly locality-based social networks, cultural formations, grassroots movements, and business activities extend across national boundaries, becoming binational if not multinational in spatial scale, urban research needs to be literally "re-placed" from the local to the translocal and transnational scales. As Schein's study illustrates, this will be no easy task.

Comparative Transnationalisms

Another current constraint upon existing knowledge about transnational networks, translocalities, and transnational urbanism is the dearth of comparative urban studies. In my view, future urban research ought to focus considerable attention on comparatively analyzing diverse cases of transnational network formation and translocality construction. Such studies may take several different forms, offering insight concerning different modes of transnational urbanism.

Three particularly useful modes of comparison come to mind. These are (a) comparing different transnational networks operating in the same city; (b) comparing transnational network practices across different nations and cities; and (c) comparing efforts by global governance devotees to implement a neoliberal political agenda in different national and urban formations. Let us consider how each of these approaches might be advanced.

Comparing different transnational networks in the same city

To more fully explicate the parameters of transnational urbanism it is important to compare and contrast transnational practices undertaken by different social networks in the same city. This will enable us to examine both (a) different local effects of different modes of transnational social organization and (b) different impacts the social and political organization of a particular city has on the networks. How, for example, do the translocal social networks of Dominicans and Mexicans who orchestrate part of their lives in New York City, interpret, accommodate to, or resist the current urban racial hierarchy, local political system, and economic niches available in the Big Apple? (compare Guarnizo, 1998, and R. Smith, 1998). How do the different ethnic networks currently linking Los Angeles to other Latin American and Pacific Rim metropoles relate to each other within LA? (see Matthei and Smith, 1998; Waldinger and Bozorgmehr, 1996). Are such localized intergroup relations antagonistic or accommodative? In what respects are they both or neither? (see, for example, Rodriguez, 1995). Once the dynamics of transnational urbanism are more fully understood in particular urban formations, it will doubtless be easier to address research questions of transnational urbanism comparatively across cities.

Comparing network practices across space

A useful starting point in pursuit of this second research strategy would be to compare the practices of the same or a similar transnational network in different cities. The network in question might be a migrant group, a business investment network, or a participating component of a transnational social movement. The goal of such an approach would be to determine the effect of the local on the transnational.

In the case of migration, for example, we might study the practices of groups sharing the same national origin or urban background who migrate to different transnational cities. Ninna Sørensen (1998) has insightfully completed just such a comparative ethnographic study of Dominican transnational migrants in Santo Domingo, New York, and Madrid. Sørensen discusses comparatively social constructions of group identity derived from the personal migration narratives of Dominican women and men in New York and Madrid, textual analysis of "native" novels about Dominican transnational migration experiences written "from a US-based room with a view" (ibid.: 243), and interpretations of the transnational, gender-coded, symbolic content of "local" television commercials linking New York and Santo Domingo. Reflecting on the relationship between spoken, written, and read identities, Sørensen is able to develop a highly differentiated conceptualization of transnationalism that deconstructs relationships, not only between metropolitan majorities in North American and European cities and different types of Dominican "minority others," but also relationships *within* the groups of transmigrants she studies, based on emergent counter-narratives of gender relations. Everyday stories organize the transformation of space into place as Dominican migrants interpret their situatedness in old and new urban contexts and thereby culturally construct their histories and "herstories" (Sørensen, 1993, 1996, 1998). Far from essentializing their identities under the homogenizing discourse of the "migrant community," migrants, even those within the same migrating group (e.g. those moving back and forth between Santo Domingo and New York), construct different, often competing, and gender-inflected identity narratives. While relying upon an essentializing "migratory legend" of collective experience to positively differentiate themselves from other transmigrant groups in US society, these migrants also articulate a parallel, individualized, and gendered migration narrative to situate themselves and their personal experiences of displacement and relocation in the context of this collective legend. In New York, their individualized narratives are articulated in an institutional context of other competing narratives, including the transnational organizational practices of "migrant" organizations, some of whose leaders are engaged in projecting "national" traditions that construct and reinforce particular racial and gender roles inscribed in a mythic "Hispanic"

patriarchal family, while others resist the exclusion of "blackness" from Dominican national identity and in the process create a space for the inclusion
of less patriarchal Afro-Caribbean family practices in Dominican migratory
legend. Cultural and political identity are constantly (re)negotiated in these
complex cross-national institutional contexts.

Gender politics play out differently in New York and Madrid. The differences are due not only to national differences in state policies and gender
relations in the two transnational metropoles, but also to differences between
the two migratory streams in terms of class and gender composition, network
ties, and cultural differences between localities and regions of origin. Moreover, migrant organizations are less developed in Madrid than in New York
owing, in part, to the recency of the translocal migration network there.
Thus, such mediating institutions do not play an important role in the development of Dominican identity narratives in Madrid, while they continue
to matter in the Big Apple. Although the two translocalities both involve
Dominican transmigrants, the different translocal social spaces encapsulate different transnational networks, generate different identity discourses, produce
different degrees of political mobilization, and thus constitute quite different
contested terrains.

Turning next to the case of transnational business investment networks,
two useful modes of comparison come to mind. Business enterprises generate
abundant activities, forms of advertising, and other interventions that constitute forms of "self presentation" in different cultural and political settings.
We have seen above that ethnographic analysis of different forms of self-
presentation used by transnational Chinese business investors in Vancouver
and Shenzhen yielded interesting comparisons, underlining the continuing
importance of local cultural contexts in different transnational cities. It would
likewise be useful to compare the practices of multinational corporations like
Nike or McDonald's to legitimize their investment practices in different cities
and societies. This would enable us to separate global from national and local
discourses and practices and show how the three discursive spaces interact in
the social production of identities and social practices. It would also enable us
to begin to sort out the differences among the processes of appropriation and
localization of global consumer products and services in different urban and
national settings.

An excellent example of this sort of comparative urban research may be
found in James. L Watson's (1997) useful collection of case studies. Watson
and his collaborators compare the processes of marketing, appropriation, and
localization of McDonald's food and its restaurant settings in Beijing, Hong
Kong, Taipei, Seoul, and various Japanese cities. Remarkable differences in
local responses to McDonald's global reach are revealed in these fascinating
ethnographically grounded studies. For example, in Beijing a new class of
yuppies views McDonald's as a way to connect to the world outside China,

while many residents of Seoul, steeped in economic nationalism, regard eating a Big Mac as a form of cultural and economic treason (compare the studies by Yan and Bak in Watson, 1997). The studies in this book are especially useful because they avoid the essentialism often found in discussions of national appropriation of global commodities and commodity-signs. These ethnographies highlight notable class, gender, and status differences in consumption practices found within each of the East Asian social formations. Thus, in several of the East Asian transnational cities studied, women have begun to appropriate the space of the McDonald's restaurants as a kind of sanctuary from other male-dominated public settings. Likewise, while many Koreans of both sexes avoid McDonald's out of a sense of patriotism, an emergent yuppie stratum in Seoul, like their counterparts in Beijing, treats McDonald's outlets as arenas for conspicuous consumption (Watson, 1997: 9).

Another case in point is the stimulating study by David Andrews (1997) of efforts by the National Basketball Association to deploy US commodity-sign culture to create a global market for its products and media packages and become what Andrews characterizes as a "(Trans)National Basketball Association." Andrews finds that not only the NBA's media message, but also its popular reception, varies from place to place. In an effort to create local markets for their global wares, the NBA downplays the over-representation of African-American athletes in US metropolitan markets in order to appeal to white hegemony in the American marketplace, while virtually celebrating the energy and achievements of American blackness when targeting British urban youth culture. Because of these differences the mere consumption of American commodity-signs is not identical to the Americanization of local cultures. Indeed, Andrews (ibid.: 94) concludes that the appropriation of the blackness imaginary the NBA projects in Britain creates a space for resistance by young people of color in British metropoles to "the lingering racism of British imperial discourse," while in the US positive aspects of blackness and black achievement found in the British NBA advertising are unavailable for consumption and redeployment. While Andrews does not offer sufficient evidence about the consequences of differences in media reception to fully support this last conclusion, it is nonetheless clear that the way in which he frames his analysis is quite suggestive of the fruitful insights about "global localization" that can be derived by comparing the heterogeneous local ways in which corporate global media messages are received and consumed in different places. (See also Lash and Urry, 1994: 308ff.)

Turning now to the case of the networks that constitute transnational social movements, several interrelated modes of comparison come to mind. One fruitful research strategy is to investigate comparatively the dynamics of political mobilization by "global" grassroots movements like Greenpeace or Amnesty International in different transnational cities, in order to tease out the local inflections, networks, and practices which movements having global reach rely on to pursue their agendas in different cities and state formations. The same approach could be used to study the local and regional inflections of non-issue based cultural and religious movements like Islamic fundamentalism. (For studies with which to begin such comparisons see Wapner, 1995; Imig and Tarrow, 1996; Princen and Finger, 1994; Eikelman, 1997; Kane; 1997.) Relatedly, it is important to determine if transnational social movements operating in parts of the world like Western Europe, which are regulated by a network of supranational institutions, operate differently when they engage in political action in parts of the world that are not so regulated (see Tarrow, 1998: 177). It is equally important to realize, as my analysis of transnational grassroots movements in chapter 7 makes clear, that not all such transnational movements have global reach. Many, such as the Mixtec transnational leagues discussed in that chapter (see also Nagengast and Kearney, 1990; Smith, 1994), define their goals and objectives quite locally, but use new transnational public spheres and means of communication and travel to forge coalitions that encompass the entire Western hemisphere. Viewing such "local to global" movements in comparative perspective would require developing a nuanced understanding of how different local cultural and political practices change as they are deployed in extra-local arenas containing different political opportunities and constraints.

Comparing localizations of the neoliberal project

To explore the scope and limits of the neoliberal and global governance agendas it is important to consider the heterogeneous consequences of neoliberal economic policies in different cities and state formations where they have become localized (e.g. Bangkok, Jakarta, and Singapore). This type of comparative historical research would focus on the interplay of the "global" and the "local" in producing new spaces of domination, accommodation, and resistance. To highlight the usefulness of this third approach I will briefly compare the impact of neoliberal politics in San Jose, Costa Rica and Mexico City.

Richard Tardanico (1992) has analyzed the role of Costa Rica's social democratic state in mediating the impact of global economic restructuring in San Jose. Tardanico points out that cities in Latin America have displayed striking diversity in the ways in which local conditions interact with global economic restructuring processes. These diverse local differences account for a wide variety of distributional outcomes among Latin American cities, as well as different class, gender, and generational variations within cities. Unlike other Central American states, Costa Rica has had a modernizing political elite with social democratic values, that has used state policies to abolish the standing army, nationalize banks, dampen the labor movement, and incorporate the poor as social program clientele. Yet the global economic crisis has seriously disrupted this modernist arrangement. The social democratic state has been required to introduce fiscal austerity measures. In response, San Jose's urban households have pursued work-related survival strategies. The urban households have mobilized what Tardanico terms "reserve income producers," primarily middle-aged and elderly women. These women have entered informal work structures to offset job and real-income losses by other household members and general cuts in the social wage by the state.

Nevertheless, Costa Rica's political elites have tempered the negative impact of neoliberal fiscal austerity by measures such as food assistance, temporary public employment, and selective price controls, which favored the poor. This has enabled them to maintain a delicate political balance. The austerity policies have allowed them to obtain significant aid and debt relief from the US, while their social policy initiatives thus far have enabled them to maintain political stability in the face of austerity policies that have produced food riots (see Walton, 1987) and other forms of popular protest elsewhere. The structural adjustment policies pursued by the Costa Rican political formation have softened the blow of general retrenchment, while the reorganization of urban households and the expansion of informal work at the community level have mediated both the economic crisis and the state restructuring. In the face of the ongoing project of neoliberalism, the question of the social conditions and responses of displaced households in other cities and societies where welfare-state political and economic arrangements have been weakened, but where social policies to buffer the ensuing decline in living standards are absent, remains important.

This is nowhere more apparent than in the case of the implementation of neoliberalism in Mexico. The unrelenting pursuit of neoliberal policies by the PRI-dominated Mexican state has been undertaken in collaboration with the Clinton Administration and the transnational agencies of neoliberalism and global governance. State policy changes in the past decade have abrogated peasant rights to communal lands (*ejido*), deregulated commodity markets, sold large-scale public assets, reduced the social wage, and dramatically increased interest rates. To legitimate these austerity measures and integrate Mexican state policies into the global governance agenda, the PRI began to open up electoral processes that had been closed for nearly seven decades. The co-operation of the PRI-dominated state in the tri-national passage of the North American Free Trade Agreement (NAFTA) in January, 1994 triggered the Zapatista rebellion in rural Chiapas. This collision contributed significantly to an ensuing peso crisis that destabilized social and economic relations throughout Mexico. Since then, the PRI-dominated Mexican state has faced a seemingly permanent political crisis, as the political opening required by transnational actors "from above" was taken seriously by a wide variety of oppositional voices "from below," including transnational supporters of the Zapatista rebellion.

Untempered neoliberalism in Mexico increased social inequalities, swelled Mexico City's barrios with ever more rounds of landless peasants, and squeezed the urban working and middle classes to a point of no return (McMichael, 1996: 43–4). State-sponsored neoliberal policies created more billionaires than Mexico had ever anticipated. At the same time they unleashed a popular revolt against the politics of globalization and neoliberalism. Ignited by the Zapatista rebellion in rural Chiapas, and facilitated by the electoral opening initiated by PRI, this popular revolt has been multidimensional. It has included debtor protests against banks by homeowners and small business people in Mexico City and elsewhere in urban Mexico; grassroots challenges to the corruption of local and regional patronage politics throughout Mexico; widespread rural community mobilizations in support of human and communal rights; and the emergence of widespread support for the Zapatista movement's democratization agenda, ranging from mass mobilizations in Mexico City, to the social construction of a transnational coalition of Zapatista support groups linked by the internet. The politicization of the issues of globalization, neoliberalism, and governance in Mexico has ended one-party rule in three Mexican states and the national legislature and has resulted in the election of the first non-PRI Mayor of Mexico City, leftist Cothumec Cardenas (see Barkin, Ortiz, and Rosen, 1997). These developments have increased the divisions within the PRI between its authoritarian, technocratic, and populist factions. The PRI's response to the unraveling of its previously hegemonic political position has been improvisational, alternating between accommodation to and repression of the grassroots pressures for greater democratization of local communities, the state, and civil society.

In sum, while San Jose, Costa Rica is relatively quiescent politically as a result of the urban, national, and transnational responses to neoliberalism localized there, the political crisis in Mexico has been prolonged, bitter, and often violent. A different set of urban, national, and transnational networks, actions, and power relations have come together in Mexico City. These collusions and collisions have culminated in Mexico City's political transformation and in the ongoing struggle to democratize Mexican society. Globalization thus clearly takes different forms and has different effects in the cities and nation-states in which it is localized. The global and the local are not separate containers but mutually constitutive social processes.

Summing Up

The optic of transnational urbanism is preferable to the time-space compression, global cities, and postmodern urbanism approaches to urban research for several related reasons. It is an agency-oriented perspective that enables us to see how "globalization" is socially constructed by the historically specific social practices that constitute transnational networks. The "postnational" assumptions of more economistic frameworks are replaced by an approach in which the nation-state is given its due as an institutional actor implicated in the process of forming and reconstituting transnational ties. Ordinary people are viewed as creative actors involved in the social construction of transnational urbanism by the social networks they form, rather than being ignored or represented as passive objects propelled by underlying economic or cultural logics. Local forms of socioeconomic organization, political culture, and identity formation are taken into account without being erased or essentialized as backwaters of reactionary nostalgia. The rise of translocalities and the meaning-making practices that occur in these new social spaces are shown to be central to the social organization of transnational urbanism.

In this book I have sought to demonstrate that the study of transnational urbanism allows us to expand our vision to encompass the full range of cities implicated in the political–economic and sociocultural practices of transnational migrants, entrepreneurs, political activists, and institutions. It moves us beyond approaches to globalization that attribute too much power to capital, too much uniformity to urbanization, too much hierarchy to inter-urban relations, and too little autonomy to culture. In its place transnational urbanism offers an approach capable of grasping the complex differences intersecting within and between the world's cities. These differences are socially produced by the networks and circuits of social interaction intersecting in particular cities and in particular lives.

Transnational urbanism is complex and multifaceted. Although in this respect it may resemble a diamond, it is neither a thing nor a continuum of events that can easily be grasped. It is a complex process of meaning-making involving global, transnational, and local dynamics. A useful starting point along this path is to study the effects that global policies and transnational networks have on cities, local power structures, and ordinary people's lives, and the effects that particular cities and their people have on these networks of power, meaning, and identity. To execute this double move, global policies and transnational networks must be localized; localities must be transnationalized; and the criss-crossing connections among the various scales of social practice must be historicized. To envision cities as sites of transnational urbanism is a central task for present and future urban research.

Epilogue: The City as Crossroads

A Good Traveler has no fixed plans and is not intent on arriving.
Lao Tzu, 570–490 BC

I became an immigrant the day I was forbidden to remember. . . . To arrive is just an illusion.
Guillermo Gómez-Peña, field notes, Sproul Plaza, Berkeley, 1993

Societal evolutionism is still quite evident in the globalization discourses that have dominated urban theory in the past two decades. In this book I have sought to displace these evolutionary discourses with a social constructionist urban theory in which globalization is treated as an unfinished product of politically and culturally constructed social practices, rather than a structural force operating behind people's backs and inexorably determining their futures. I began this book by deconstructing three key globalization discourses that, by focusing resolutely on perceived structural transformations in world capitalism and privileging economic over sociocultural and political processes, have caused us to lose sight of this world of social practice.

The turn to the realm of social practice does not mean that urban researchers must move from a global to a purely local gaze when conducting urban research. Indeed, this book also has been about the need to include a transnational dimension in agency-oriented urban studies. By deploying the metaphor of transnational urbanism I have tried to capture the notion of the city as a crossroads of social relations constituted by the interactions of local, national, and transnational actors and the networks through which they operate. The optic of transnational urbanism brings into focus historically specific activities and projects instituted, reproduced, or transformed by these social interactions. Viewed in this light, the diversity of place-making practices, the dynamics of political conflict and accommodation, the variety of state policy-making projects, and the agency of social networks come to the forefront of urban analysis.

In Part II of this book I sought to show that as we move closer to the ground, using the methods of historicized political economy and transnational ethnography, we are rendered capable of discerning the culture and politics of specific cities, the transnational web of relations to other localities in which they are embedded, the social and spatial practices of their residents, the social organization of their everyday life, and even the identities of their subjects. As we listen to representations made in these micro-worlds we unavoidably hear many voices and thence begin to discern the full complexity of the politics of difference. This, in turn, requires us to contextualize the voices within a historicized analysis. I have therefore framed my critique of evolutionary urban theories of globalization within a historicized political–economic analysis of the spread of neoliberalism as a globalizing project of specific political, economic, and institutional agencies and networks. Perhaps the chief advantage of combining comparative historical methods with transnational ethnography in urban studies is that it forces us to consider the transnational in the local, to grasp the tension between universalizing and particularizing social forces, to discern the interplay of criss-crossing social worlds, and thus to expand the boundaries of our human imaginations.

I would like to end this book by returning to the concrete realm of "everyday life" that I have sought to redefine: the everyday viewed not as a sedentary, nostalgic site of "local culture," but as a dynamic crossroads of local, national, and transnational place-making practices. I first give the reader a tour of a few of the new social spaces of urban research that the transnational imaginary allows us to see, think about, and research under conditions of transnational urbanism. To illustrate the fruitfulness of the transnational urbanism optic, I close with a series of vignettes teasing out several of the transnational political connections that are an inseparable part of urban political life in contemporary Los Angeles and New York.

As the twentieth century has drawn to a close, the range and complexity of transnational connections constituting the terrain of transnational urbanism have come into sharper focus. These transnational connections, once largely sociocultural, have become more explicitly political, transforming the boundaries of political campaigning and social movement politics, and redefining the scope and character of community economic development. Transnational connections increasingly affect the dynamics of national electoral politics. In May, 1998, a Filipino police officer volunteered to provide advice with security and crowd logistics at political rallies in Manila, Philippines, held by his preferred presidential candidate Joseph Estrada. When Estrada eventually won, the police officer returned to his normal beat as a Filipino-American police officer in San Francisco, California (*San Francisco Chronicle*, May 9, 1998: A13). In February, 1999, an opposition member of the Guatemalan Congress got an early start on the November elections in Guatemala by actively campaigning in four major Guatemalan population centers: Miami, Chicago, San Francisco, and Los Angeles. The Congressperson reasoned that, because Guatemala had allowed dual citizenship since 1996 and over 1 million of Guatemala's 11 million citizens now live in the US, largely concentrated in these four cities, her transnational political campaigning was a reasonable expenditure of her scarce resources and time (Dolinsky, 1999).

Such transnational electoral connections are not merely found in major US "immigrant" cities. They are increasingly common throughout the world. In Jakarta, and elsewhere in Indonesia, the first free elections in 44 years were held in June, 1999. The Indonesian election was closely monitored by a transnational coalition of grassroots organizations drawn largely from other newly democratized nation-states. Organizations participating in the monitor-ing process included representatives from the National Movement for Free Elections (Namfrel) from the Philippines, the Fair Election Monitoring Alli-ance from Bangladesh, a transnational pro-democracy activist leader from Guyana, and scores of local monitoring groups from Indonesia itself, all coa-lescing around this localized transnational project. In the last years of the twentieth century similar transnational alliances have helped monitor elections in many far-flung places across the globe, including Sri Lanka, the West Bank, Cambodia, Yemen, Panama, Taiwan, Bulgaria, Chile, Kenya, and South Africa (Mydans, 1999).

Beyond the electoral arena, transnational connections increasingly shape the once largely localist field of community economic development. In 1999 a small sewing-machine factory opened in the village of Timbinal, Mexico, thanks to a "transnational public–private partnership" forged between planners for the Mexican state of Guanajuato and a group of 23 Mexican transmigrants who came to Napa, California, from Timbinal in the 1980s to work in the wine industry. This joint venture was initiated by the state planners who, aware that Mexicans living in the US send "home" between $5 billion and $6 billion annually, actively sought out investment from the migrants under the auspices of a state-sponsored program. The program, "Mi Comunidad," was created in 1997 to tap into the translocal loyalties of the state's transnational migrant communities. The joint venture provided for a resource-matching arrangement which combined migrant investment capital and state-financed training for workers and managers. The 23 transmigrant investors put $4,000 each into the plant, which now employs 35 people in a transnational com-munity economic development scheme that one commentator has described as creating "perhaps the first full-time jobs . . . in Timbinal" in the twentieth century (Quinones, 1999: A1, A6).

The collaboration I have just described is one of nine such transnational "public–private partnerships" that have established sewing-machine factories in other translocalities in Guanajuato state. "Mi Comunidad" now links these localities to such places as Atlanta, Georgia, Elgin, Illinois, and La Habra, Orange County, California, among others. The state planners point out that similar transnational development of micro-industries is occurring in other regions of Mexico, as well as in Spain. For their part, the Mexican transmigrant investors from Napa have not limited their translocal connections to the economic sphere. They have also contributed $50,000 to renovate Timbinal's church and town plaza and to build a kindergarten. Timbinal now also has a water supply financed by a combination of transmigrant contributions and a small grant from a Napa Valley winery where 12 of the transmigrants have worked for the past two decades (ibid.: A6).

Such reconfigured loyalties, identities, and place-making practices are increasingly common in the world in which we are living. Just as Mexican state planners have tapped into residual home-town loyalties by pursuing their local economic development projects on a transnational scale of social practice, so too have other social actors tapped into a complex array of cross-cutting networks, loyalties, and identities that the neoliberal discourse on globalization has sough to erase, but that the transnational scale of social practice has vividly inscribed. This practical political and geographic jumping of scale that I have termed transnational urbanism, is perhaps nowhere more materially "real" than in contemporary Los Angeles and New York. It is therefore at these two nodal points of transnational social practice that I choose to end this book.

Transnational urbanism in Los Angeles is complex and multidimensional, encompassing myriad translocal and transnational circuits in a sometimes dizzying array of criss-crossing articulations on the ground. In chapter 4 we drew a picture of the transnational entrepreneurialism involved in the formation of the ethnic economy in Los Angeles, the transnational ties implicated in the social construction of LA's Koreatown as an urban place, and the transnational political and information exchanges supporting the political organization of the Korean Immigrant Workers Advocates (KIWA) as a local political force aimed at reconfiguring the character of Korean transnationalism in Los Angeles and providing a voice to the Latino and Asian working classes who now constitute the backbone of the service sector in greater Los Angeles. These, and other flows of people, resources, and cultural practices that now link Los Angels to diverse localities in Mexico, Guatemala, El Salvador, Southeast Asia, and elsewhere, have fundamentally reconstituted the city's working-class landscape. It is important to situate these transnational migration flows in their specific historical contexts, as I have tried to do by underlining the significance of US Cold War imperial pretensions, US–Mexican bilateral relations, US labor migration and refugee policies, and the politically constructed neoliberal globalization project.

But historical contexts tell us little of what is happening on the ground as a result of these criss-crossing articulations of transnational networks of people "from between" and "from below." Peter Olney, a key organizer of the highly successful "Justice for Janitors" labor organizing campaign in Southern

California, has shown that quite a bit is indeed happening to reshape urban political life in contemporary Los Angeles as a direct result of its transnational connections. According to Olney (1993: 13), "some of the most dramatic union victories through prolonged struggle have been won by majority un-documented workforces." Many of the transnational workers engaged in these struggles have brought with them a legacy of past political and trade union experience, social capital, and of course the vast numbers that have made Los Angeles the second largest city in the world for Mexicans, Salvadorans, and Guatemalans. Moreover, in Los Angeles, union organizers have chosen a successful strategy to leverage this transnational political experience by organizing entire occupational sectors rather than single firms. This strategy worked during the 1990s precisely because the initial attraction of employers of low-paid work for largely undocumented transnational migrants had tended to concentrate them in entire occupational sectors such as janitorial work, construction, and the garment trades.

For these reasons, far from being docile or afraid of political visibility, undocumented transnational migrant workers, particularly from Mexico and Central America, have proven to be the backbone of grassroots labor organizing campaigns in Los Angeles in the past decade. In the "Justice for Janitors" campaign it was these undocumented workers that provided the militancy and political skills that enabled the Service Employees International Union (SEIU) to gain better pay and working conditions in the janitorial sector by targeting large real estate developers and the large Danish-based transnational contracting company, International Service Systems, that held the contract to clean the entertainment, financial, and legal office complex of LA's Century City. Similar militant organizing campaigns in the LA region have won dramatic victories for Latino dry-wallers who were heavily concentrated in this occupational niche within the construction sector. In another labor organizing campaign in the 1990s, a group of 1,200, largely Mexican-origin workers at an auto parts factory in greater Los Angeles, were successfully organized thanks to the self-organizing abilities of "a cadre of Mexican workers from the Federal District with experience in the trade union movement in Mexico's capital city" (ibid.: 14).

Numerous transnational sociopolitical connections beyond labor organizing have emerged in contemporary Los Angeles in the late twentieth century as elements of its transnational urbanism. The interplay of transnationalism from above (by sending states) and below (by migrant groups) is evident in the practices of numerous Mexican and Central American "home-state" and "home-town" associations in Los Angeles, now forging dual identities and promoting community development projects in various "communities of origin" south of the US border (see, for example, Goldring, 1998). Other agendas and projects inform the transnational practices "from the middle" of a wide variety of social, political, religious, and charitable organizations from Central American localities that have established affiliates in Los Angeles (Chinchilla and Hamilton, 1992: 86).

Still other transnational connections between "the middle" and the grass-roots are being sought by the numerous politicians from Mexico, Guatemala, and El Salvador who now regularly include Los Angeles among their campaign stops. Similar transnational electoral connections are now being forged on the streets of Los Angeles under various discourses and practices of "dual citizenship," which link political practices in Los Angeles to national politics in South Korea and Israel. During a week-long "state visit" to Los Angeles in 1998, South Korean President Kim Dae-jung reached out to the hundreds of thousands of Koreans and Korean-Americans living in the Los Angeles region. He announced that he was preparing legislation to empower Korean trans-national migrants to enjoy the full rights and privileges of dual-citizenship, including work, property ownership, travel, and inheritance rights. Kim urged "Koreans who live in America" to learn English well, so that they might become fully bilingual and bicultural, and thus "become valuable bridges in the future of the two nations," while conveying to their children "their ancestral history, culture, and language". In the same vein, prior to the parliamentary elections in Israel in the spring of 1999, an organization backing losing candidate Benjamin Netanyahu offered extremely cheap round-trip air fares to Tel Aviv from several US cities, including Los Angeles. Its goal was to allow likely supporters of Netanyahu who enjoyed dual citizenship to vote for him for prime minister and to support members of the Knesset from other rightist parties. Not to be outdone, transnational activist supporters of winning candidate Ehud Barak prepared to offer cheap flights for the second round of voting. Each transnational faction expected to send 5,000 voters to the polls by this method (Merl, 1999).

Transnational urbanism in Los Angeles is evident as well in the political practices of transnational social movements. On March 19, 1999, a contingent of supporters of the Zapatista Army for National Liberation (EZLN) traveled south from Los Angeles to the San Diego–Tijuana border zone to participate in a cross-border rally in support of a *consulta*, or national referendum, which the Zapatistas were sponsoring throughout Mexico on March 21. One of the participants in the rally was Jesus Corona, a representative of a Los Angeles-based organization, the Zapatista Front for National Liberation. Corona, a self-described "Mexican residing abroad," stood on the US side of the border for two hours clad in peasant garb and waving a massive Zapatista banner. He and his compatriots shouted slogans of support to four Zapatista delegates and several dozen banner-waving and slogan-chanting US and Mexican supporters of the Zapatistas who stood on the Mexican side of the 15-feet high border fence.

This rally was part of a transnational effort by the Zapatistas to mobilize supporters from outside Mexico to bring pressure to bear on the Mexican state

and society. The widest and deepest support for the Zapatista cause in the US
is concentrated in the Southern California region in general, and Los Angeles
in particular. Numerous polling places for the *consulta* were set up throughout
the region. The polling places included the downtown Los Angeles headquarters of Local 11 of the Hotel and Restaurant Employees Union, the Peace
Center located on Third Street in Los Angeles, and the LA and Santa Ana
offices of Hermanidad Mexicana Nacional.

Lydia Brazon is the Executive Director of the Chiapas '98 Coalition, an
alliance of 65 of the over 100 "brigades" organized in the US to support the
Zapatista cause. According to Brazon these transnational voting arrangements
in the *consulta* came about as a result of the translocal connections forged
between Los Angeles transnational activists and the Zapatista leadership in
Chiapas. In her words: "There were some serious objections up here because
only people living in Mexico could vote in the *consulta*. . . . The Chicanos got
all upset . . . so they got that restriction changed by the Zapatistas" (Schou,
1999: 4). As a result of these interactions, any Mexican citizen was allowed to
vote in the *consulta,* regardless of where they lived or whether or not they
possessed an official Mexican voting certificate. In a final transnational twist to
this story, the ballots cast in the "national" referendum by "Mexicans residing
abroad" were gathered by pro-Zapatista organizations in the US with assistance from the Humanitarian Law Project, a UN-registered NGO whose
regular activities include election monitoring in Mexico and elsewhere.

Transnational urbanism in New York, as in Los Angeles, is equally complex
and multidimensional, encompassing myriad transnational ties and translocal
circuits of communication. Consider the following. At the India Day Parade
in New York City, in August, 1998, the State Bank of India set up a booth to
advertise the selling of a bond offering a state-guaranteed 7.75 percent rate of
interest to Indian transmigrants and Indian-Americans, both officially recognized in India as "non-resident Indians." The activity was part of a worldwide
two-week campaign by bank officers to raise at least $2 billion from members
of the Indian diaspora through the bond offering. The bonds were made
available at local branches of the State Bank of India and at Citibank branches
that offer services to non-resident Indians. The State Bank of India officials
advertised the bond sale in the "local" Indian media in New York, sponsored
dinners at Indian restaurants in midtown Manhattan, and set up booths at
shopping strips, all designed to promote the discourse: "Make money. Help
the motherland." Their $2 billion transnational goal was reached in less than
two weeks and the banking officials set their sights on $3 billion by the
campaign's end. The proceeds from the bond sale were earmarked to finance
major infrastructure development projects in India, including road construction and the extension of telephone lines (Sengupta, 1998). By this means the
transnational scale of social practice was used to finance a nationalist developmental agenda by mobilizing worldwide diasporic loyalties. This story illustrates

that, on the ground, nationalism and transnationalism are mutually constitutive rather than antagonistic social processes. Neither has been erased by an abstract logic of globalization operating behind people's backs or in a dematerialized space of flows.

This is only one pointed example of the multidimensional transnational urbanism now an inseparable part of everyday urban life in New York City. In this book we have discussed other dimensions of New York's transnational urbanism. The Big Apple's employment opportunity structure has generated the collective resources that have enabled indigenous Mexican migrants from Ticuani to form a "home-town" association in New York, send funds to their village of origin to finance community development projects, and thereby become key players in the local community power structure "back home." Within the Big Apple these same translocal social actors have secured their occupational niches in the New York labor market by inserting themselves into a place within the prevailing local racial hierarchy. They have done so by constructing an ethnic identity as "hard-working indigenous Mexicans," a discursive and practical move which positions them slightly above their fellow "Latinos" from Puerto Rico (see R. Smith, 1998). These male transmigrants improve their power and status in Ticuani, while fitting into the local racial hierarchy in New York, at the same time that transmigrant women orchestrating their lives between Santo Domingo, Dominican Republic, and New York City, construct migratory legends which empower them to transgress local gendered boundaries at both ends of their transmigrant circuit (see Sørensen, 1998).

In the arena of transnational electoral politics mentioned above, New York City Mayor Rudy Giuliani makes regular trips to Santo Domingo, Dominican Republic to campaign for re-election. Under the aegis of various dual-citizenship and dual-nationality arrangements, political candidates from Guatemala, the Dominican Republic, Haiti, Colombia, Mexico, and elsewhere return the favor. In the arena of social movement politics, the Big Apple is a site of transnational social mobilizations such as those linking labor activists in El Salvador with activists in New York who have organized consumer boycotts against The Gap clothing chain in order to change sweatshop conditions in the textile factories in El Salvador that supply clothing to The Gap.

The reconstruction of New York's Chinatown in the past two decades is a paradigm case of the contested politics of place-making that is a further hallmark of New York's transnational urbanism. In Chinatown, heterogeneous "Chinese" transnational networks of investment, migration, power, and cultural production from Guangdong, Fujian, Hong Kong, and Taiwan intersect with each other and interact with local institutional and organizational actors and agents of the local and national state in a variety of localized struggles for power, space, place, and identity. The complex social relations of power and meaning intersecting in Chinatown reconstruct its urban space and sense of place and confound all attempts to homogenize and essentialize this "ethnic neighborhood" and frame it within conventional discourses of urban ethnic politics.

To underline the complexity of the social relations of transnational urbanism, I will end my narration of transnational urbanism and this book by amplifying upon my previous discussion of the complex political discourses and conflicts triggered by the shooting of Amadou Diallo. Recall that Diallo was the unarmed transnational migrant street peddler from Guinea who was killed while standing in his doorway by the Street Crime Unit of the New York Police Department. I previously stressed the central political role played by Amadou Diallo's mother, Kadiatou Diallo, who may be seen as a kind of quintessential transnational multipositional, multilingual, and multicultural subject, whose shifting social locations in different discursive domains enabled her to engage in the politics of representation quite differently in different socially structured networks of meaning and power. In New York City, immediately following the shooting, Kadiatou lent her transnational voice and her symbolic presence as a grieving mother to a civil disobedience campaign against police brutality organized by the Reverend Al Sharpton, a campaign that otherwise might have been interpreted as a largely local protest, led by various political enemies of Mayor Rudy Giuliani, who regarded the Diallo incident as a political opportunity to embarrass the controversial mayor. When she returned to her native Guinea to bury her son, Kadiatou Diallo became a kind of instant national celebrity, gracefully adapting to a variety of religious ceremonies and political rituals organized there in reaction to the killing of her son. The Government of Guinea put a fleet of cars at the Diallo family's disposal, surrounded Kadiatou with prominent government officials, and arranged prayer services, motorcades, state television and radio appearances by the family, and formal ceremonies in its honor. In these ways, the Diallo killing in New York City was appropriated as part of a nationalist discourse in Guinea. Thus, at a prayer service for Amadou Diallo held at the country's largest mosque in Conakry, the nation's capital, Foreign Minister Lamine Kamara declared that "Guinea decided this was not just a family affair but a national affair." Part of the political agenda of the Foreign Ministry was to assuage the fears of the many other transnational families that are part of the current reality of everyday life in Guinea. As Fanta Kouyat, a Foreign Ministry official who had herself lived in New York City as a child, explained: "We all know that in this or that family there is a cousin or a brother who is in America. . . . So we think that what happened to this family could happen to any family here" (Sachs, 1999a).

Explaining her ability to adapt serenely yet firmly to the new political roles that have been thrust upon her by the play of circumstances surrounding her son's death, Kadiatou Diallo stated simply: "Leadership is not something I can impose on myself, but sacrificing myself and being an example would be very good – to change bad into good" (quoted in Sachs, 1999a). As part of this role, Kadiatou re-entered the political arena of US civil rights politics on a national scale several months after burying her son in Guinea. When she returned to New York she was honored by New York City religious leaders at an interdenominational prayer service devoted to her son's memory organized by John Cardinal O'Connor (Wilgoren, 1999). She then traveled to Chicago to participate in a rally that was an element of a multi-city civil rights campaign against police brutality triggered by the Diallo shooting. During this stage of her political journey, she appeared in Chicago with the Reverend Jesse Jackson at a meeting of his political organization, Operation PUSH/ Rainbow Coalition. Jackson termed the Diallo case "the caboose of a long train of abuses" and expressed his belief that Kadiatou Diallo could serve as an icon to "mobilize a national consciousness" about abusive police practices (Sachs, 1999b).

Lest it be thought that Kadiatou Diallo has become an empty signifier, a malleable icon of other people's discursive agendas rather than an acting political subject in her own right, it is important to add a bit more detail to the picture. Mrs. Diallo is a complex multipositional subject who possesses considerable social and cultural capital and worldly experience. She spent many years outside of Guinea, with her first husband, Saikou Amad Diallo, who was a trader in commodities in neighboring Liberia. There she became trilingual by adding English to French and her native language at a private college. The couple had four children, including Amadou, the eldest. The family eventually moved to Thailand and Singapore, where she and her husband ran a business importing gemstones. Following her divorce in 1994 she remained in Thailand for a time to enable her children to continue their studies at an international school where classes were conducted in English and French. She eventually returned to Guinea and later remarried. She now runs a gem trading company in Guinea while working out arrangements for a joint venture with an investor from Australia in the mining sector (ibid.). On the day that her son Amadou was killed, her first husband, Saikou, was in Vietnam, where he now lives and works (Harden, 1999). Throughout the various stages of her personal and political journey, Kadiatou and her relatives have stressed that theirs is a family of education and means that is counted as part of the Guinean elite. The Foreign Minister mentioned earlier in my narrative is a close friend of the family. Although Guinea is one of the poorest countries in Africa, Kadiatou lives with all the conveniences of global communications: e-mail, fax, satellite television, and cellular telephones.

In her discursive interventions into the political worlds in which she has recently moved, Mrs. Diallo has selectively entered the battlefield. She steadfastly resisted initial media representations of her son as a poor immigrant, calling attention to her own relatively privileged family background (Sachs,

1999b). She forcefully rebutted charges by Mayor Giuliani that she had spurned his offer of help after the shooting at the behest of Reverend Al Sharpton, rather than because of her awareness that the mayor had defended the police actions that resulted in the killing of her son. In her words: "I'm a woman, a mother, and I understand who he is. I saw him on TV when I got here and he said the cops were good cops. So with or without Reverend Al, I would say to the Mayor the same thing. He could not get to me" (quoted in Sachs, 1999b; see also Wilgoren, 1999). Kadiatou Diallo's public rhetoric has been decidedly free of racial divisiveness as she casts her own calls for accountability for the death of her son in more universalistic, at times even religious, terms (see Wilgoren, 1999; Sachs, 1999b). She has insisted that it is her son and not she that is iconic and that she wants him to live on as a symbol of youth and of "all the innocent people who are victims of police brutality" (Sachs, 1999a).

In the last instance, the complex causes and effects of this "temporarily sutured" transnational political subject, and the patterned local, national, and transnational networks through which she moves, embody my social theory of transnational urbanism. The protean transnationalism of this single social actor, Kadiatou Diallo, recalls a key insight of Jean-François Lyotard that urban theorists and researchers would do well to keep in mind as they think about the social relations of power and meaning intersecting in particular cities and in particular lives. Each "self," Lyotard (1984: 15) tells us,

> exists in a fabric of relations that is now more complex and mobile than ever before. Young or old, man or woman, rich or poor, a person is always located at 'nodal points' of specific communication circuits. . . . Or better: one is always located at a post through which various kinds of messages pass. No one . . . is ever entirely powerless over the messages that traverse and position him [or her] at the post of sender, addressee, or referent.

To understand the future of urban change we must therefore focus our attention upon the communication circuits, no matter how complex, by which people are connected to each other, make sense of their lives, and act upon the worlds that they see, in which they dwell, and through which they travel.

References

Abu-Lughod, Janet Lippman (1995) "Comparing Chicago, New York, and Los Angeles: Testing Some World City Hypotheses," in Paul L. Knox and Peter J. Taylor (eds) *World Cities in a World System*. Cambridge and New York: Cambridge University Press, pp. 171–91.

Ahmad, Aijaz (1987) "Jameson's Rhetoric of Otherness and the National Allegory," *Social Text*, 17 (6): 3–25.

Albrow, Martin, John Eade, Jorg Dürrschmidt, and Neil Washbourne (1997) "The Impact of Globalization on Sociological Concepts: Community, Culture and Milieu," in John Eade (ed.) *Living the Global City*. New York and London: Routledge, pp. 20–36.

Anderson, Benedict (1983) *Imagined Communities: Reflections on the Growth and Spread of Nationalism*. New York and London: Verso. Reprinted 1991.

Anderson, J. (1993) "Worldwide Freedom in Grim Decline," *San Francisco Examiner* (December 17): A23.

Andrews, David L. (1997) "The (Trans)National Basketball Association: American Commodity-sign Culture and Global–Local Conjuncturalism," in Ann Cvetkovich and Douglas Kellner (eds) *Articulating the Global and the Local: Globalization and Cultural Studies*. Boulder, Col. and Oxford: Westview Press, pp. 72–101.

Anzaldúa, Gloria (1987) *Borderlands: La Frontera: The New Mestiza*. San Francisco: Spinsters/aunt lute.

Appadurai, Arjun (1990) "Disjuncture and Difference in the Global Cultural Economy," *Public Culture*, 2 (2): 1–24.

—— (1991) "Global Ethnoscapes: Notes and Queries for a Transnational Anthropology," in R. G. Fox (ed.) *Recapturing Anthropology: Working in the Present*. Santa Fe, N. Mex.: School of American Research Press, pp. 191–210.

—— (1996) *Modernity at Large: Cultural Dimensions of Globalization*. Minneapolis: University of Minnesota Press.

Arvidson, Enid (1995) "Cognitive Mapping and Class Politics: Toward a Nondeterminist Image of the City," *Rethinking Marxism*, 8 (2): 8–23.

Barber, Benjamin R. (1995) *Jihad vs. McWorld*. New York: Times Books.

Barkin, David, Irene Ortiz, and Fred Rosen (1997) "Globalization and Resistance: The Remaking of Mexico," *NACLA Report on the Americas*, 30 (4) (summer): 14–27.

Barry, Dan (1999) "In Police Shooting, Civil Disobedience On a Tight Schedule," *New York Times* (March 19): A1, A17.

Basch, Linda, Nina Glick Schiller, and Cristina Szanton Blanc (1994) *Nations Unbound: Transnational Projects, Postcolonial Predicaments and the Deterritorialized Nation-State.* New York: Gordon and Breach.

Bauman, Zygmunt (1998) *Globalization: The Human Consequences.* New York: Columbia University Press.

Beauregard, Robert A. and Anne Haila (1997) "The Unavoidable Incompleteness of the City," *American Behavioral Scientist*, 41 (3) (Nov./Dec.): 327–41.

Beinart, Peter (1997) "An Illusion for our Time," *New Republic* (October 20): 20–4.

Benton, Lauren (1996) "From the World Systems Perspective to Institutional World History: Culture and Economy in Global Theory," *Journal of World History*, 7 (2): 261–95.

Bernstein, Charles (1987) "Centering the Postmodern," *Socialist Review*, 17 (6): 48–56.

Bird, Jon (1993) "Dystopia on the Thames," in Jon Bird, Barry Curtis, Tim Putnam, George Robertson, and Lisa Tickner (eds) *Mapping the Futures: Local Cultures, Global Change.* London and New York: Routledge, pp. 120–35.

Blanc, Cristina Szanton (1997) "The Thoroughly Modern 'Asian': Capital, Culture and Nation in Thailand and the Philippines," in Aihwa Ong and Donald Nonini (eds) *Ungrounded Empires.* New York: Routledge, pp. 261–86.

Boggs, Carl (1986) *Social Movements and Political Power.* Philadelphia: Temple University Press.

Bondi, Liz (1990) "Feminism, Postmodernism, and Geography: Space for Women," *Antipode*, 22 (2): 156–67.

Brecher, Jeremy and Tim Costello (1994) *Global Village or Global Pillage.* Boston: South End Press.

Brysk, Alison (1995) "Hearts and Minds: Bringing Symbolic Politics Back In," *Polity* 27 (4) (summer): 559–85.

Buroway, Michael (1991) "The Extended Case Method," in Michael Buroway, et al. *Ethnography Unbound: Power and Resistance in the Modern Metropolis.* Berkeley, Los Angeles, and London: University of California Press, pp. 271–87.

Campbell, David (1996) "Political Processes, Transversal Politics, and the Anarchical World," in Michael J. Shapiro and Hayward R. Alker (eds) *Challenging Boundaries.* Minneapolis: University of Minnesota Press, pp. 7–31.

Castells, Manuel (1983) *The City and the Grassroots.* Berkeley and Los Angeles: University of California Press.

—— (1984) "Space and Society: Managing the New Historical Relationships," in Michael Peter Smith (ed.) *Cities in Transformation.* Beverly Hills, Calif. and London: Sage, pp. 235–60.

—— (1996) *The Rise of the Network Society.* Oxford: Blackwell Publishers.

—— (1997) *The Power of Identity.* Oxford: Blackwell Publishers.

—— (1998) *End of Millennium.* Oxford: Blackwell Publishers.

de Certeau, Michel (1984) *The Practice of Everyday Life.* Berkeley: University of California Press.

Chase-Dunn, Christopher (1984) "Urbanization in the World System: New Directions for Research," in Michael Peter Smith (ed.) *Cities in Transformation.* Beverly Hills, Calif. and London: Sage, pp. 111–20.

Chinchilla, Norma Stolz and Nora Hamilton (1992) "Seeking Refuge in the City of Angels: The Central American Community," in Gerry Riposa and Carolyn Dersch (eds) *City of Angels*. Dubuque, Iowa: Kendall/Hunt, pp. 83–100.

Cho, Sumi K. (1993) "Korean Americans vs. African Americans: Conflict and Construction," in Robert Gooding-Williams (ed.) *Reading Rodney King – Reading Urban Uprising*. New York and London: Routledge, pp. 196–211.

Clements, Mike (1992) "Drywallers' Strike Nails Down a Principle," *Los Angeles Times* (November 16): B7.

Clifford, James (1987) "Of Other Peoples: Beyond the 'Salvage' Paradigm," in Hal Foster (ed.) *Discussions in Contemporary Culture*. Seattle: Bay Press, pp. 121–30.

—— (1992) "Traveling Cultures," in Lawrence Grossberg, Cary Nelson, and Paula Treicher (eds) *Cultural Studies*. New York: Routledge, pp. 96–116.

Clifford, James and George E. Marcus (eds) (1986) *Writing Culture: The Politics and Poetics of Ethnography*. Berkeley and Los Angeles: University of California Press.

Comision Economica para America Latina y el Caribe (1991) *Remesas y Economia Familiar en El Salvador, Guatemala y Nicaragua* (Junio).

Connor, Steven (1989) *Postmodernist Culture*. Oxford: Blackwell Publishers.

—— (1993) "Between Earth and Air: Value, Culture, and Futurity," in Jon Bird, Barry Curtis, Tim Putnam, George Robertson, and Lisa Tickner (eds) *Mapping the Futures*. London and New York: Routledge, pp. 229–36.

Cooke, Philip (1986) "Modernity, Postmodernity, and the City," *Theory, Culture and Society*, 5: 475–92.

—— (1988) "The Postmodern Condition and the City," *Comparative Urban and Community Research*, 1: 62–80.

Coombe, Rosemary J. and Paul Stoller (1994) "X Marks the Spot: Ambiguities of African Trading in the Commerce of the Black Public Sphere," *Public Culture*, 7: 249–74.

Cox, Kevin (ed.) (1997a) *Spaces of Globalization*. New York: Guilford Press.

—— (1997b) "Introduction: Globalization and Its Politics in Question," in Kevin Cox (ed.) *Spaces of Globalization*. New York: Guilford Press, pp. 1–18.

—— (1997c) "Globalization and the Politics of Distribution: A Critical Assessment," in Kevin Cox (ed.) *Spaces of Globalization*. New York: Guilford Press, pp. 115–36.

—— (1998) "Spaces of Dependence, Spaces of Engagement, and the Politics of Scale, or: Looking for Local Politics," *Political Geography*, 17 (1) (January): 1–23.

Crotty, James and Gary Dymski (1998) "Can the Korean Labor Movement Defeat the IMF?" *Dollars and Sense* (Nov./Dec.): 16–20.

Curry, James and Martin Kenney (1999) "The Paradigmatic City: Postindustrial Illusion and the Los Angeles School," *Antipode*, 31 (1): 1–28.

Cvetkovich, Ann and Douglas Kellner (eds) (1997) *Articulating the Global and the Local: Globalization and Cultural Studies*. Boulder, Col. and Oxford: Westview Press.

Davis, Mike (1990) *City of Quartz*. London: Verso.

—— (1992) "Burning All Illusions in LA," in Don Hazen (ed.) *Inside the LA Riots*. New York: Institute for Alternative Journalism, pp. 97–100.

Dear, Michael (1986) "Postmodernism and Planning," *Society and Space*, 4: 367–84.

—— (1991a) "The Premature Demise of Postmodern Urbanism," *Cultural Anthropology*, 6 (4) (Nov.): 538–52.

—— (1991b) "Taking Los Angeles Seriously: Time and Space in the Postmodern City," *Architecture California*, 13 (2): 36–42.

Dear, Michael and Steven Flusty (1999) "Postmodern Urbanism," *Annals of the Association of American Geographers*, 88 (1): 50–72.

Deutsche, Rosalyn (1991) "Boy's Town," *Society and Space*, 9: 5–30.

Derrida, Jacques (1978) *Writing and Difference*. London: Routledge and Kegan Paul.

—— (1981) *Positions*. Chicago: University of Chicago Press.

—— (1985) *The Ear of the Other*. New York: Schocken.

Dicken, Peter (1997) "Transnational Corporations and Nation-States," *International Social Science Journal*, 151: 77–89.

Dolinsky, Lewis (1999) "Guatemalan Campaign Goes North," *San Francisco Chronicle* (February 19): A12.

Drainville, Andre (1998) "The Fetishism of Global Civil Society," in M. P. Smith and L. E. Guarnizo (eds) *Transnationalism from Below*. New Brunswick, NJ: Transaction, pp. 35–63.

Eade, John (ed.) (1997) *Living the Global City: Globalization as a Local Process*. London and New York: Routledge.

Eikelman, Dale (1997) "Trans-state Islam and Security," in S. Rudolph and J. Piscatori (eds) *Transitional Religion and Fading States*. Boulder, Col. and Oxford: Westview Press, pp. 27–46.

Elizondo, Sergio (1989) "ABS: Aztlan, the Borderlands, and Chicago," in Rudolfo Anaya and Francisco Lomerli (eds) *Aztlan: Essays on the Chicano Homeland*. Albuquerque: University of New Mexico Press, pp. 205–18.

Espinoza, S. (1993) "Remembering the Pain: Female Immigrants Tell of Abuse," *San Francisco Chronicle* (March 9): A11.

Farley, Maggie (1998) "Indonesians Scapegoat Ethnic Chinese," *San Francisco Examiner* (February 1): A23.

Feagin, Joe R. and Michael Peter Smith (1987) "Cities and the New International Division of Labor: An Overview," in M. P. Smith and J. R. Feagin (eds) *The Capitalist City*. Oxford: Blackwell Publishers, pp. 3–34.

Feagin, Joe R., Anthony M. Orum, and Gideon Sjoberg (1991) *A Case for the Case Study*. Chapel Hill and London: University of North Carolina Press.

Featherstone, Mike (ed.) (1990) *Global Culture: Nationalism, Globalization and Modernity*. London: Sage.

Fisher, Robert and Joe Kling (1989) "Community Mobilization: Prospects for the Future," *Urban Affairs Quarterly*, 25 (Dec.): 200–11.

Foucault, Michel (1977) *Power/Knowledge*, ed. Colin Gordon. New York: Pantheon Books.

Freeman, James M. (1989) *Hearts of Sorrow: Vietnamese-American Lives*. Stanford, Calif.: Stanford University Press.

Friedmann, John (1986) "The World City Hypothesis," *Development and Change*, 17 (1): 69–84.

—— (1995) "Where We Stand: A Decade of World City Research," in P. L. Knox and P. J. Taylor (eds) *World Cities in a World System*. Cambridge: Cambridge University Press, pp. 21–47.

Friedmann, John and Goetz Wolff (1982) "World City Formation: An Agenda for Research and Action," *International Journal of Urban and Regional Research*, 6 (2): 309–39.

Garcia, Kenneth J. (1992) "After Years of Boom, Los Angeles Hits Skids," *San Francisco Chronicle* (December 21): A1, A8.

—— (1994) "State's History of Intolerance to Immigrants," *San Francisco Chronicle* (December 28): A13.

Garfinkle, Harold (1991) "Respecification," in Graham Button (ed.) *Ethnomethodology and the Human Sciences*. New York: Cambridge University Press, pp. 10–19.

Geertz, Clifford (1983) *Local Knowledge: Further Essays in Interpretive Anthropology*. New York: Basic Books.

Gertler, Meric S. (1997) "Between the Global and the Local: The Spatial Limits to Productive Capital," in K. Cox (ed.) *Spaces of Globalization*. New York: Guilford Press, pp. 45–63.

Gibson-Graham, J. K. (1996/1997) "Querying Globalization," *Rethinking Marxism*, 9 (1) (spring): 1–27.

Giddens, Anthony (1991) *Modernity and Self-identity: Self and Society in the Late Modern Age*. Stanford, Calif.: Stanford University Press.

Gilbert, Melissa R. (1997) "Feminism and Difference in Urban Geography," *Urban Geography*, 18 (2): 166–79.

Glick Schiller, Nina and Georges Fouron (1998) "Transnational Lives and National Identities: The Identity Politics of Haitian Immigrants," in M. P. Smith and L. E. Guarnizo (eds.) *Transnationalism from Below*. New Brunswick, NJ: Transaction, pp. 130–63.

Goldring, Luin (1998) "The Power of Status in Transnational Social Fields," in M. P. Smith and L. E. Guarnizo (eds) *Transnationalism from Below*. New Brunswick, NJ: Transaction, pp. 165–95.

Gordon, David (1988) "The Global Economy: New Edifice or Crumbling Foundations?" *New Left Review* (March/April): 24–64.

Goss, Jan (1997) "Representing and Re-presenting the Contemporary City," *Urban Geography*, 18: 180–8.

Gray, John (1998) *False Dawn: The Delusions of Global Capitalism*. London: Granta Books.

Gregory, Steven (1998) *Black Corona: Race and the Politics of Place in an Urban Community*. Princeton, NJ: Princeton University Press.

Grosfoguel, Ramón (1995) "Global Logics in the Caribbean City System: The Case of Miami," in Paul L. Knox and Peter J. Taylor (eds) *World Cities in a World System*. Cambridge and New York: Cambridge University Press, pp. 156–70.

Gross, Jane (1993) "Los Angeles Schools: Hobbled and Hurting," *New York Times* (February 16): C11.

Grossberg, Lawrence (1988) "Putting the Pop Back in Postmodernism," in Andrew Ross (ed.) *Universal Abandon? The Politics of Postmodernism*. Minneapolis: University of Minnesota Press, pp. 166–90.

Guarnizo, Luis Eduardo (1994) "Los Dominicanyork: The Making of a Binational Society," *Annals of the American Academy of Political and Social Science* (May).

—— (1996) "The Nation-state and Grassroots Transnationalism: Comparing Mexican and Dominican Transmigration." Paper presented at 118th Annual American Ethnological Association Meeting, San Juan, Puerto Rico, April.

—— (1998) "The Rise of Transnational Social Formations: Mexican and Dominican State Responses to Transnational Migration," *Political Power and Social Theory*, 12: 45–94.

—— (1999) Personal conversations on transnational migrant networks.

Guarnizo, Luis Eduardo and Michael Peter Smith (1998) "The Locations of Trans-nationalism," in M. P. Smith and L. E. Guarnizo (eds) *Transnationalism from Below*. New Brunswick, NJ: Transaction, pp. 3–34.

Gupta, Akhil and James Ferguson (1997a) "Beyond 'Culture': Space, Identity, and the Politics of Difference," in A. Gupta and J. Ferguson (eds) *Culture, Power and Place*. Durham, NC and London: Duke University Press, pp. 33–51.

—— (eds) (1997b) *Culture, Power, Place: Explorations in Critical Anthropology*. Durham, NC and London: Duke University Press.

—— (1997c) "Culture, Power, and Place: Ethnography at the End of an Era," in A. Gupta and J. Ferguson (eds) *Culture, Power and Place*. Durham, NC and London: Duke University Press, pp. 3–29.

Gurr, Ted Robert and Desmond S. King (1987) *The State and the City*. London: Macmillan.

Hagan, Jacqueline (1994) *Deciding to be Legal: A Maya Community in Houston*. Philadelphia: Temple University Press.

Hall, Stuart (1988) "Brave New World," *Marxism Today*, 24–9.

—— (1991) "Old and New Identities, Old and New Ethnicities," in Anthony King (ed.) *Culture, Globalization, and the World System*. Current Debates in Art History 3, State University of New York at Binghampton: 41–68.

Hannerz, Ulf (1996) *Transnational Connections*. London and New York: Routledge.

Harden, Elaine (1999) "Slain Man's Mother Rejects Mayor's Aid," *New York Times* (February 11): B8.

Harloe, Michael, C. G. Pickvance, and John Urry (eds) (1990) *Place, Policy, and Politics: Do Localities Matter?* London: Unwin Hyman.

Harris, Richard and Robert Lewis (1999) "Constructing a Fault(y) Zone: Misrepresentations of American Cities and Suburbs, 1900–1950," *Annals of the American Association of Geographers*, 88 (4): 622–39.

Hart, Nicky (1989) "Gender and the Rise and Fall of Class Politics," *New Left Review*, 175 (May/June): 19–47.

Harvey, David (1973) *Social Justice and the City*. Baltimore: Johns Hopkins University Press.

—— (1978) "The Urban Process Under Capitalism," *International Journal of Urban and Regional Research*, 2 (1): 101–32.

—— (1985a) *Consciousness and the Urban Experience*. Oxford: Blackwell Publishers.

—— (1985b) *The Urbanization of Capital*. Oxford: Blackwell Publishers.

—— (1987) "Three Myths in Search of a Reality in Urban Studies," *Society and Space*, 5: 367–76.

—— (1989) *The Condition of Postmodernity*. Oxford: Blackwell Publishers.

—— (1990) "Between Space and Time: Reflections on the Geographical Imagination," *Annals of the Association of American Geographers*, 80: 418–34.

—— (1992) "Postmodern Morality Plays," *Antipode*, 25 (4): 300–26.

—— (1993) "From Space to Place and Back Again: Reflections on the Condition of Postmodernity," in Jon Bird, Barry Curtis, Tim Putnam, George Robertson, and Lisa Tickner (eds) *Mapping the Futures*. New York and London: Routledge, pp. 3–29.

—— (1995) "Nature, Politics and Possibilities: A Debate and Discussion with David Harvey and Donna Haraway," *Environment and Planning D: Society and Space*, 13: 507–27.

—— (1996) *Justice, Nature and the Geography of Difference.* Oxford: Blackwell Publishers.

Hazen, Don (ed.) (1993) *Inside the LA Riots.* New York: Institute for Alternative Journalism.

Hegman, Susan (1989) "History, Ethnography, Myth: Some Notes on the 'Indian Centered' Narrative," *Social Text,* 23 (fall/winter): 145–58.

Henderson, Jeffrey (1989) "The Political Economy of Technological Transformation in Hong Kong," in Michael Peter Smith (ed.) *Pacific Rim Cities in the World Economy.* New Brunswick, NJ: Transaction, pp. 102–55.

Herod, Andrew (1997) "Labor as Agent of Globalization and as a Global Agent," in Kevin Cox (ed.) *Spaces of Globalization.* New York: Guilford Press, pp. 167–200.

Herzog, Lawrence A. (1990) *Where North Meets South: Cities, Space, and Politics on the US–Mexico Border.* Austin: Center for Mexican American Studies, University of Texas.

Hill, Richard Child and Kuniko Fujita (1995) "Osaka's Tokyo Problem," *International Journal of Urban and Regional Research,* 19 (2): 181–93.

Hirschman, Albert O. (1970) *Exit, Voice and Loyalty.* Cambridge, Mass.: Harvard University Press.

Hirst, Paul and Grahame Thompson (1995) "Globalization and the Future of the Nation-state," *Economy and Society,* 24 (3) (Aug.): 408–42.

—— (1996) *Globalization in Question.* Cambridge: Polity Press.

Holmes, Steven A. (1999) "New York City Faces a Study of Police Acts," *New York Times* (March 6): A1, A12.

Hsing, You-tien (1997) "Building *Guanzxi* Across the Straits: Taiwanese Capital and Local Chinese Bureaucrats," in Aihwa Ong and Donald Nonini (eds) *Ungrounded Empires.* New York: Routledge, pp. 143–64.

Hutcheon, Linda (1988) *A Poetics of Postmodernism.* New York and London: Routledge.

—— (1989) *The Politics of Postmodernism.* New York and London: Routledge.

Imig, Doug and Sidney Tarrow (1996) "The Europeanizaton of Movements?" Ithaca, NY: Institute for European Studies Working Paper No. 96, Cornell University.

International Monetary Fund (1991) *Balance of Payments Statistics Yearbook,* Vol. 42, Part I.

Jackson, Peter (1991) "Mapping Meanings: A Cultural Critique of Locality Studies," *Environment and Planning A,* (23): 215–28.

—— (1992) *Maps of Meaning.* London and New York: Routledge.

Jameson, Frederic (1983) "Postmodernism and Consumer Society," in Hal Foster (ed.) *The Anti-Aesthetic.* Port Townsend, Washington: Bay Press, pp. 111–25.

—— (1984) "Postmodernism, or the Cultural Logic of Late Capitalism," *New Left Review,* 146: 53–92.

—— (1989) "Marxism and Postmodernism," *New Left Review,* 176 (July/Aug.): 31–46.

—— (1991) *Postmodernism: Or, the Cultural Logic of Late Capitalism.* Durham, NC: Duke University Press.

—— (1998) *The Cultural Turn.* London and New York: Verso.

Jenson, Jane (1990) "Different But Not Exceptional: The Feminism of Permeable Fordism," *New Left Review,* 184 (Nov./Dec.): 58–68.

Johnson, James H., Walter Farrell, and Melvin Oliver (1993) "Seeds of the Los Angeles Rebellion of 1992," *International Journal of Urban and Regional Research,* 17: 115–19.

Johnson, James H., Cloyzelle K. Jones, Walter C. Farrell, and Melvin Oliver (1992) "The Los Angeles Rebellion: A Retrospective View," *Economic Development Quarterly*, 6 (4) (November): 356–72.

Kane, Ousmane (1997) "Muslim Missionaries and African States," in S. Rudolph and J. Piscatori (eds) *Transnational Religion and Fading States*. Boulder, Col. and Oxford: Westview Press, pp. 47–62.

Kang, Connie (1998a) "Dual Citizenship Plans for Korean Americans," *San Francisco Examiner* (June 14): 10.

—— (1998b) "Activism Opens Generational Rift in Koreatown Workplaces," *Los Angeles Times* (September 6): A1.

Katznelson, Ira (1981) *City Trenches*. New York: Pantheon Books.

Kayatenik, Serap A. and David F. Ruccio (1998) "Global Fragments: Subjectivity and Class Politics in Discourses of Globalization," *Economy and Society*, 27 (Feb.): 74–96.

Kearney, Michael (1991) "Borders and Boundaries of State and Self at the End of Empire," *Journal of Historical Sociology*, 4 (March): 52–74.

—— (1995) "The Effects of Transnational Culture, Economy, and Migration on Mixtec Identity in Oaxacalifornia," in M. P. Smith and J. R. Feagin (eds) *The Bubbling Cauldron: Race, Ethnicity, and the Urban Crisis*. Minneapolis: University of Minnesota Press, pp. 226–43.

Keck, Margaret E. and Kathryn Sikkink (1998) *Activists Beyond Borders: Advocacy Networks in International Politics*. Ithaca, NY and London: Cornell University Press.

Kellner, Douglas (1997) *Media Culture*. London and New York: Routledge.

Kern, Stephen (1983) *The Culture of Time and Space*. Cambridge, Mass.: Harvard University Press.

Kidder, Thalia and Mary McGinn (1995) "In the Wake of NAFTA: Transnational Workers Networks," *Social Policy* (summer): 14–21.

Kim, Elaine H. (1993) "Home is Where the *Han* Is: A Korean American Perspective on the Los Angeles Upheavals," *Social Justice*, 20 (1–2) (spring–summer): 1–21.

—— (1999) "'At Least You're Not Black': Asian Americans in US Race Relations," *Social Justice*, 25 (3): 3–12.

King, Anthony D. (1996) "Introduction: Cities, Texts, and Paradigms," in A. D. King (ed.) *Representing the City*. New York: New York University Press, pp. 1–20.

Knox, Paul (1995) "World Cities and the Organization of Global Space," in R. J. Johnston, Peter J. Taylor, and Michael J. Watts (eds) *Geographies of Global Change*. Oxford: Blackwell Publishers, pp. 232–47.

Kristof, Nicholas D. (1998) "Pols Find Rural Japan Resistant to Fiscal Reform," *San Francisco Examiner* (July 5): A16.

—— (1999) "Empty Isles are Signs Japan's Sun Might Dim," *New York Times* (August 1): 1, 4.

Kusno, Abidin (1998) Personal conversations on the crisis in Indonesia.

Kwong, Peter (1992) "The First Multicultural Riots," in Don Hazen (ed.) *Inside the LA Riots*. New York: Institute for Alternative Journalism, pp. 88–93.

Laclau, Ernesto (1990) *New Reflections on the Revolution of Our Time*. New York and London: Verso.

Laclau, Ernesto and Chantal Mouffe (1985) *Hegemony and Socialist Strategy*. London and New York: Verso.

—— (1987) "Post-Marxism without Apologies," *New Left Review*, 166 (Nov./Dec.): 79–106.

Lash, Scott and John Urry (1994) *Economies of Signs & Space*. London, Thousand Oaks, and New Delhi.

Lauria, Mickey (ed.) (1997) *Reconstructing Urban Regime Theory: Regulating Urban Politics in a Global Economy*. Thousand Oaks, Calif.: Sage.

Lee, Dong Ok (1995) "Responses to Spatial Rigidity in Urban Transformation: Korean Business Experience in Los Angeles," *International Journal of Urban and Regional Research*, 19 (1): 40–54.

Lee, Hoon (1996) "Building Class Solidarity Across Racial Lines: Korean-American Workers in Los Angeles," in John Anner (ed.) *Beyond Identity Politics: Emerging Social Justice Movements in Communities of Color*. Boston: South End Press, pp. 47–61.

Lee, Susan K. (1993) "Koreans in America," *Crossroads* (July/Aug.): 17–18.

Lefebvre, Henri (1971) *Everyday Life in the Modern World*. New York: Harper and Row.

—— (1991) *The Production of Space*. Oxford: Blackwell Publishers.

Lessinger, Johanna (1992) "Investing or Going Home? A Transnational Strategy Among Indian Immigrants in the United States," in N. Glick Schiller, L. Basch, and C. Szanton Blanc (eds) *Toward a Transnational Perspective on Migration: Race, Class, Ethnicity, and Nationalism Reconsidered*. New York: Annals of the New York Academy of Sciences, 645: 53–80.

Ley, David (1998) Review of Knox and Taylor (eds) *World Cities in a World System*, in *Environment and Planning A*, pp. 181–2.

Lie, John (1995) "American Sociology in a Transnational World: Against Parochialism," *Teaching Sociology*, 25 (April): 136–44.

Light, Ivan and Edna Bonacich (1988) *Immigrant Entrepreneurs: Koreans in Los Angeles, 1965–1982*. Los Angeles and Berkeley: University of California Press.

Light, Ivan, Richard B. Bernard, and Rebecca Kim (1999) "Immigrant Incorporation in the Garment Industry of Los Angeles," *International Migration Review*, 33 (1): 5–25.

Lin, Jan (1998) *Reconstructing Chinatown: Ethnic Enclave, Global Change*. Minneapolis: University of Minnesota Press.

Lipietz, Alain (1986) "New Tendencies in the International Division of Labor," in Alan J. Scott and Michael Storper (eds) *Production, Work, and Territory*. Boston: Allyn and Bacon, pp. 16–40.

Logan, John R. and Harvey L. Molotch (1987) *Urban Fortunes*. Berkeley: University of California Press.

Louis, Arthur M. (1993) "Mortgage Forclosures Still Soaring," *San Francisco Chronicle* (December 9): D1.

Low, Murray (1997) "Representation Unbound: Globalization and Democracy," in Kevin Cox (ed.) *Spaces of Globalization*. New York: Guilford Press, pp. 240–80.

Lyotard, Jean-François (1984) *The Postmodern Condition*. Minneapolis: University of Minnesota Press.

McAdam, Doug, John D. McCarthy, and Mayer Zald (eds) (1996) *Comparative Perspectives on Social Movements*. Cambridge: Cambridge University Press.

Machimura, Takashi (1998) "Symbolic Uses of Globalization in Urban Politics in Tokyo," *International Journal of Urban and Regional Research*, 22 (2): 183–94.

McMichael, Philip (1996) "Globalization: Myths and Realities," *Rural Sociology*, 61 (1): 25–55.

Mahler, Sarah J. (1996) *American Dreaming: Immigrant Life on the Margins*. Princeton, NJ: Princeton University Press.

—— (1998) "Theoretical and Empirical Contributions Towards a Research Agenda for Transnationalism," in M. P. Smith and L. E. Guarnizo (eds) *Transnationalism from Below*. New Brunswick, NJ: Transaction, pp. 64–100.

Mair, Andrew (1997) "Strategic Localization: The Myth of the Postnational Enterprise," in Kevin Cox (ed.) *Spaces of Globalization*. New York: Guilford Press, pp. 64–88.

Malkki, Lisa (1995) *Purity and Exile: Violence, Memory, and National Cosmology Among Hutu Refugees in Tanzania*. Chicago: University of Chicago Press.

Mander, Jerry and Edward Goldsmith (eds) (1996) *The Case Against the Global Economy*. San Francisco: Sierra Club Books.

Mann, Eric (1993) "Los Angeles – A Year After (I): The Poverty of Corporatism," *The Nation* (March 29): 406–11.

Marcus, George E. and Michael M. J. Fischer (1986) *Anthropology as Cultural Critique: An Experimental Moment in the Human Sciences*. Chicago and London: University of Chicago Press.

Martinez, Oscar J. (1994) *Border People: Life and Society in the US–Mexico Borderlands*. Tucson and London: University of Arizona Press.

Martinez, Ruben (1993) *The Other Side: Notes from the New LA, Mexico City, and Beyond*. New York: Vintage.

—— (1995) "Meet the Future in the Past," *NACLA Report on the Americas*, 28 (4) (Jan./Feb.): 35–7.

Mascia-Lees, Frances E., Patricia Sharpe, and Colleen Ballerino Cohen (1989) "The Postmodern Turn in Anthropology," *Signs*, 1 (autumn): 7–33.

Massey, Doreen (1991a) "A Global Sense of Place," *Marxism Today* (June): 24–8.

—— (1991b) "Flexible Sexism," *Space and Society*, 9: 31–57.

—— (1991c) "The Political Place of Locality Studies," *Environment and Planning: A*, (23): 267–81.

—— (1993) "Power-geometry and a Progressive Sense of Place," in Jon Bird, Barry Curtis, Tim Putnam, George Robertson, and Lisa Tickner (eds) *Mapping the Futures: Local Cultures, Global Change*. New York and London: Routledge, pp. 59–69.

—— (1994a) "Double Articulation: A Place in the World," in A. Bammer (ed.) *Displacements: Cultural Identities in Question*. Bloomington: Indiana University Press, pp. 111–21.

—— (1994b) *Space, Place, and Gender*. Minneapolis: University of Minnesota Press.

Matthei, Linda and David Smith (1998) "'Belizean Boyz 'n the Hood'? Garifuna Labor Migration and Transnational Identity," in M. P. Smith and L. E. Guarnizo (eds) *Transnationalism from Below*. New Brunswick, NJ: Transaction. pp. 270–90.

Melucci, Alberto (1995) "The Global Planet and the Internal Planet," in Marcy Darnovsky, Barbara Epstein, and Richard Flacks (eds) *Cultural Politics and Social Movements*. Philadelphia: Temple University Press, pp. 287–98.

Merl, Jean (1999) "Groups to Help Emigres Fly to Israel for Elections," *Los Angeles Times* (May 9): B1, B5.

Mintz, Sidney (1985) *Sweetness and Power: The Place of Sugar in Modern History*. New York: Viking.

Miranda, G. (1993) "Women's Rights are Human Rights," *The Bay Guardian* (March 3): 18–19.

Mitchell, Katharyne (1993) "Multiculturalism, or the United Colors of Capitalism?" *Antipode*, 25: 263–94.

—— (1996) "In Whose Interest? Transnational Capital and the Production of Multiculturalism in Canada," in R. Wilson and W. Dissanayake (eds) *Global/Local: Cultural Production and the Transnational Imaginary*. Durham, NC and London: Duke University Press, pp. 219–54.

—— (1997) "Transnational Discourse: Bringing Geography Back In," *Antipode*, 29 (2): 101–14.

Mollenkopf, John H. (1983) *The Contested City*. Princeton, NJ: Princeton University Press.

Morris, Meaghan (1992) "On the Beach," in L. Grossberg, C. Nelson, and P. Treichler (eds) *Cultural Studies*. New York and London: Routledge, pp. 450–78.

—— (1993) "Future Fear," in Jon Bird, Barry Curtis, Tim Putnam, George Robertson, and Lisa Tickner (eds) *Mapping the Futures*. New York and London: Routledge, pp. 30–46.

Mouffe, Chantal (1988) "Radical Democracy: Modern or Postmodern?" in Andrew Ross (ed.) *Universal Abandon? The Politics of Postmodernism*. Minneapolis: University of Minnesota Press, pp. 31–45.

Mouzelis, Nicos (1988) "Marxism or Post-Marxism?" *New Left Review*, 167 (Jan./ Feb.): 107–23.

Mullings, Leith (ed.) (1987) *Cities of the United States: Studies in Urban Anthropology*. New York: Columbia University Press.

Mydans, Seth (1992) "Separateness Grows in Scarred Los Angeles," *New York Times* (November 15): 1, 19.

—— (1995) "Los Angeles Official Seeks to Close Major Hospital," *New York Times* (June 20): A8.

—— (1999) "Nurturing Democracy from the Grass Roots," *New York Times* (June 13): WK 5.

Nagengast, Carole and Michael Kearney (1990) "Mixtec Ethnicity: Social Identity, Political Consciousness, and Political Activism," *Latin American Research Review*, 25 (2): 61–91.

Nonini, Donald (1997) "Shifting Identities, Positioned Imaginaries: Transnational Traversals and Reversals by Malaysian Chinese," in Aihwa Ong and Donald Nonini (eds) *Ungrounded Empires: The Cultural Politics of Modern Chinese Transnationalism*. New York: Routledge, pp. 203–27.

Nonini, Donald and Aihwa Ong (1997) "Chinese Transnationalism as an Alternative Modernity," in Aihwa Ong and Donald Nonini (eds) *Ungrounded Empires: The Cultural Politics of Modern Chinese Transnationalism*. New York: Routledge, pp. 3–38.

Olney, Peter (1993) "The Rising of the Million," *Crossroads* (July/August): 13–16.

Ong, Aihwa (1997) "Chinese Modernities: Narratives of Nation and of Capitalism," in A. Ong and D. Nonini (eds) *Ungrounded Empires: The Cultural Politics of Modern Chinese Transnationalism*. New York: Routledge, pp. 171–203.

—— (1999) *Flexible Citizenship: The Cultural Logics of Globalization*. Durham, NC and London: Duke University Press.

Ong, Aihwa and Donald Nonini (eds) (1997) *Ungrounded Empires: The Cultural Politics of Modern Chinese Transnationalism.* New York: Routledge.

Ong, Paul, et al. (1989) *The Widening Divide: Income Inequality and Poverty in Los Angeles.* Los Angeles: UCLA Graduate School of Architecture and Urban Planning.

—— (1993) *Beyond Asian-American Poverty: Community Economic Development Policies and Strategies.* Los Angeles: Asian American Public Policy Institute.

Pahl, Ray E. (1990) "Is the Emperor Naked? Some Questions on the Adequacy of Sociological Theory in Urban and Regional Research," *International Journal Of Urban And Regional Research*, 13 (4) (December): 709–20.

Pastor, Manuel, Jr (1993) *Latinos and the Los Angeles Uprising: The Economic Context.* Claremont, Calif.: Thomas Rivera Center.

Pearlstone, Zena (1990) *Ethnic LA.* Beverly Hills, CA: Hillcrest Press.

Pintak, Lawrence (1998) "Near-anarchy in Indonesia: Armed Forces Trying to Find Way to Tell Suharto to Go," *San Francisco Chronicle* (May 15): A1, A17.

Portes, Alejandro (1987) "The Social Origins of the Cuban Enclave Economy of Miami," *Sociological Perspectives*, 30 (October): 340–72.

—— (1996a) "Transnational Communities: Their Emergence and Significance in the Contemporary World System," Working Papers Series, No. 16. Program in Comparative and International Development, Department of Sociology, Johns Hopkins University.

—— (1996b) "Global Villagers: The Rise of Transnational Communities," *The American Prospect*, 2: 74–7.

Portes, Alejandro and Robert D. Manning (1986) "The Immigrant Enclave: Theory and Empirical Examples," in Joane Nagel and Susan Olzak (eds) *Competitive Ethnic Relations.* Orlando: Academic Press, pp. 47–68.

Portes, Alejandro and John Walton (1981) *Labor, Class, and the International System.* New York: Academic Press.

Pratt, A. C. (1991) "Discourses of Locality," *Environment and Planning A*, (23): 257–66.

Princen, Thomas and Matthias Finger (1994) *Environmental NGOs in World Politics: Linking the Local and the Global.* London and New York: Routledge.

Quiñones, Sam (1999) "Mexico Emigrants Spin a Bold Idea," *San Francisco Examiner* (June 20): A1, A6.

Reinhold, Robert (1993) "Rebuilding Lags in Los Angeles a Year After Riots," *New York Times* (May 10): A1, A10.

Ritchie, Mark (1996) "Cross-border Organizing," in Jerry Mander and Edward Goldsmith (eds) *The Case Against the Global Economy.* San Francisco: Sierra Club Books, pp. 494–500.

Robbertson, T. (1993) "Thousands of Guatemala Exiles Return," *San Francisco Chronicle* (January 21): A10.

Robbins, Bruce (1993) "Comparative Cosmopolitanisms," in B. Robbins, *Secular Vocations: Intellectuals, Professionalism, Culture.* London: Verso, pp. 180–211.

Rodriguez, Nestor (1995) "The Real 'New World Order': The Globalization of Racial and Ethnic Relations in the Late Twentieth Century," in M. P. Smith and J. R. Feagin (eds) *The Bubbling Cauldron: Race, Ethnicity and the Urban Crisis.* Minneapolis: University of Minnesota Press, pp. 211–25.

—— (1996) "The Battle for the Border: Notes on Autonomous Migration, Transnational Communities, and the State," *Social Justice*, 23 (3): 21–37.

Rodriguez, Nestor P. and Jacqueline Maria Hagan (1992) "Apartment Restructuring and Latino Immigrant Tenant Struggles: A Case Study of Human Agency," in M. P. Smith (ed.) *After Modernism: Global Restructuring and the Changing Boundaries of City Life*. New Brunswick, NJ: Transaction Publishers, pp. 164–80.

Rosaldo, Renato (1989) *Culture and Truth: The Remaking of Social Analysis*. Boston: Beacon Press.

Rose, Gillian (1993) "Some Notes Towards Thinking About the Spaces of the Future," in Jon Bird, Barry Curtis, Tim Putnam, George Robertson, and Lisa Tickner (eds) *Mapping the Futures: Local Cultures, Global Change*. London and New York: Routledge, pp. 70–83.

Rosenthal, John (1988) "Who Practices Hegemony? Class Division and the Subject of Politics," *Cultural Critique* (spring): 29.

Rouse, Roger (1990) "Men in Space: Power and the Appropriation of Urban Form Among Mexican Migrants in the United States." Paper presented at the Residential College, University of Michigan, Ann Arbor (March 14).

—— (1991) "Mexican Migration and the Social Space of Postmodernism," *Diaspora*, 1 (1) (spring): 8–23.

—— (1995) "Thinking Through Transnationalism," *Public Culture*, 7 (2): 353–402.

Ruiz, A. (1992) "Peace Caravan Heads South," *The Daily Californian* (August 7): 1, 3.

Sachs, Susan (1999a) "Slain Man's Mother is Center of Attention in Guinea," *New York Times* (February 17): B1.

—— (1999b) "From Grieving Mother to Forceful Celebrity," *New York Times* (April 12): A1.

Sahlins, Marshall (1976) *Culture and Practical Reason*. Chicago: University of Chicago Press.

San Francisco Chronicle, 1998 (May 9) "Support for Estrada Extends Beyond Bay Area": A13.

Sanger, David E. (1998) "World Bank, A Bit Nervous, Resumes Aid to Indonesia," *New York Times* (July 3): A5.

Sassen, Saskia (1988) *The Mobility of Labor and Capital*. Cambridge: Cambridge University Press.

—— (1991) *The Global City: New York, London, Tokyo*. Princeton, NJ: Princeton University Press.

—— (1995) *Losing Control: Sovereignty in an Age of Gobalization*. New York: Columbia University Press.

—— (1998) *Globalization and its Discontents*. New York: New Press.

Sassen, Saskia and Alejandro Portes (1993) "Miami: A New Global City?" *Contemporary Sociology*, 22 (4): 471–80.

Sassen-Koob, Saskia (1982) "Recomposition and Peripheralization at the Core," *Contemporary Marxism*, 5: 88–100.

—— (1984a) "Capital Mobility and Labor Migration: Their Expression in Core Cities," in M. Timberlake (ed.) *Urbanization in the World System*. New York: Academic Press.

—— (1984b) "The New Labor Demand in Global Cities," in Michael Peter Smith (ed.) *Cities in Transformation*. Beverly Hills, Calif.: Sage, pp. 139–71.

—— (1986) "New York City: Economic Restructuring and Immigration," *Development and Change*, 17 (1): 85–119.

—— (1987) "Growth and Informalization at the Core: A Preliminary Report on New York City," in Michael Peter Smith and Joe R. Feagin (eds) *The Capitalist City*. Oxford: Backwell Publishers, pp. 138–54.

Savage, L. (1998) "Shifting Gears: Union Organizing in the Low Wage Service Sector," in L. Herod (ed.) *Organizing the Landscape*. Minneapolis: University of Minnesota Press, pp. 225–54.

Sayer, Andrew (1987) "Hard Work and its Alternatives," *Society and Space*, 5: 395–9.

—— (1989) "The 'New' Regional Geography and Problems of Narrative," *Society and Space*, 7: 253–76.

—— (1991) "Behind the Locality Debate: Deconstructing Geography's Dualisms," *Environment and Planning A* (23): 283–308.

Schein, Louisa (1998a) "Forged Transnationality and Oppositional Cosmopolitanism," in M. P. Smith and L. E. Guarnizo (eds) *Transnationalism from Below*. New Brunswick, NJ: Transaction, pp. 291–313.

—— (1998b) "Importing Miao Brethren to Hmong America: A Not So Stateless Transnationalism," in Pheng Cheah and Bruce Robbins (eds) *Cosmopolitics: Thinking and Feeling Beyond the Nation*. Minneapolis: University of Minnesota Press, pp. 163–91.

Schlesinger, Arthur (1992) *The Disuniting of America*. New York: Norton.

Schou, Nick (1999) "The Northern Factor," *LA Weekly* (March 19): Lexis–Nexis, 1–4.

Scott, Alan (ed.) (1997) *The Limits of Globalization*. London and New York: Routledge.

Scott, Allen J. (1993) *Technopolis: High Technology Industry and Regional Development in Southern California*. Berkeley and Los Angeles: University of California Press.

—— (1995) "Industrial Urbanism in Southern California: Post-Fordist Civic Dilemmas and Opportunities," *Contention*, 5: 39–65.

Scott, Allen J. and Edward Soja (1986) "Editorial," *Society and Space*, 4: 249–56.

Sengupta, Somini (1998) "India Taps Into Its Diaspora," *New York Times* (August 19): A31.

Shapiro, Michael (1992) *Reading the Postmodern Polity*. Minneapolis: University of Minnesota Press.

Sikkink, Kathryn (1993) "Human Rights, Principled Issue Networks, and Sovereignty in Latin America," *International Organization*, 47 (3): 411–41.

Simonsen, Kirsten (1990) "Planning on 'Postmodern' Conditions," *Acta Sociologica*, 33: 51–62.

Sims, Calvin (1994) "Who Said Los Angeles Could Be Rebuilt in a Day," *New York Times* (May 22): 5.

Sklair, Leslie (1998) "The Transnational Capitalist Class and Global Capitalism," *Political Power and Social Theory*, 12: 3–43.

Smart, Alan and Josephine Smart (1998) "Transnational Social Networks and Negotiated Identities in Interactions between Hong Kong and China," in M. P. Smith and L. E. Guarnizo (eds) *Transnationalism from Below*. New Brunswick, NJ: Transaction, pp. 103–29.

Smith, Jackie, Ron Pagnucco, and Charles Chatfield (1997) "Social Movements and World Politics: A Theoretical Framework," in Jackie Smith, Charles Chatfield, and Ron Pagnucco (eds) *Transnational Social Movements and Global Politics*. Syracuse: Syracuse University Press, pp. 59–79.

Smith, Michael Peter (1980) *The City and Social Theory*. Oxford: Blackwell Publishers.
—— (ed.) (1984) *Cities in Transformation*. Beverly Hills, Calif. and London: Sage.
—— (1988) *City, State, and Market*. Oxford: Blackwell Publishers.
—— (1989) "Urbanism: Medium or Outcome of Human Agency?" *Urban Affairs Quarterly* (March): 353–8.
——(1992) "Postmodernism, Urban Ethnography, and the New Social Space of Ethnic Identity," *Theory and Society*, 21: 493–531.
—— (1994) "Can You Imagine? Transnational Migration and the Globalization of Grassroots Politics," *Social Text*, 39: 15–33.
—— (1997) "Looking for Globality in Los Angeles," in A. Cvetkovich and D. Kellner (eds) *Articulating the Global and the Local: Globalization and Cultural Studies*. Boulder, Col. and Oxford: Westview Press, pp. 55–7.
Smith, Michael Peter and Joe R. Feagin (eds) (1987) *The Capitalist City: Global Restructuring and Community Politics*. Oxford: Blackwell Publishers.
—— (1995) "Putting Race in its Place," in Michael Peter Smith and Joe R. Feagin (eds) *The Bubbling Cauldron: Race, Ethnicity and the Urban Crisis*. Minneapolis: University of Minnesota Press, pp. 3–27.
Smith, Michael Peter and Luis Eduardo Guarnizo (eds) (1998) *Transnationalism from Below*. New Brunswick, NJ: Transaction.
Smith, Michael Peter and Bernadette Tarallo (1993a) *California's Changing Faces: New Immigrant Survival Strategies and State Policy*. Berkeley: California Policy Seminar.
—— (1993b) "The Postmodern City and the Social Construction of Ethnicity in California," in Malcom Cross and Michael Keith (eds) *Racism, the City, and the State*. London and New York: Routledge, pp. 61–76.
—— (1995) "Who are the 'Good Guys'?: The Social Construction of the Vietnamese 'Other'," in M. P. Smith and J. R. Feagin (eds) *The Bubbling Cauldron: Race, Ethnicity and the Urban Crisis*. Minneapolis: University of Minnesota Press.
Smith, Michael Peter and Richard Tardanico (1987) "Urban Theory Reconsidered: Production, Reproduction, and Collective Action," in M. P. Smith and J. R. Feagin (eds) *The Capitalist City*. Oxford: Blackwell Publishers, pp. 87–110.
Smith, Michael Peter, Bernadette Tarallo, and G. Kagiwada (1991) "Colouring California: New Asian Immigrant Households, Social Networks and the Local State," *International Journal of Urban and Regional Research*, 15 (2): 250–68.
Smith, Robert (1996) "The Flower Sellers of Manhattan," *NACLA Report on the Americas*, 20 (3) (Nov./Dec.): 41–3.
—— (1998) "Transnational Localities: Community, Technology and the Politics of Membership within the Context of Mexico and US Migration," in M. P. Smith and L. E. Guarnizo (eds) *Transnationalism from Below*. New Brunswick, NJ: Transaction, pp. 196–239.
Soja, Edward J. (1986) "Taking Los Angeles Apart: Some Fragments of a Critical Human Geography," *Society and Space*, 4: 255–72.
—— (1989) *Postmodern Geographies*. London and New York: Verso.
—— (1996) *Thirdspace: Journeys to Los Angeles and Other Real and Imagined Places*. Oxford: Blackwell Publishers.
Sørensen, Ninna (1993) "Ethnicity and Gender," in H. Lindholm (ed.) *Ethnicity and Nationalism*, Goteborg: Nordic Network of Ethnic Studies.

—— (1996) "There are No Indians in the Dominican Republic," in K. Hastrup and K. Olwig (eds) *Siting Culture*. London: Routledge, pp. 142–64.

—— (1998) "Narrating Identity Across Dominican Worlds," in M. P. Smith and L. E. Guarnizo (eds) *Transnationalism from Below*. New Brunswick, NJ: Transaction, pp. 241–69.

Stone, Clarence N. (1989) *Regime Politics: Governing Atlanta*. Lawrence: University Press of Kansas.

Storper, Michael (1997) "Territories, Flows, and Hierarchies in the Global Economy," in Kevin Cox (ed.) *Spaces of Globalization*. New York: Guilford Press, pp. 19–44.

—— (1999) "The Poverty of Paleo-Leftism," *Antipode*, 31 (1): 37–44.

Strom, Stephanie (1998) "South Koreans Protest Spread of Layoffs in IMF Plan," *New York Times* (May 28): A7.

Sturgeon, Noël (1997) *Ecofeminist Natures: Race, Gender, Feminist Theory and Political Action*. New York and London: Routledge.

Tajbakhsh, Kian (1991) "Marxisms and Crisis of Communist Ideology," *Economic and Political Weekly* (August 17): 1,934.

Tardanico, Richard (1992) "Economic Crisis and Structural Adjustment: The Changing Labor Market of San Jose, Costa Rica," in M. P. Smith (ed.) *After Modernism: Global Restructuring and the Changing Boundaries of City Life*. New Brunswick: Transaction, pp. 70–104.

Tarrow, Sidney (1998) *Power in Movement: Social Movements and Contentious Politics*. Cambridge: Cambridge University Press.

Thompson, John B. (1995) *The Media and Modernity: A Social Theory of the Media*. Stanford, Calif.: Stanford University Press.

Tiebout, Charles M. (1956) "A Pure Theory of Local Expenditures," *Journal of Political Economy*, 64 (October): 416–24.

Tilly, Charles (1978) *From Mobilization to Revolution*. Reading, Mass.: Addison–Wesley.

—— (1983) "Flows of Capital and Forms of Industry in Europe, 1500–1900," *Theory and Society*, 12 (2): 123–42.

—— (1984) *Big Structures, Large Processes, Huge Comparisons*. New York: Russell Sage.

—— (1988) "What's Left of the City?" *Journal of Urban History*, 14 (3) (May): 394–8.

Tyler, Stephen A. (1986) "Postmodern Ethnography: From Document of the Occult to Occult Document," in James Clifford and George Marcus (eds) *Writing Culture: The Politics and Poetics of Ethnography*. Berkeley and Los Angeles: University of California Press, pp. 122–40.

—— (1987) *The Unspeakable*. Madison: University of Wisconsin Press.

Urry, John (1986) "Locality Research: The Case of Lancaster," *Regional Studies*, 20: 233–42.

Vertovec, Steven (1999) "Conceiving and Researching Transnationalism," *Ethnic and Racial Studies*, 22 (2): 447–62.

Wade, Robert (1996) "Globalization and its Limits: Reports on the Death of the National Economy are Greatly Exaggerated," in Suzanne Berger and Ronald Dore (eds) *National Diversity and Global Capitalism*. Ithaca, NY and London: Cornell University Press, pp. 60–88.

Waldinger, Roger and Mehdi Bozorgmehr (eds) (1996) *Ethnic Los Angeles*. New York: Russell Sage Foundation.

Wallerstein, Immanuel (1979) *The Capitalist World Economy*. New York: Cambridge University Press.

—— (1980) *The Modern World System*, vol. 2. New York: Academic Press.

Walton, John (1987) "Urban Protest and the Global Political Economy: The IMF Riots," in Michael Peter Smith and Joe R. Feagin (eds) *The Capitalist City: Global Restructuring and Community Politics*. Oxford: Blackwell Publishers, pp. 364–86.

Walton, John and David Seddon (1996) *Free Markets and Food Riots*. Oxford: Blackwell Publishers.

Wapner, Paul (1995) "Bringing Society Back In: Environmental Activism and World Civic Politics," *World Politics*, 47: 311–40.

Ward, Peter (1995) "The Successful Management and Administration of World Cities: Mission Impossible?" in Paul L. Knox and Peter J. Taylor (eds) *World Cities in a World System*. New York: Cambridge University Press, pp. 298–314.

Watson, Sophie (1991) "Guilding the Smokestacks: The New Symbolic Representations of Deindustrialized Regions," *Environment and Planning D: Society and Space*, 9: 59–70.

White, James W. (1998) "Old Wine, Cracked Bottle?: Tokyo, Paris, and the Global City Hypothesis," *Urban Affairs Review*, 33 (4) (March): 451–77.

Wilgoren, Jodi (1999) "Cardinal and Parents of Diallo Share Hopes," *New York Times* (April 7): A21.

Wilson, Rob and Wimal Dissanayake (eds) (1996) *Global/Local: Cultural Production and the Transnational Imaginary*. Durham, NC and London: Duke University Press.

Wolf, Eric (1982) *People Without History*. Berkeley: University of California Press.

World Bank (1991) *World Development Report 1991: The Challenge of Development*.

Young, Iris Marion (1998) "Harvey's Complaint with Race and Gender Struggles: A Critical Response," *Antipode*, 30 (1): 36–42.

Zabin, Carol (1995) "Mixtecs and Mestizos in California Agriculture: Ethnic Displacement and Hierarchy among Mexican Farm Workers," in M. P. Smith (ed.) *Marginal Spaces*. New Brunswick, NJ: Transaction, pp. 113–43.

Zukin, Sharon (1988) "The Postmodern Debate over Urban Form," *Theory, Culture & Society*, 5: 431–46.

—— (1991) *Landscapes of Power*. Berkeley: University of California Press.

Index